CAMBRIDGE
EDUCATION

UNLOCK

LISTENING & SPEAKING SKILLS 2

Alison Ramage Patterson

CAMBRIDGE
UNIVERSITY PRESS

CAMBRIDGE
UNIVERSITY PRESS

University Printing House, Cambridge CB2 8BS, United Kingdom

Cambridge University Press is part of the University of Cambridge.

It furthers the University's mission by disseminating knowledge in the pursuit of education, learning and research at the highest international levels of excellence.

www.cambridge.org
Information on this title: www.cambridge.org/9781107642805

© Cambridge University Press 2014

It is normally necessary for written permission for copying to be obtained in advance from a publisher. The worksheets, role-play cards, tests, and tapescripts at the back of this book are designed to be copied and distributed in class. The normal requirements are waived here and it is not necessary to write to Cambridge University Press for permission for an individual teacher to make copies for use within his or her own classroom. Only those pages that carry the wording '© Cambridge University Press' may be copied.

First published 2014

Printed in the United Kingdom by Latimer Trend

A catalogue record for this publication is available from the British Library

ISBN 978-1-107-68232-0 Listening and Speaking 2 Student's Book with Online Workbook
ISBN 978-1-107-64280-5 Listening and Speaking 2 Teacher's Book with DVD
ISBN 978-1-107-61400-0 Reading and Writing 2 Student's Book with Online Workbook
ISBN 978-1-107-61403-1 Reading and Writing 2 Teacher's Book with DVD

Additional resources for this publication at www.cambridge.org/unlock

Cambridge University Press has no responsibility for the persistence or accuracy of URLs for external or third-party internet websites referred to in this publication, and does not guarantee that any content on such websites is, or will remain, accurate or appropriate. Information regarding prices, travel timetables, and other factual information given in this work is correct at the time of first printing but Cambridge University Press does not guarantee the accuracy of such information thereafter.

CONTENTS

UNL⊘CK UNIT STRUCTURE

The units in *Unlock Listening and Speaking Skills* are carefully scaffolded so that students build the skills and language they need throughout the unit in order to produce a successful Speaking task.

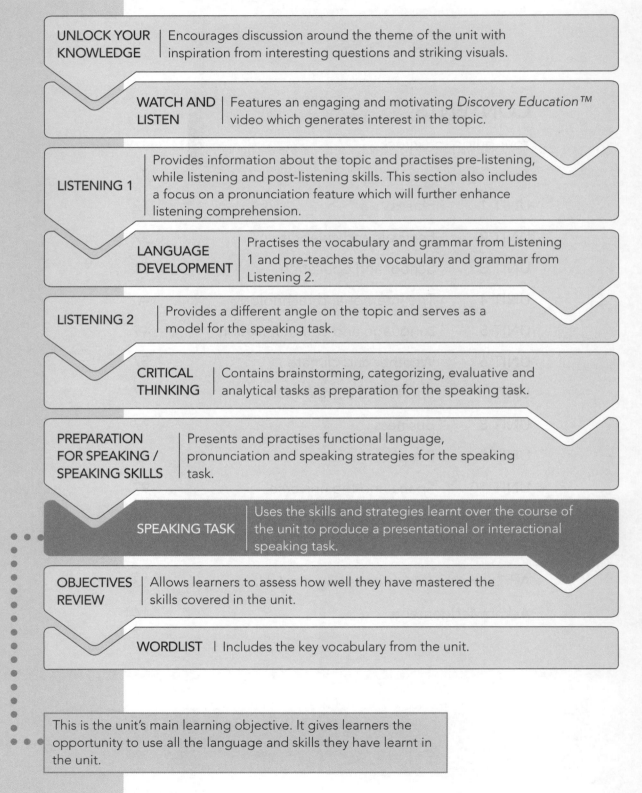

| UNLOCK YOUR KNOWLEDGE | Encourages discussion around the theme of the unit with inspiration from interesting questions and striking visuals. |

| WATCH AND LISTEN | Features an engaging and motivating *Discovery Education*™ video which generates interest in the topic. |

| LISTENING 1 | Provides information about the topic and practises pre-listening, while listening and post-listening skills. This section also includes a focus on a pronunciation feature which will further enhance listening comprehension. |

| LANGUAGE DEVELOPMENT | Practises the vocabulary and grammar from Listening 1 and pre-teaches the vocabulary and grammar from Listening 2. |

| LISTENING 2 | Provides a different angle on the topic and serves as a model for the speaking task. |

| CRITICAL THINKING | Contains brainstorming, categorizing, evaluative and analytical tasks as preparation for the speaking task. |

| PREPARATION FOR SPEAKING / SPEAKING SKILLS | Presents and practises functional language, pronunciation and speaking strategies for the speaking task. |

| SPEAKING TASK | Uses the skills and strategies learnt over the course of the unit to produce a presentational or interactional speaking task. |

| OBJECTIVES REVIEW | Allows learners to assess how well they have mastered the skills covered in the unit. |

| WORDLIST | Includes the key vocabulary from the unit. |

This is the unit's main learning objective. It gives learners the opportunity to use all the language and skills they have learnt in the unit.

UNLOCK MOTIVATION

UNLOCK YOUR KNOWLEDGE

Work in pairs. Look at the photograph and answer the questions.

1 Have you ever learnt something in the way you can see in the photograph? Was it a good way to learn?

2 Talk about something you learnt outside of the classroom. How did you learn? Did you enjoy it? Why?

3 Do you plan to learn something new? If yes, what would you like to learn?

4 What do you think will happen to schools and learning in the future?

PERSONALIZE

Unlock encourages students to bring their own knowledge, experiences and opinions to the topics. This **motivates** students to relate the topics to their own contexts.

DISCOVERY EDUCATION™ VIDEO

Thought-provoking videos from *Discovery Education™* are included in every unit throughout the course to introduce topics, promote discussion and motivate learners. The videos provide a new angle on a wide range of academic subjects.

> The video was excellent! It helped with raising students' interest in the topic. It was well-structured and the language level was appropriate.
>
> Maria Agata Szczerbik, United Arab Emirates University, Al-Ain, UAE

UNL⌀CK CRITICAL THINKING

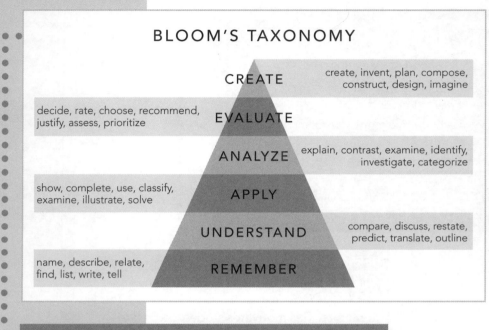

BLOOM'S TAXONOMY

CREATE — create, invent, plan, compose, construct, design, imagine

decide, rate, choose, recommend, justify, assess, prioritize — **EVALUATE**

ANALYZE — explain, contrast, examine, identify, investigate, categorize

show, complete, use, classify, examine, illustrate, solve — **APPLY**

UNDERSTAND — compare, discuss, restate, predict, translate, outline

name, describe, relate, find, list, write, tell — **REMEMBER**

> [...] with different styles of visual aids such as mind maps, grids, tables and pictures, this [critical thinking] section [provides] very crucial tools that can encourage learners to develop their speaking skills.
>
> Dr. Panidnad Chulerk, Rangit University, Thailand

BLOOM'S TAXONOMY

The Critical thinking sections in *Unlock* are based on Benjamin Bloom's classification of learning objectives. This ensures learners develop their **lower-** and **higher-order thinking skills**, ranging from demonstrating **knowledge** and **understanding** to in-depth **evaluation**.

The margin headings in the Critical thinking sections highlight the exercises which develop Bloom's concepts.

LEARN TO THINK

Learners engage in **evaluative** and **analytical tasks** that are designed to ensure they do all of the thinking and information-gathering required for the end-of-unit speaking task.

CRITICAL THINKING

At the end of this unit you are going to do the speaking task below.

Plan and give a set of instructions.

Giving instructions

To give instructions, use a simple flow chart to help you think of the actions you will need to describe the process.

APPLY

2 Complete the instructions for setting the alarm on a mobile phone. Write the verbs in the box in the flow chart.

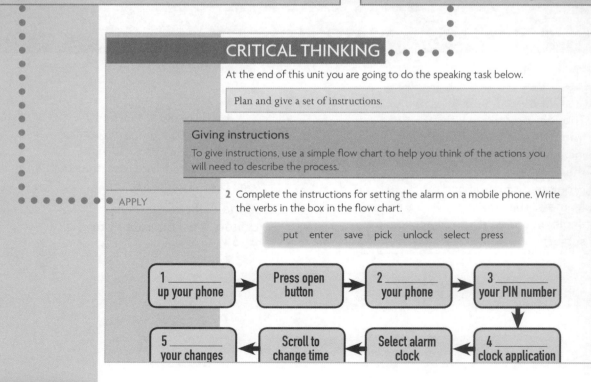

put   enter   save   pick   unlock   select   press

1 _____ up your phone → Press open button → 2 _____ your phone → 3 _____ your PIN number

5 _____ your changes ← Scroll to change time ← Select alarm clock ← 4 _____ clock application

UNL🔒CK RESEARCH

THE CAMBRIDGE LEARNER CORPUS ◉

The **Cambridge Learner Corpus** is a bank of official Cambridge English exam papers. Our exclusive access means we can use the corpus to carry out unique research and identify the most common errors that learners make. That information is used to ensure the *Unlock* syllabus teaches the most **relevant language**.

THE WORDS YOU NEED

Language Development sections provide vocabulary and grammar-building tasks that are further practised in the 🔒 UNL🔒CK ONLINE Workbook. The glossary provides definitions and pronunciation, and the end-of-unit wordlists provide useful summaries of key vocabulary.

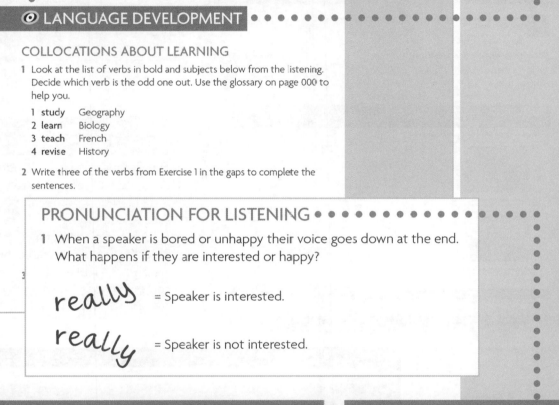

◉ LANGUAGE DEVELOPMENT

COLLOCATIONS ABOUT LEARNING

1 Look at the list of verbs in bold and subjects below from the listening. Decide which verb is the odd one out. Use the glossary on page 000 to help you.

1 **study**   Geography
2 **learn**   Biology
3 **teach**   French
4 **revise** History

2 Write three of the verbs from Exercise 1 in the gaps to complete the sentences.

PRONUNCIATION FOR LISTENING

1 When a speaker is bored or unhappy their voice goes down at the end. What happens if they are interested or happy?

really = Speaker is interested.

really = Speaker is not interested.

ACADEMIC LANGUAGE

Unique research using the **Cambridge English Corpus** has been carried out into academic language, in order to provide learners with relevant, academic vocabulary from the start (CEFR A1 and above). This addresses a gap in current academic vocabulary mapping and ensures learners are presented with carefully selected words which they will find essential during their studies.

PRONUNCIATION FOR LISTENING

This unique feature of *Unlock* focuses on aspects of pronunciation which may inhibit listening comprehension. This means that learners are primed to understand detail and nuance while listening.

> "The language development is clear and the strong lexical focus is positive as learners feel they make more progress when they learn more vocabulary."
> Colleen Wackrow,
> Princess Nourah Bint Abdulrahman University, Al-Riyadh, Kingdom of Saudi Arabia"

UNL**O**CK SOLUTIONS

FLEXIBLE

Unlock is available in a range of print and digital components, so teachers can mix and match according to their requirements.

UNL**O**CK ONLINE WORKBOOKS

The **UNLOCK ONLINE** Workbooks are accessed via activation codes packaged with the Student's Books. These **easy-to-use** workbooks provide interactive exercises, games, tasks, and further practice of the language and skills from the Student's Books in the Cambridge LMS, an engaging and modern learning environment.

CAMBRIDGE LEARNING MANAGEMENT SYSTEM (LMS)

The Cambridge LMS provides teachers with the ability to track learner progress and save valuable time thanks to automated marking functionality. Blogs, forums and other tools are also available to facilitate communication between students and teachers.

UNL**O**CK EBOOKS

The *Unlock* Student's Books and Teacher's Books are also available as interactive eBooks. With answers and *Discovery Education™* videos embedded, the eBooks provide a great alternative to the printed materials.

UNL☮CK TEACHING TIPS

1 Using video in the classroom

The *Watch and listen* sections in *Unlock* are based on documentary-style videos from *Discovery Education*™. Each one provides a fresh angle on the unit topic and a stimulating lead-in to the unit.

There are many different ways of using the video in class. For example, you could ask learners to listen to the audio track of the video without viewing the images and ask learners what the video is about. Then show the whole video and check whether the learners were correct. You could ask learners to reconstruct the voiceover or record their own commentary to the video. Try not to interrupt the first viewing of a new video, you can go back and watch sections again or explain things for struggling learners. You can also watch with the subtitles turned on when the learners have done all the listening comprehension work required of them. For less-controlled listening practice, use the video for free note-taking and ask learners to compare their notes to the video script.

See also: Goldstein, B. and Driver, P. (2014) *Language Learning with Digital Video*, Cambridge University Press, and the *Unlock* website www.cambridge.org/unlock for more ideas on using video in the classroom.

2 Teaching listening skills

Learners who aim to study at university will need to be comfortable listening to long, complex listening texts in a number of different genres. The listening texts in *Unlock Listening & Speaking Skills* provide learners with practice in the different listening sub-skills and also provide topic-related ideas and functional language needed for the *Speaking task*. Every unit focuses on one key listening skill, which is highlighted in a box, as well as various sub-skills, so that learners build on their listening skills throughout.

Before listening for the first time, use the *Preparing to listen* skills boxes to draw on learners' background knowledge and expectations of the listening text. Use the *While listening* skills boxes to focus students on listening sub-skills. Use the *Pronunciation for listening* activities to raise awareness of pronunciation features which can help listeners

decode speech. Learners have an opportunity for reflection on what they have listened to in the *Discussion* activities.

3 Teaching pronunciation

Unlock features *Pronunciation for listening* and *Pronunciation for speaking* sections. In *Pronunciation for listening*, learners focus on aspects of pronunciation which can enhance their listening comprehension, such as linking words, intonation, strong and weak forms in connected speech, homophones, etc. This will help learners to obtain more meaning from the listening text and in real life. Encourage learners to try using these pronunciation features in their own speaking so that they will be primed to hear them.

In *Pronunciation for speaking*, learners focus on aspects of pronunciation which they can put into practice in the *Speaking task*, such as consonant clusters, vowel sounds, connected speech, sentence stress and using intonation and tone. Practise pronunciation with your learners by recording them and giving feedback on the clarity, pace and stress in the *Speaking task*. Encourage your learners to record themselves and reflect on their own pronunciation.

4 Teaching speaking skills

Learners work towards the *Speaking task* throughout the unit by learning vocabulary and grammar relevant for the task, and then by listening to the key issues involved in the topic. Learners gather, organize and evaluate this information in the *Critical thinking* section and use it to prepare the *Speaking task*. *Unlock* includes two types of *Speaking task* – presentational and interactional. In the presentational tasks, learners will be required to give a presentation or monologue about the topic, often as part of a team. The interactional tasks require learners to role-play or interact with another person or persons.

There is an *Additional speaking task* for every unit in the Teacher's Book. This can be used as extra speaking practice to be prepared at home and done in class or as part of an end-of-unit test/evaluation. The *Additional speaking task* is also available on the Online Workbook. See section 8 for more details.

If your learners require IELTS test practice, point out that the discussion questions in the *Unlock your knowledge* sections provide practice of *IELTS Part 1 and 3* and the *Speaking tasks* provide practice of *IELTS Part 2*. Set the *Speaking task* as a timed test with a minimum time of two minutes and grade the learners on their overall fluency, vocabulary and grammar and the quality and clarity of their pronunciation.

5 Managing discussions in the classroom

There are opportunities for free discussion throughout *Unlock Listening & Speaking Skills*. The photographs and the *Unlock your knowledge* boxes on the first page of each unit provide the first discussion opportunity. Learners could be asked to guess what is happening in the photographs or predict what is going to happen or they could investigate the questions for homework in preparation for the lesson.

Throughout the rest of the unit, the heading *Discussion* indicates a set of questions which can be an opportunity for free speaking practice. Learners can use these questions to develop their ideas about the topic and gain confidence in the arguments they will put forward in the *Speaking task*.

To maximize speaking practice, learners could complete the discussion sections in pairs. Monitor each pair to check they can find enough to say and help where necessary. Encourage learners to minimize their use of L1 (their first language) and make notes for any error correction and feedback after the learners have finished speaking.

An alternative approach might be to ask learners to role-play discussions in the character of one of the people in the unit. This may free the learners from the responsibility to provide the correct answer and allow them to see an argument from another perspective.

- **Task checklists**

  Encourage your learners to reflect on their performance in the *Speaking task* by referring to the Task checklist at the end of the unit. The checklists can also be used by learners to reflect on each other's performance, if you feel that your learners will be comfortable doing so.

- **Additional speaking tasks**

  There are ten Additional speaking tasks in the Teacher's Book, one for each unit. These provide another opportunity to practise the skills and language learnt in the unit.

- **Model language**

  Model language in the form of functional expressions and conversation gambits follow the *Additional speaking tasks* to help learners develop confidence in their speaking ability by providing chunks of language they can use during the *Speaking task*. Photocopy the *Model language* and hand this to your learners when they plan and perform their writing task. Make sure learners practise saying them before they begin their task.

6 Teaching vocabulary

The *Wordlist* at the end of each unit includes topic vocabulary and academic vocabulary. There are many ways that you can work with the vocabulary. During the early units, encourage the learners to learn the new words by setting regular review tests. You could ask the learners to choose, e.g. five words from the unit vocabulary to learn. Encourage your learners to keep a vocabulary notebook and use new words as much as possible in their speaking.

7 Using the Research projects with your class

There is an opportunity for students to investigate and explore the unit topic further in the *Research projects* which feature at the end of each unit in the Teacher's Books. These are optional activities which will allow your learners to work in groups (or individually) to discover more about a particular aspect of the topic, carry out a problem-solving activity or engage in a task which takes their learning outside the classroom.

Learners can make use of the Cambridge LMS tools to share their work with the teacher or with the class as a whole. See section 8 for more ideas.

8 Using UNLOCK digital components: Online Workbook and the Cambridge Learning Management System (LMS)

The Online Workbook provides:

- additional practice of the key skills and language covered in the Student's Book through interactive exercises. The **UNLOCK ONLINE** symbol next to a section or activity in the Student's Book means that there is additional practice of that language or skill in the Online Workbook. These exercises are ideal as homework.

- *Additional speaking tasks* from the Teacher's Books. You can ask your learners to carry out the *Additional speaking tasks* in the Online Workbook for homework. Learners can record their response to the task and upload the file for the teacher.

- a gradebook which allows you to track your learners' progress throughout the course. This can help structure a one-to-one review with the learner or be used as a record of learning. You can also use this to help you decide what to review in class.

- games for vocabulary and language practice which are not scored in the gradebook.

The Cambridge LMS provides the following tools:

- **Blogs**

The class blog can be used for free writing practice to consolidate learning and share ideas. For example, you could ask each learner to post a description of their holiday (or another event linked to a topic covered in class). You could ask them to read and comment on two other learners' posts.

- **Forums**

The forums can be used for discussions. You could post a discussion question and encourage learners to post their thoughts on the question for homework.

- **Wikis**

In each class there is a Wiki. You can set up pages within this. The wikis are ideal for whole-class project work. You can use the wiki to practise process writing and to train the students to redraft and proofread. Try not to correct students online. Take note of common errors and use these to create a fun activity to review the language in class.

See www.cambridge.org/unlock for more ideas on using these tools with your class.

> **How to access the Cambridge LMS and setup classes**
> Go to www.cambridge.org/unlock for more information for teachers on accessing and using the Cambridge LMS and Online Workbooks.

9 Using Unlock interactive eBooks

Unlock Listening & Speaking Skills Student's Books are available as fully interactive eBooks. The content of the printed Student's Book and the Student's eBook is the same. However, there will be a number of differences in the way some content appears.

If you are using the interactive eBooks on tablet devices in the classroom, you may want to consider how this affects your class structure. For example, your learners will be able to independently access the video and audio content via the eBook. This means learners could do video activities at home and class time could be optimized on discussion activities and other productive tasks. Learners can compare their responses to the answer key in their eBooks which means the teacher may need to spend less time on checking answers with the whole class, leaving more time to monitor learner progress and help individual learners.

10 Using mobile technology in the language learning classroom

By Michael Pazinas, Curriculum and assessment coordinator for the Foundation Program at the United Arab Emirates University.

The presiding learning paradigm for mobile technology in the language classroom should be to create as many meaningful learning opportunities as possible for its users. What should be at the core of this thinking is that while modern mobile technology can be a 21st century 'super-toolbox', it should be there to support a larger learning strategy. Physical and virtual learning spaces, content and pedagogy all need to be factored in before deciding on delivery and ultimately the technological tools needed.

It is with these factors in mind that the research projects featured in this Teacher's Book aim to add elements of hands-on enquiry, collaboration, critical thinking and analysis. They have real challenges, which learners have to research and find solutions for. In an ideal world, they can become tangible, important solutions. While they are designed with groups in mind, there is nothing to stop them being used with individuals. They can be fully enriching experiences, used as starting points or simply ideas to be adapted and streamlined. When used in these ways, learner devices can become research libraries, film, art and music studios, podcast stations, marketing offices and blog creation tools.

Michael has first-hand experience of developing materials for the paperless classroom. He is the author of the Research projects *which feature in the Teacher's Books.*

1 PLACES

Learning objectives

Before you start the Unlock your knowledge section, ask students to read the Learning objectives box so that they have a clear idea of what they are going to learn in this unit. Tell them that you will come back to these objectives at the end of the unit when they review what they have learned. Give them the opportunity to ask you any questions they might have.

UNLOCK YOUR KNOWLEDGE

Lead-in

👥👥👥 Ask students for a show of hands as to who lives in a flat/an apartment or a house. Put students into groups of 3 or 4. Ask students to think of the advantages and disadvantages of living in these different types of home. Allow 2–3 minutes for this, before inviting feedback from the class.

👥👥 Allow 4–5 minutes for students to discuss the questions in pairs and then invite feedback from the class. Select one pair and ask them for a summary of their response to question 1, and then invite feedback from other pairs on this. Continue through to question 4.

Answers

1 Answers will vary, but reasons for wanting to live in a block of flats could include: cheaper, better for small families, easier to clean, views if the block is tall. Reasons for wanting to live in a house could include: more spacious for a family, has a garden, maybe in a better part of the city.
2 Yes, because they are made of mud.
3 Possible reasons: They live there because their families always have. They have to live there for their work. They might like the snow, sea, mountains, etc.
4 Answers will vary.

Background note

Flat and *apartment* mean the same thing; *flat* is specifically British English. A block of flats, or apartment block, is a building containing flats/apartments.

Optional activity

👥👥 👥👥👥 Put students into pairs/groups with other students who chose the same place they would like to live. Ask them to research this place to find out some information about why it is a good place to live and/or why they would like to live there. This could be done in class if time/facilities allow or as homework. Alternatively, brainstorm what students would like in their ideal place to live and then ask students to research on the internet a place that matches their criteria.

WATCH AND LISTEN

Video script

▶ Alaska: the largest state in the United States of America. It has the fewest people living in it, with a population of only seven hundred and twenty two thousand people. Why do so few people live here? One reason is the long winter. Winter lasts eight months in Alaska. In some places the temperature can drop as low as −60 ° Celcius. Everyone is waiting for winter to come: the people, wolves, bears and moose.

Kachemak Bay is on the Kenai Peninsula on the south coast of Alaska.

People in this part of Alaska live from the land. They are not close to shops or other services that are normally in towns. And they don't go to the supermarket and buy food from the shelves.

The Kilcher family has lived in the bay for many years. They know that they have to prepare their home for the long winter. They have to chop wood and save it for the winter months. It is important to store the pieces of wood next to their house because in winter there is too much snow to do this job. The wood is used for fuel to heat the house for the whole of the winter. The wood is put into a fire called a stove. The stove is in the middle of the kitchen.

Another job to do before winter is to move all their cows. In the summer months the cows live in Kachemak bay. But the men must move the cows before winter comes. Moving the cows is called 'driving the cattle home'. It is not an easy job. The two brothers, Otto and Atz, have to get the cattle home before the weather gets too bad.

It is also important to collect all the vegetables from the garden. The vegetables are put into boxes and stored in the house to keep them safe. They store fruit in cans and jars.

A big storm is coming. Brothers Otto and Atz are still driving the cattle home. The brothers will have to spend the night outdoors. Atz's son Atz Lee is worried. Winter has come early. Luckily, Otto and Atz make it home with the cattle after two days and everyone is safe.

PREPARING TO WATCH

UNDERSTANDING KEY VOCABULARY

1 👤👥 Students work individually to match the verbs to the phrases. Point out the example and, if appropriate, do the second one together. Allow 2–3 minutes for this. Ask students to check with a partner, before inviting feedback from the class.

Answers

1 d 2 e 3 g 4 a 5 h 6 f 7 c 8 b

2 👤 Students work individually to write down three ideas about the difficulties of living in Alaska. Allow about 2 minutes for this. Then put students into pairs and ask them to compare ideas. Allow a further 2 minutes for this, before inviting feedback from the class.

Answers

Answers will vary, but could include: winter in Alaska is very hard, the weather is very cold, there is not much daylight.

Background note

Alaska is the northernmost and coldest state of the USA, separated from the rest of the country by Canada. It is the largest American state.

WHILE WATCHING

LISTENING FOR KEY INFORMATION

3 ▶👤👥 Play the video and ask students to see how many of their ideas from Exercise 2 were correct. Ask students to check with a partner, before inviting feedback from the class. You could point out that the USA uses Fahrenheit not Celsius to measure temperature and that −60 ° Celsius is −80 ° Fahrenheit. Ask students if they know which one is used in their country.

Answers will vary.

4 ▶👤 Ask students to look at the photographs. Tell them they are going to watch a video and that they should put the photographs in the order they see them in the video. Play the video. If this is a strong class, Exercises 4 and 5 could be done together, with answer checking after Exercise 5. If the class is weaker, check answers to Exercise 4 before going on to Exercise 5.

Answers

a 5 b 1 c 4 d 2 e 6 f 3

5 👥 Students work with a partner to decide what is happening in each photograph. Highlight the vocabulary from Exercise 1 and encourage students to use it. If the class is weak, do the first one together. Allow about 3 minutes for this, before inviting feedback from the class.

Answers

The Kilchers are: a collecting vegetables from the garden b chopping wood c driving the cattle home d storing wood e storing vegetables f putting wood in the stove

6 👤👥 Students work individually to match the questions to the answers. Allow about 2 minutes. If the class is weak, ask students to check with a partner. Do not check answers at this stage.

7 ▶ Play the video again while students check their answers individually. Invite feedback from the class.

Answers

1 e 2 c 3 f 4 b 5 d 6 a

DISCUSSION

8 👥 Students work with a partner to discuss the questions. Allow 2–3 minutes for student discussion, and then invite feedback from the class. Encourage students to give reasons for question 2 in particular.

9 👥👥 Tell the class that they are going to spend next winter in Alaska. If you think your class needs more support, start by eliciting what things they need to take with them to make life comfortable. Put the suggestions on the board, e.g. very warm clothes, lots of heaters, transport that can survive the cold. Then put students into groups and ask them to choose just three items from the list on the board and to give reasons for their choice. Allow about 5 minutes for this. Put students into pairs, with each partner coming from a different group. Ask students to tell each other about the things they have chosen. Have they chosen the same or different things? Allow about 5 minutes for this, before inviting feedback from the class. If there is a wide variety of things that students wish to take, write them on the board and then have a vote to decide which three things the class will take with them to Alaska.

LISTENING 1

PREPARING TO LISTEN

PREDICTING CONTENT USING VISUALS

> **Optional lead-in**
>
> Refer students back to the lead-in on page 12 when you asked about where they live, and ask students if they can think of other interesting places where people can live. Encourage students to be as creative as possible and put all reasonable ideas on the board. Suggested ideas: in an ice house (igloo), in caves, in trees, on a boat, underground, in tents, in skyscrapers.

1 👥 Read the Predicting keywords and activating knowledge box while students read along. Students then work with a partner to match the pictures to the words in the box. Point out that some words will be used more than once. Do this without dictionaries if you think students can manage. Allow 2–3 minutes for this, before inviting feedback from the class.

> **Answers**
>
> a cave, ancient, rock b cave, rock, mushroom-shaped c bridge d industrial, bridge

2 👤👥 Students work individually to match the words to their definitions. Allow about 1 minute for this. If appropriate, ask students to check with a partner, before inviting feedback from the class.

> **Answers**
>
> 1 recognize b 2 strange a 3 located c

3 👥 Students work with a partner to answer the questions in Exercise 2 for the photographs in Exercise 1. Allow about 3 minutes for this, before inviting feedback from the class. Tell students the names of the places but not the countries they are in as this is checked when they listen in Exercise 10.

> **Answers**
>
> Answers will vary, but the places are: a Matmata, Tunisia b Cappadocia, Turkey c Ponte Vecchio, Florence, Italy d Neft Dashlari, Azerbaijan

PRONUNCIATION FOR LISTENING

4 🔊 1.1 Tell students to listen to the words in the table and repeat them, noticing how the vowel sounds correspond to the IPA symbols in the column headings. Play the audio.

> **Optional activity**
>
> Copy the table onto the board and drill students through the IPA sounds and the words, firstly by modelling the sound/word for them to repeat. Point out the first vowel sound is long and the other three are short. Demonstrate this by exaggerating the lengths. Then point to a sound/word and ask students to repeat. Encourage students to say the sound/word clearly and confidently. Gradually increase the speed at which you point, encouraging students to keep up by calling out the sounds/words as fast as you point to them. This gives students less time to think and helps with learning.

5 👥 Students work in pairs to practise saying the words in Exercise 4 and then put the words from Exercise 1 in the correct column, according to the underlined letters there. Allow 3–4 minutes for this, before inviting feedback from the class.

> **Answers**
>
> (The words in brackets are the answers to Exercise 6.)
>
> | /eɪ/ | /ɒ/ | /ɪ/ | /ʌ/ |
> |---|---|---|---|
> | place cave ancient (strange) | hot rock (long) | quick bridge (beautiful) | up mushroom-shaped industrial (lovely) |

6 Ask students to work on their own and put the four words in the box in the correct column in the table, according to the underlined letters there. If appropriate, ask students to check with a partner, before inviting feedback from the class.

> **Answers**
> See the words in brackets in the table above.

7 To illustrate the importance of the vowel sounds, tell students to imagine that you are all in a café and you'd like 'a *hit* coffee'. Do they know what you want? Give them a clue: *hit* is supposed to be the opposite of *cold*, to elicit that it should be *hot*. Give another example: 'I'd like a coffee with *lets* of milk'. Clue: *lets* is supposed to be the opposite of *a little*, to elicit that it should be *lots*. Demonstrate this activity with a strong student. Students then work with a partner to say the words from the table while the other students guess the row and the column.

WHILE LISTENING

LISTENING FOR MAIN IDEAS

8 🔊 1.2 Before you play the audio, refer students back to the pictures in Exercise 1 and ask students what they think the listening will be about. Play the audio. Students work individually to answer the questions. If appropriate, ask students to check with a partner, before inviting feedback from the class.

> **Answers**
> 1 c 2 b

LISTENING FOR DETAIL

9 Ask students to look at the table in Exercise 10 and allow them about 2 minutes to circle the correct words in sentences 1–3. If appropriate, do these with the class, eliciting answers from the students. Ask students what clues there are in the table, e.g. *years*, *kilometres* are likely to have a number before them.

> **Answers**
> 1 names 2 numbers 3 place; numbers

10 🔊 1.2 Play the audio again. Students work individually to answer the questions. If appropriate, pause the audio after each section/number to allow them time to write. Check in pairs, before inviting feedback from the class.

> **Answers**
> 1 Tunisia 2 700 3 355 4 Turkey 5 8,000 6 Italy
> 7 1345 8 Azerbaijan 9 30 10 5,000

DISCUSSION

11 To avoid students all choosing the same question, randomly assign numbers 1, 2 and 3 to different students. Ask them to think about answers to the question they have been given. Give them 1 minute thinking time. Circulate and help with any vocabulary.

12 Put students into pairs, with each student having a different question to talk about. Encourage the student listening to ask follow-up questions. Allow 5 minutes for this, before inviting feedback from the class.

◉ LANGUAGE DEVELOPMENT

REVIEW OF THE PAST SIMPLE

> **Optional lead-in**
>
> To focus students' attention on the Past simple, say: 'Every day I come to class by bus but yesterday I "mmmm" by taxi.' to elicit came. 'I usually have coffee for breakfast but yesterday I "mmmm" tea.' to elicit had. Say a few more examples applicable to you to allow students to call out the Past simple form that is needed.

1 Students work in pairs and circle the Past simple verbs in the sentences. Allow about 1 minute for this, before inviting feedback from the class.

> **Answers**
> 1 started 2 went 3 did … know 4 changed
> 5 was, destroyed 6 decided, needed, built 7 put

2 👥 Students work in pairs to answer the questions. Allow about 2 minutes for this. If the class is weak, do this with the whole class and put answers on the board.

> ### Answers
>
> 1 3: Did you know …? *did* (past of *do*) is the auxiliary verb used 2 the infinitive form

3 👥 Students work in pairs to complete the table. Allow about 2 minutes for this, before inviting feedback from the class.

> ### Answers
>
> | Past simple verbs: regular | Past simple verbs: irregular |
> |---|---|
> | *started* (x 2) | went |
> | changed | *knew* |
> | destroyed | was |
> | decided | built |
> | needed | put |

4 👤 Students work on their own to complete the questions. Allow about 2 minutes for this, before inviting feedback from the class.

> ### Answers
>
> 1 did you start 2 was 3 did you go 4 did you know 5 did you change

5 👥 Students work in pairs. If time allows, they should ask and answer all the questions rather than just two of them. Allow about 4 minutes for this, before inviting feedback from the class. Finish by asking a few students the same questions about their partner if it is a strong class, and about themselves if it is a weaker class.

PLACES WE LIVE AND WORK

6 Ask students where they would expect to find the places given.

> ### Answers
>
> in a town

7 👥 Students work in pairs to match the words in the box to the correct pictures. Allow 5 minutes for this, before inviting feedback from the class. As you check answers, write the words on the board.

> ### Answers
>
> a traffic lights b river c bus stop d cottage
> e tourist information office f street g forest
> h mountain i lake j field k coffee shop l wildlife

8 👥 Start this exercise by doing the first question together as a class. Put students into small groups of 3 or 4 to complete the activity. Allow about 5 minutes for this. Circulate and monitor, giving assistance where appropriate.

> ### Possible answers
>
> 1 at a bus stop for a bus, at a coffee shop for your friend, at traffic lights for them to go green 2 **Town**: street, river; **Countryside**: river, field, lake, mountain 3 tourist information office 4 coffee shop, lake, mountain, field 5 Answers will vary.

9 👥 Students work in pairs to choose five words or objects from the pictures. Tell students that they are going to describe the words/objects they have chosen to their partner, who has to guess what each one is. Read aloud the example and check understanding. Allow 1 minute thinking time for students to decide what they are going to say. Which partner is able to guess most correctly? Allow about 8 minutes for this, before inviting feedback from the class about how good they were at guessing their partner's objects.

Optional activity

As an alternative to Exercise 9, make a set of cards, with each card having one of the words/objects in the box in Exercise 7. If you have pictures of these things, you can use these instead. Put students into small groups of 3 or 4. Put the cards face down in the middle of the group. Students take it in turns to pick up a card and describe the word or object on the card to the rest of the group. The student who guesses the word/object keeps the card. The winner is the student who has the most cards at the end. Allow about 10 minutes for this. Circulate and monitor, giving assistance where appropriate.

10 Students work in small groups of 3 or 4 and tell each other about the places. Remind them to give reasons for their answers. Tell students to ask as many questions about each place as possible. Which are the most interesting places? Allow about 8–10 minutes for this, depending on the size of the groups. Finish by inviting feedback from the class and deciding which is the most interesting place for each of the three questions.

LISTENING 2

PREPARING TO LISTEN

UNDERSTANDING KEY VOCABULARY

Optional lead-in

Books closed. Ask students if any of them have got lost when they were driving (or being driven) in a new place or even in their own city. Ask: 'What did you do?' Then ask students: 'What can we use so that we don't get lost?' to elicit *street signs, maps, satnav, asking other people for directions*, etc.

1 Ask students to open their books at page 23 and tell students that the words in colour are called a word cloud. Explain that it is an image made up from words in a text, where the more often the word is used in the text, the bigger it is in the word cloud. People can make their own word clouds using *wordle* on the internet. Tell students that they are going to listen to a teacher giving a lecture and ask: 'Which two words are used most often in the lecture you are going to hear?' to elicit *satnav* and *GPS*. Students work in pairs to make predictions about the lecture. Allow about 2 minutes for this, before inviting feedback from the class. Write predictions on the board for checking later.

2 Students work individually to match the sentence halves. Allow about 2 minutes for this, before asking students to check with a partner. Invite feedback from the class and then concept-check the vocabulary by asking the following questions: 'When we *process* information, does it mean that we just understand it?' to elicit *no, we organize it as well*. 'What does *organize* mean?' to elicit *putting things in an order so that we can understand them*. 'Is something that is *complicated* or *complex* easy to understand?' to elicit *no, it is difficult to understand*. 'Do we use *obviously* with a *fact* or an *opinion*?' to elicit *fact*. 'What is an *opinion*?' to elicit *something we feel, think or believe*.

Answers

1 c 2 a 3 b 4 d

WHILE LISTENING

LISTENING FOR GIST

3 (1.3) Highlight the three options before students listen and refer to the predictions that they made in Exercise 1 which you have written on the board. Play the audio. After listening, invite feedback from the class and refer to the predictions on the board. Were any of them correct?

Answers

b

4 Tell students to decide about the sentences based on what they can remember from the lecture. Do the first question with the class and point out the phrase that tells us that it is a fact (*are usually*). Ask the class to think of any phrases that could suggest opinion to elicit *I think, I believe*. Tell students that they should think about who is speaking and to what purpose (why?). Are they giving information or ideas about the topic? Do they want you to agree with them? Allow about 3 minutes for this. Do not check answers at this stage.

5 (◀ **1.3**) Either listen again to check or read from the audioscript on pages 209–210 if the class is weak.

> **Answers**
> 1 F 2 F 3 DK 4 F 5 F 6 F 7 F 8 O

POST-LISTENING

DISTINGUISHING FACT FROM OPINION

6 👥 If this is a strong class, ask students to work with a partner to guess which words go in the gaps, before checking with the audioscript. If the class is not so strong, ask students to work with a partner and to look at the audioscript on pages 209–210 to find the answers. Allow about 5 minutes for this, before inviting feedback from the class.

> **Answers**
> 1 Obviously 2 we know 3 have found 4 I think
> 5 believe 6 personally feel 7 my opinion 8 seems to me

7 Elicit answers to the questions from the whole class.

> **Answers**
> **Opinions:** I think, I believe, I personally feel, in my opinion, it seems to me
> **Facts:** obviously, as we know, have found.
> The tense often used to give facts is the Present simple.

8 👤 Allow 2–3 minutes for students to fill in the Fact and Opinions grouping diagrams with phrases from Exercise 6.

DISCUSSION

9 👥 Students work in pairs to discuss how they find out where to go when they are travelling to new places. Ask students to give reasons for their choices. Allow about 2 minutes for this, before inviting feedback from the class. Alternatively, if there are a number of students who don't drive or have a car, they could talk about what their friends or relations use, or what they would prefer to use if they had a car. Ask students to give reasons for their choices. Allow about 2 minutes for this, before inviting feedback from the class.

CRITICAL THINKING

At this point in each unit students are asked to begin to think about the Speaking task they will do at the end of the unit (*Create a presentation for your classmates about an interesting place. Give factual information and your opinion about the place you choose.*) Give them a minute to look at the box. Then explain that the place could be either a location or a type of home.

REMEMBER

1 👤👥 You could introduce this activity by describing your home, giving two facts and two opinions. Write key words on the board and ask students: 'Which are the facts? Which are the opinions?' Refer students back to Exercise 8 on Student's Book page 25 for the language they need for giving facts and opinions. Students then work individually to plan their own descriptions. Allow 2–3 minutes for this. They then work with a partner and describe their homes to each other. Encourage them to ask questions about each other's homes. Allow about 4 minutes speaking time, before inviting feedback from the class.

> **Answers will vary.**

2 👥 Remind students of the places in Listening 1 and any notes they made about them. Read out each piece of information given about the Ponte Vecchio (b). Students then work individually or with a partner to label the other three photos. When students have done as much as they can, they could use the audioscript 1.2 on page 209 to complete and check their answers.

> **Answers**
> a 700 years old; in Tunisia 355 kilometres south of the capital, Tunis; houses in caves c 8,000 years old; in Cappadocia in the centre of Turkey; cave houses like mushrooms d new; Neft Dashlari in Azerbaijan; it is a city on a bridge above the sea that is 30 miles long

EVALUATE

3 👥 Do the Ponte Vecchio example (b) as a class, eliciting opinions from students first. Students work in pairs to add two opinions to the other three photographs (a, c, d). Allow about 3 minutes for this, before inviting feedback from the class.

| Answers will vary.

CREATE

4 👤 Read out the Planning a presentation box while students read along. Then give each student a letter to correspond with the places in Exercise 2 (a–d). Allow 1 minute for students to make notes about their place.

5 👤 Students work alone. Allow 1 minute for them to check their ideas against the information in the table.

6 👤 Students work alone to put the headings in the correct place in the table.

| **Answers**
| 1 Introduction and general facts 2 History 3 Opinion
| (advantages) 4 Opinion (disadvantages) 5 Summary

7 👤 Students work alone to complete the table. Allow about 6 minutes for this. Circulate and monitor, giving assistance where required.

8 👥 Students work in pairs. Make sure the two people in each pair are not describing the same place. Allow about 4 minutes to complete the task, before inviting feedback from the class. Did everyone guess which place their partner was describing?

SPEAKING

PREPARATION FOR SPEAKING

Optional lead-in

Refer students to the table in Exercise 6 on page 27 and ask: 'What is this table helping us to do?' Elicit, '*to organize our presentation*' Then ask: 'Is organization important?' (Yes) 'Why?' (*It makes it easier for the listener to understand what we are saying*).

1 👤 Students work individually to match the topics to the sentences. Allow about 1 minute for this, before inviting feedback from the class.

| **Answers**
| 1 d 2 a 3 b 4 c

2 (◀ 1.4) 👤 Play the audio and stop after the first sentence and check the answer with the class. Play the rest of the audio. Students work individually to complete the exercise.

| **Answers**
| 1 I'd like to talk about 2 First of all
| 3 I'd also like to talk about 4 Finally

PRONUNCIATION FOR SPEAKING

3 (◀ 1.5) Play the audio or model the sentence yourself. Write *talk about* on the board and then add the link between the *talk* and *about* to show that they are linked. Drill *talk_about* with the class and then the whole sentence so they can pick up the rhythm.

4 👥 Students work in pairs to complete the rule. Allow about 1 minute for this.

| **Answers**
| consonant; vowel

5 👤 Write the sentence *First of all let's look at the advantages.* on the board. Ask students to work on their own to draw links between the words.

| **Answers**
| *First_of_all* let's *look_at* the advantages.

6 (◀ 1.6) Either play the audio or model the sentence. First, drill *first_of_all*. Then drill *look_at*. Then drill the whole sentence.

7 👥 Students work in pairs to mark the links. Write the phrases on the board and invite students to add the links. Drill each phrase with students, starting first with the linked words and then expanding to the whole phrase. Point out that the -e in *some* is silent so the link is from the -m in *some* to the i- in *information*. Keep these phrases on the board to help students with the next activity.

> **Answers**
>
> 1 I'd like to give so*me␣information␣about* …
> 2 Now let's tal*k␣about* … 3 The next topi*c␣is* …
> 4 Finally let's loo*k␣at*.

ORGANIZING INFORMATION FOR A PRESENTATION

8 Put students into pairs and nominate each student A or B. Tell Student A to look at the information on page 194 and Student B to look at the information on page 196. Allow students 4 minutes to complete their table with the correct information. Students should decide what they want to say in the Summary. Circulate and monitor. When students have completed their table, remind them of the phrases on the board which will help them organize their presentation. Allow about 2 minutes for this.

> **Answers**
>
> **Student A**
> Introduction (name of place and location): Sentenil de Las Bodegas; located 157 miles northeast of Cádiz, in Spain
> General facts / history: people lived there – Roman times; first people – in caves then built into mountain side; castle built – 12th century
> Opinion – advantages: unusual; nice building
> Opinion – disadvantages: houses – dark?
> Summary: answers will vary.
> **Student B**
> Introduction (name of place and location): Hadhramaut; in Shibam, centre of Yemen; in the desert of Ramlat al sab'atayn
> General facts / history: mud houses – built 16th century; rebuilt many times over last hundred years; some of the mud houses – 30 metres high
> Opinion – advantages: unusual; very interesting place to live
> Opinion – disadvantages: dangerous in rain
> Summary: answers will vary.

SPEAKING TASK

PREPARE

1 Give students a minute to read the box and remind themselves of the Speaking task they are going to do. If students have problems thinking of interesting places or to avoid all of them choosing the same place. You could write the names of some unusual places on small pieces of paper which students select at random. Suggestions: Beppu, Japan; Mount Roraima, South America; Lake Nakuru, Kenya; Death Valley, California; Pamukkale, Turkey; Perito Moreno Glacier, Argentina; Rotorua, New Zealand; Plitvice Lakes, Croatia; Chocolate Hills in Bohol, Philippines. Additional suggestions could include places that are the opposite of where your students live, e.g. capital cities if they live in small towns, cold places if they live in hot places, wet places if they live in dry places.

2 This is best done for homework, but if the internet is available in the class and students have access to it via laptops or tablets, then it can be done in class, and this would work well if students are going to give group presentations (see alternative below).

3 Students work individually to prepare their talks, using the table to make notes. They should plan to talk for 1 minute. While students are preparing their presentations, circulate and give assistance where needed.

PRESENT

4 Put students into small groups of 3 or 4, making sure that no two students are going to talk about the same place. Students present their place to the rest of their group, speaking for about 1 minute each. Encourage those listening to ask questions at the end.

5 Finish by asking for feedback from the class about the most interesting place. Have a vote for the place students would most like to visit.

Alternatively, if the class is small enough and/or you have the time, this can be done as a group presentation to the whole class. Put students into groups of 3 and let them choose a place or give them one from the suggestions in Exercise 1 above. Tell students to divide their presentation into three sections, with each student preparing to speak for about 1 minute. Preparation can be done for homework. If appropriate, allow visual aids to be included in the presentation. When presenting to the class, impose a time limit of 3 minutes for each group's presentation. At the end of the presentations, take a vote on which place most students would like to visit.

ADDITIONAL SPEAKING TASK

See page 134 for the Additional speaking task (*Describing an interesting home*) and Model language for this unit.

Make a photocopy of page 134 for each student but cut off the details about homes (A, B, C) at the foot of the page. Cut up the details about the homes into 3 (A, B or C).

👥 Divide the class into 3 groups (A, B, C) and give each member of the group the details about one of the homes. Tell the students that they are going to describe 'their' home to other students. They should use the table on their sheet to plan their talks. Encourage students to be as creative as possible and to add new details (e.g. *It has 15 rooms.*) and opinions (e.g. *It's really beautiful.*). Allow about 10 minutes for this.

👥 Put students into new groups of 3 (A, B and C), so that each student will talk about a different home. Ask students to present their homes to each other. Encourage them to ask questions. They should then decide which home they like best. Allow 10 minutes for this.

Finish off by inviting feedback from the class. Which is the most popular home?

TASK CHECKLIST AND OBJECTIVES

REVIEW

Refer students to the end of the unit for the Task checklist and Objectives review. Students complete the tables individually to reflect on their learning and identify areas for improvement.

WORDLIST

See Teaching tips page 10, section 6, for ideas about how to make the most of the Wordlist with your students.

REVIEW TEST

See pages 114–115 for the photocopiable Review test for this unit and page 107 for ideas about when and how to administer the Review test.

RESEARCH PROJECT

Create a documentary about Alaska

Divide the class into groups and ask each group to investigate a different aspect of Alaska, e.g. its geography, nature, history, industry or literature. Tell students that they need to find images, sounds, music and videos to create a class documentary entitled *Alaskan life: Past and present*. Students could use the Cambridge LMS to create a wiki to share their research with the rest of the class.

The class will use the information from each group to create a short documentary film about Alaska. To plan the documentary, students will need to create a script or storyboard. They will also have to think about who in the class will direct the documentary, who will work the camera, who will edit the video, and who will present or narrate the documentary. They could then upload the film to a video-sharing website.

2 FESTIVALS AND CELEBRATIONS

Learning objectives

Before you start the Unlock your knowledge section, ask students to read the Learning objectives box so that they have a clear idea of what they are going to learn in this unit. Tell them that you will come back to these objectives at the end of the unit when they review what they have learned. Give them the opportunity to ask you any questions they might have.

UNLOCK YOUR KNOWLEDGE

Optional lead-in

Write festival on the board and ask anyone if they know what it means or can give an example. If students have problems thinking of examples, then think of an important celebration in the country you are in, for example, Eid al-Fitr in Islamic countries, Christmas in Christian countries or use a well-known local festival. Ask students why we have festivals and elicit to celebrate and point out that this is the verb and that celebration is the noun.

👥 👥👥 Ask students to open their books at page 33 and to work in pairs to answer questions 1–3. Allow about 3 minutes for this, before inviting feedback from the class. Alternatively, if students come from the same country, put them into groups and ask them to rank their country's festivals by how much they enjoy them and why. Invite feedback from each group to see if each group has the same rankings. If students come from different countries, put them into groups with each student from a different country and ask them to tell each other about different festivals in their countries. Each group should decide which festival is the most fun. Invite feedback from students. Is there one festival that everyone thinks is the most fun?

Answers
1 India or Nepal 2 Answers will vary. 3 Answers will vary.

Background note

The photograph shows the Hindu festival of Holi which is celebrated in the spring.

Optional activity

👤 👥👥 Ask students individually to research on the internet a festival from a different country. Alternatively, students can work in groups looking at either countries or some specific festivals. Some of the most famous festivals worldwide include: Carnaval, Brazil; Diwali, India; Burning Man, USA; La Tomatina, Spain; Mardi Gras, USA; Carnevale Venezia, Venice, Italy; Land diving, Vanuatu; Durbar, Nigeria. Ask students to be prepared to tell the rest of the class about 'their' country or festival. This can then be done in groups as either a warmer or an end-of-class activity.

WATCH AND LISTEN

Video script

▶ Festivals are celebrated all around the world. In China, people are getting ready to celebrate one of the world's biggest festivals. This is Chinese New Year. For 15 days in spring, eight hundred million people travel across China to be with their friends and family. People decorate their homes with red lanterns. They paint red paper banners with good luck phrases like 'Happiness' and 'Wealth' and hang them outside the front door.

Across the country, there are parades in every town. People wear bright costumes, dance and play music. In the famous dragon dance, young men carry a dragon made of paper, silk and wood in the air and dance through the streets, collecting money.

On New Year's Eve, everyone sits down together for a traditional meal with their family. This meal has 22 courses. They exchange gifts of money, put inside a red envelope for luck. People also take small gifts of food to their friends, like oranges or sweets. At night, the streets fill with people.

But no Chinese New Year celebration is complete without fireworks. All across the country, the New Year is welcomed with firework displays, big and small. One of the biggest displays is in the city of Hong Kong. Over one million people come to watch the display, which uses several tonnes of fireworks.

PREPARING TO WATCH

UNDERSTANDING KEY VOCABULARY

1 👥 Allow about 2 minutes for students to work in pairs to match the words to the photographs.

Answers
1 d 2 f 3 b 4 a 5 e 6 c

2 👤 Ask students to work on their own to complete the sentences with the verbs in the box. Do not check answers at this stage.

WHILE WATCHING

UNDERSTANDING MAIN IDEAS

3 ▶️ 👤 👥 Play the video and ask students to check their answers to Exercise 2. Ask students to check with a partner, before inviting feedback from the class.

> **Answers**
>
> 1 celebrate 2 travel 3 decorate 4 paint 5 wear
> 6 exchange 7 welcomed

LISTENING FOR KEY INFORMATION

4 ▶️ 👤 👥 Play the video again and ask students to circle the correct answer. Ask students to check with a partner, before inviting feedback from the class.

> **Answers**
>
> 1 15 2 spring 3 happiness and wealth
> 4 outside the house 5 men 6 22 7 red envelopes
> 8 sweets 9 1 million

DISCUSSION

5 👥 👥👥 Put students into different pairs or into groups for these discussions. Allow about 3 minutes for this, before inviting feedback from the class. To finish, have a vote on how many students would like to visit China for New Year and why, and how many students wouldn't and why. Invite feedback from some students about what their partner does to celebrate New Year. Find out who has the most fun.

> **Optional activity**
>
> 👤 👥👥 For many parts of the world, New Year falls on the night of the 31st December but there are other cultures, like China, where the New Year falls on a different date. Ask students individually to research on the internet how many different 'New Years' they can find. Alternatively, put students into groups and give them a specific New Year to find some information about. Suggested New Years include: Eastern Orthodox Church, 14th January; Vietnamese New Year, same as the Chinese New Year, between 21st January and 21st February; Tibetan New Year, between January and March; Sikh New Year, 14th March; Uzbek, Kazakh and other Central Asian countries' New Year, 22nd March; Bengali New Year, mid-April; Coptic Orthodox Church New Year, 11th September.

LISTENING 1

PREPARING TO LISTEN

UNDERSTANDING KEY VOCABULARY

> **Optional lead-in**
>
> Elicit the festivals students have already learned about. Ask: 'What type of festivals are these?' to elicit cultural. If students aren't able to answer, prompt them with some questions, for example, 'Are they music festivals?' 'Are they book festivals?' Once they have identified these festivals as cultural, ask students what other types of festivals they can think of. Accept all reasonable suggestions.

1 👥 Do the first word with the class and then ask students to work in pairs to choose the correct meaning of the word in bold. Allow about 3 minutes for this, before inviting feedback from the class.

> **Answers**
>
> 1 talk 2 something organized for enjoyment
> 3 have been done for a long time
> 4 customs, art, music and food
> 5 group of musicians
> 6 desert 7 can enjoy it

PREDICTING CONTENT USING VISUALS

2 👤 Students work on their own to match the words in Exercise 1 to the photographs.

> **Answers**
>
> a activity, culture, band, entertainment b activity, traditional, culture, camel, entertainment c lecture

3 👤 Students work on their own to match the festivals to the photographs. Do not check answers at this stage.

WHILE LISTENING

LISTENING AND TAKING NOTES

4 🔊 2.1 👤 👥 Tell students they are now going to listen to information about these three festivals and to check their answers for Exercise 3. Play the audio. Ask students to check with a partner, before inviting feedback from the class.

> **Answers**
>
> 1 c 2 b 3 a

5 👤 Explain that when we write notes, we only write the important words. Students work on their own to cross out the words that are not needed.

> **Answers**
>
> 1 the festival is in 2 you can see, you can try

6 👥 Read the Listening and taking notes box with students following in their books. Highlight the example and ask students: 'Why don't we need the words *the festival is in*?' (because, in the context, *Muscat* tells us that information, *festival* is understood, and the other words are 'grammar' words). Explain that students often attempt to write down all the words of the sentence which they know contains the answer to a question. Then they miss the next part of the listening. An important academic skill is being able to take notes accurately and quickly, and for this only the most important words are required. In this context, the most important words, those which carry the content, are the nouns. To illustrate the idea of 'grammar' words and 'content' words, write the sentence *The festival is in Muscat.* on the board twice, one above the other. In the top sentence, rub out the words *festival* and *Muscat* (the 'content' words) and then ask students if they can tell what this sentence means, to elicit *no*. Then for the second sentence, rub out *The*, *is* and *in* (the 'grammar' words) and then ask students if they can still get the meaning of the sentence, to elicit *yes*. Do the first answer with the whole class and then ask students to work in pairs to predict the information in each gap. Students often have difficulty with reading the words around the gap to help them predict what sort of word should be in the gap. This exercise helps them practise this skill as the types of word are well signposted. Give students about 5 minutes for this, before inviting feedback from the class.

> **Possible answers**
>
> 1 a country 2 a month 3 a type of activity 4 a type of activity 5 a month 6 something we listen to 7 a place 8 months 9 an activity 10 activities 11 a type of activity

7 🔊 **2.1** 👤 Play the audio again to allow students to check their answers.

> **Answers**
>
> 1 UK 2 October 3 games 4 lecture 5 October 6 music 7 museums 8 January and February 9 sport 10 dancing 11 a fashion

> **Background note**
>
> The Cambridge (UK) Festival of Ideas is an annual festival offering talks, activities, workshops, etc. to the general public.
>
> Iceland Airwaves is an annual music festival, which was originally held in an aircraft hangar in Reykjavík.
>
> The Muscat Festival celebrates all aspects of Omani culture, and is well known for being educational as well as cultural.

DISCUSSION

8 👤 Students work individually to think about a festival in their country, or one that they have learned about in this unit. Allow about 2 minutes for them to write their notes and which activities they like / would like to do most.

9 👥 Tell students to speak to three other people in the class and tell them about their festival and find out which activities they would like to do at this festival. They also listen to what the others say about their festivals and make notes about their partners' festivals and which different activities they like / would like to do. Allow about 10 minutes for this.

10 Ask students to return to their seats and allow 1 minute of silent time for them to analyze their partners' responses. Invite feedback from the class. Which festivals and activities were most popular?

PRONUNCIATION FOR LISTENING

11 Tell students to look at the sentence and ask them which the important words are. Remind them of the 'The festival is in Muscat' activity that you did earlier. Students underline the important words. Do not check answers at this stage as students will listen and check in Exercise 12.

12 🔊 **2.2** Either play the audio or model the sentence to elicit from the students the words that are stressed.

> **Answers**
>
> The important words are stressed: It is an <u>interesting</u> <u>event</u> to <u>come</u> to.

13 👥 Do the first one with the whole class by writing it on the board and then saying the sentence, putting stress on *things* and *do* to elicit that these are the important words. Underline the words as students identify them. Ask students to work in pairs to find the stressed words in the other sentences. Encourage them to say the sentences out loud to each other.

14 (◄) 2.3 👤 Play the audio for students to check their answers. Play the audio again for students to repeat, and/or drill the sentences with the class, stressing the important words.

> **Answers**
> 1 … what kind of <u>things</u> do people <u>do</u>?
> 2 Are there any <u>things</u> you <u>don't like</u> …?
> 3 Have you <u>got many people here</u> from <u>other countries</u>?

15 👥 Students work with a partner to write questions, using the key words given. If appropriate, you can either do the first one with the class and/or write the following extra words on the board to help the students: *in, your.*

> **Answers**
> 1 What activities do you do in your free time?
> 2 Have you got any hobbies?
> 3 Can you describe your last weekend?

16 👥 Before asking students to underline the important words, write the sentences on the board and drill them with students, stressing the important words, i.e. those underlined below. Allow 2 minutes for this activity, before inviting feedback from students or inviting them to come to the board and underline the words.

> **Answers**
> 1 What <u>activities</u> do you <u>do</u> in your <u>free</u> <u>time</u>? 2 Have you <u>got</u> any <u>hobbies</u>? 3 Can you <u>describe</u> your <u>last</u> <u>weekend</u>?

17 👥 Students work with a partner to ask and answer the questions.

> **Optional activity**
> 👥 Remind students of the note-taking they did earlier. Ask students to make notes of their partner's answers in Exercise 17. Put students into new pairs and ask them to ask and answer on behalf of their first partner.

⊙ LANGUAGE DEVELOPMENT

REVIEW OF PRESENT TENSE QUESTION FORMS

1 👤 Ask students to open their books at page 39 and complete Exercise 1 individually.

> **Answers**
> 1 <u>learn</u> 2 <u>are</u> 3 <u>enjoying</u> (Present continuous)

2 👥 Draw students' attention to the Explanation box and give them a couple of minutes to read the information, or read it aloud with students following. Ask students in pairs to identify and correct the two incorrect statements in the Explanation box. Concept-check by asking students the following: 'What do we use in questions when the main verb is in the Present simple?' to elicit *do*; 'What auxiliaries do we use when the main verb is in the *-ing* form?' to elicit *is/are*; 'What do we use in questions with adjectives or nouns?' to elicit *is/are*.

> **Answers**
> 3 Present <u>continuous</u> 4 am/is/are

> **Language note**
> Question forms in English are often very difficult for students because of the change of word order and the use of either the auxiliary verb *to do* or the verb *to be*. More practice may be needed to help students fully assimilate the grammar rules. Particularly useful activities are those where students have to put the words in a sentence in the correct order.
>
> If you would like to give further explanation, especially to help students understand why we use the auxiliary *do/does*, write the following statements on the board, one underneath the other. *You are good at music. You are listening to music. You like music.* Ask students: 'What do you need to do to make these statements into questions?' to elicit that they need to swap the subject and verb in the first two. But for the last one, '*like you music?*' doesn't work in English. We can't have the main verb at the beginning of the sentence, so instead of changing the positions of the words, we add *do* (or *does* if it is third person singular) to the beginning of the sentence. You can tell students that *do* is a helping verb as it helps the other verbs make questions and negatives.

3 👥 Tell students that they are going to listen to an interview with the organizer of a food festival. Concept-check *interview* by asking students: 'What is the difference between a lecture and an interview?' to elicit that in an interview someone is asked questions. If appropriate, do the first one with the class. Students then work in pairs to correct the questions. Allow about 3 minutes for this. Do not check answers at this stage.

4 🔊 2.4 👤 Play the audio so that students can check their answers to Exercise 3.

> **Answers**
>
> 1 <u>Do</u> you like your job?
> 2 <u>Are</u> you a chef?
> 3 What time <u>does</u> the festival start?
> 4 What kinds of food <u>do</u> you have?
> 5 <u>Is</u> it all good?
> 6 Where <u>do</u> people eat their lunch?
> 7 <u>Are</u> the people coming here to buy food or eat it?
> 8 <u>Is</u> the work interesting?

5 👤👥 Tell students to use the prompts to make questions with either *is/are* or *do/does*. If appropriate, do the first one with the class. Ask students to check with a partner, before inviting feedback from the class.

> **Answers**
>
> 1 Do you like fish and meat? 2 Do other people like your food? 3 Are you a good cook? 4 Do you feel hungry now?

6 👥 Students work with a partner to ask and answer the questions in Exercise 5. Allow about 4 minutes for this. To extend the activity, put students into new pairs and ask them to ask about their previous partners. Model this with one of the students.

COLLOCATIONS

7 👥 Read the Explanation box aloud while students follow. If they need more help, explain that collocations are two words that usually go together to form word partnerships. They can be any combination of word categories. Collocations form a key part of the English language and it is good for students to be aware of them and to learn words as part of collocations. Simple examples to illustrate

this with students are *make a mistake* (not *do a mistake*), *have a cup of coffee* (not *take a cup of coffee*). Highlight how we use the verb *go to* with *talks, classes* and *class*. Point out the example with each circle and ask students to make a sentence for each phrase, e.g. *Can I take a photograph of you with my new camera?* Ask students to work with a partner to complete the task.

> **Answers**
>
> **go to:** a festival, a concert, a celebration, an exam, a lecture, a party, school, university
> **take:** a photograph, a test, an exam, advice, care, notes, your time
> **have:** a nice time, a test, a celebration, an exam, a lecture, a party, fun, a problem

8 👤👥 Students work individually to fill in the gaps with the correct form of *go, have* or *take*. If appropriate, do the first one with the class. Ask students to check with a partner, before inviting feedback from the class.

> **Answers**
>
> 1 take 2 go 3 take 4 Have 5 take

9 👤👥 Students work individually to complete the sentences, using words from Exercise 7 in the correct form. Highlight that more than one answer may be possible. Ask students to check with a partner, before inviting feedback from the class.

> **Answers**
>
> 1 lectures 2 an exam / a test 3 university 4 problem 5 party/celebration

10 👥 Ask students to work with a partner to ask and answer the questions. Allow about 6 minutes for this, before inviting feedback from the class. To extend this activity, ask students to make notes of their partner's answers and then move to work with a different partner, asking and answering questions about their first partner. Do not invite feedback after the first part and allow another 5 minutes for this, before inviting feedback from the class.

LISTENING 2

PREPARING TO LISTEN

UNDERSTANDING KEY VOCABULARY

Optional lead-in

Books closed. Ask students: 'Do you eat any special food during celebrations in your country?' Encourage as many ideas as possible and ask follow-up questions, such as: 'Do you eat this at home or in a restaurant?' 'Do you invite family or friends to share it?' 'Do you stay in your home or go to other people's homes?'

---

1 👥 Tell students that they are going to listen to a talk about celebrations and food and ask them to open their books at page 42. Ask them to work with a partner to match the words to their definitions. Allow about 3 minutes for this, before inviting feedback from the class.

| Answers
| 1 f 2 e 3 g 4 h 5 b 6 c 7 d 8 a

2 👥 Students work with a partner to see which of the words in Exercise 1 they can see in the photographs. Allow 2 minutes for this, before inviting feedback from the class.

| Answers
| a dish b dish c layers, decorations d noodles

WHILE LISTENING

LISTENING FOR MAIN IDEAS

Language note

Point out that, in order to test students' understanding of the English language, questions may not have the same content words that are used in the text. Therefore it is important to be aware of the use of words with similar meanings, or synonyms, which will help students to answer the question. To concept-check that students understand *words with a similar meaning*, write the following words on the board and ask students to find the three pairs of words: *food, university, day, college, meal, 24 hours* (food – meal, university – college, day – 24 hours).

---

3 👥 Students work with a partner to match the phrases to the underlined words with similar meanings. If appropriate, do the first one with the class.

| Answers
| 1 f 2 d 3 a 4 c 5 g 6 e 7 h 8 b

4 🔊 2.5 👤👥 Tell students to look at phrases a–h in Exercise 3, listen to the audio and tick the categories they hear about. If appropriate, ask students to check with a partner, before inviting feedback from the class.

| Answers
| a, c, d, e

LISTENING FOR EXAMPLES

5 🔊 2.5 👤👥 Explain that when people are giving a talk, they will usually give examples to make the talk more interesting. Tell students that in this section they are going to learn how to recognize examples. Play the audio again. Students work on their own to match the country to the wedding food. If appropriate, ask students to check with a partner, before inviting feedback from the class.

| Answers
| 1 e 2 a 3 d 4 c 5 b

POST-LISTENING

RECOGNIZING EXAMPLES

6 🔊 2.6 👤👥 Tell students that they are going to listen to parts of the audio again and they should listen for the phrases that are used to introduce examples so that they can complete the sentences. Play the audio, pausing if necessary to allow students time to write the phrases. If appropriate, ask students to check with a partner, before inviting feedback from the class.

| Answers
| 1 such as 2 like 3 for instance 4 for example

7 👥 Students work with a partner to answer the questions.

| Answers
| 1 such as, like 2 for instance, for example

8 👥 Look at the example for the first sentence and elicit other examples of sweet things that students like. Give students 1 minute of thinking time to complete the sentences. Ask students to discuss their ideas with a partner. Allow 5 minutes for this, before inviting feedback from the class.

> Answers will vary.

9 👥 Students work with a partner to discuss the food that is eaten at festivals or celebrations in their country. If you have a class of mixed nationalities, make sure that students are paired with people from a different country. Allow about 3 minutes for this, before inviting feedback from the class. Put students into groups and give each group a festival or a celebration. These can include national or religious festivals or family occasions such as weddings or graduation parties. Students work in their group to agree the food that is eaten on that occasion. Students then move to different groups where they share their ideas with the rest of the group. Ask each group to decide which festival or celebration has the best food.

CRITICAL THINKING

Students begin to think about the Speaking task that they will do at the end of the unit (*Discuss a new festival and make suggestions for events. Give a poster presentation about your festival to the rest of your group.*). Give them a minute to look at the box. As a class, you could spend a few minutes brainstorming some ideas for types of festivals for the Speaking task.

Background note

A poster presentation usually gives the results of some academic research which are made public at an academic conference. It is different from a standard presentation in that all the information is displayed on a poster, which is often attached to a movable wall. For a period of time, the authors of the research are available to answer questions. In this activity, the context could be a trade fair to promote the students' country at an international tourism event. How much time you allow for producing the poster will depend on how much time you have available, but the emphasis of this activity is on what the students say rather than what they put on the poster. The poster preparation can be given for homework.

CREATE

1 👥 Students work in pairs to look at the photographs and answer the questions. If appropriate, do the first one with the class.

Possible answers

1 a is a big sporting event (a football match) b is a motor show 2 Answers will vary. 3 a in a sports stadium b in a exhibition centre 4 a people watch sports/football b people look at and sometimes buy cars 5 a and b fast food and food in restaurants

2 👤 Students work individually to complete the table. Allow 5 minutes for this. Then elicit feedback from the class and ask students to read the Organizing ideas box.

Answers

Sports event: Time – afternoon or evening; Food – fast food and restaurant food; Activities – spectators watch the match/event; Sights and sounds – a big crowd of people/spectators cheering, shouting, singing
Motor show: Time – all day; Food – fast food and restaurant food; Activities – people look at/admire and sometimes buy cars; Sights and sounds – people talking

SPEAKING

PREPARATION FOR SPEAKING

MAKING SUGGESTIONS

Optional lead-in

Write on the board *making suggestions* and then say: 'Open the window' and ask students if this is a suggestion, to elicit *no* (it is an instruction). Then say: 'Can you open the window?' and ask if this is a suggestion, to elicit *no* (it is a question/request). Ask if anyone can make a suggestion about opening the window, to elicit *You could open the window* or *How about opening the window?* or *Why not open the window?*. You only need to accept one correct response, or if students are unable to give a correct sentence, give them one of the above.

1 👥 Tell students that these are suggestions from Listening 2 and ask them to work in pairs to put them in the correct order.

Answers

1 You could look at this online.
2 How about starting with wedding cake?
3 Why not try it yourself?

2 👤👥 Students work on their own to tick the suggestions. If appropriate, ask students to check with a partner, before inviting feedback from the class.

> **Answers**
>
> 3 4 5

3 👥 Students work with a partner to complete the table with the appropriate phrases from Exercises 1 and 2. Point out that the heading of each column is the form of the verb which follows the suggestion phrase. Do the first one with the class.

> **Answers**
>
> 1 You could 2 Why not 3 Shall we 4 How about
> 5 I'd suggest 6 Can we think about

4 👥 Tell students that they are going to complete the dialogue when two people discuss which events to go to at a festival, using phrases from Exercise 3. Ask students to work with a partner and point out that more than one phrase is possible for some gaps. They should try not to use the same expression more than once, and some words/phrases aren't exactly as in Exercise 3. Remind students of the importance of the verb form following a gap, and they should notice whether the sentence with a gap ends with a full stop or a question mark, as this will determine to some extent which phrases can be used. If appropriate, do the first one with the class. Do not check answers at this stage.

5 👥 Students work with a different partner and read the dialogue aloud to each other. It might be helpful for you to allocate the roles of 'man' and 'woman' to each student. Ask students to see if they have the same phrases. While students are doing this, circulate and monitor to check that they have correct answers. Invite feedback from the class.

> **Answers**
>
> 1 Shall 2 How about / Can we think about 3 could
> 4 how about / can we think about 5 shall / could

6 👥 Ask students to close their books with their finger at page 45 and ask them: 'Can you remember how people responded to being given suggestions?'. Prompt by asking them

if people answered just 'yes' or 'no' (no, they didn't). Explain that while we do respond with a yes, it is rarely on its own. Ask students to work with a partner and look at the dialogue to identify one way of saying 'no' and four ways of saying 'yes'. Allow 2 minutes for this, before inviting feedback from the class.

> **Answers**
>
> **no:** I am not sure if that is a good idea.
> **yes:** Yes. Fantastic; OK. Good idea; Yes, that sounds good; Yes, I'd love to! That's a great idea!

7 👤 Tell students they are all going to Singapore during the festival season and that they need to choose two things they would like to do. Encourage students to ask you if there are any words or phrases in the website text that they don't understand. Allow about 4 minutes for this.

> **Answers will vary.**

> **Background note**
>
> Mooncakes are small, sweet pastries.
> Dragon boats are long, narrow boats, typically decorated with a dragon's head at the front and tail at the back.

8 👥 Put students into groups of 3 and tell them that they must decide on two events that they would like to go to. If appropriate, make sure that the key phrases are on the board to help them use appropriate language for making and responding to suggestions. Allow about 6 minutes for this. Circulate, monitor and give assistance where needed. Do not do feedback at this stage.

SPEAKING TASK

PREPARE

1 👥 Give students a minute to read the box and remind themselves of the Speaking task they are going to do. Students then work with a partner to complete the table about their own festival together. Remind students that they can use ideas from the unit or any other ideas they can think of. If appropriate, brainstorm with the class some ideas and write them on the board before they do this activity. Do not do any feedback at this stage.

2 Tell students that they are now going to analyze the Singapore Mosaic Music Festival's poster presentation. This can be done with the whole class. After checking the answer, you could set a few questions and ask students to speed-read the poster, e.g. *When is the festival?* (March) *How long does it take to get to Sentosa Island?* (15 minutes).

> **Answers**
> five

3 and 4 👥 How much time you allow the class to spend on making the poster will depend on the size of the class, and the time and materials you have available. The poster can be something as simple as some line drawings and writing on a piece of A4 paper or something produced for homework, using pictures from the internet.

PRESENT

5 👥 Students work in pairs to make notes in the box to help with their presentations.

6 👥 Put students into groups of four and allow about 2 minutes for each pair to present their poster to the other pair, with 1 minute of speaking time each and some extra time for questions. Alternatively, if the class is large, put students into groups of 6 so there are 3 pairs. Allow about 2 minutes for each presentation, 1 minute for each partner to talk, and a little longer for questions. Tell each group that they must decide which festival they would like to go to. Finish off by inviting feedback from students about the festivals they would like to go to. If the class is small enough, allow each pair to present to the whole class. Finish off by taking a vote at the end to decide which festival students would like to go to.

ADDITIONAL SPEAKING TASK

See page 135 for the Additional speaking task (*Organizing a festival*) and Model language for this unit

Make a photocopy of page 135 for each student.

Tell the class that they are going to organize a festival about an important aspect of their culture. Write 4 topics on the board (e.g. food, literature, dance, art, music, crafts, or something else, depending on your students' interests and the country you are in).

👥 Divide the class into 4 groups. Give each student a photocopy and assign each group one of the 4 festivals on the board. Students then work to make a list of the reasons why they want to hold this festival. Each student should make a list in prepation for the next stage. Allow 5 minutes for this.

👥 Put the students into new groups of 4, one for each of the festivals on the board. Ask them to discuss each one and then to choose the best. They should be prepared to justify their choice. Allow about 10 minutes for this.

Elicit feedback from all the groups and see which festival is the most popular.

TASK CHECKLIST AND OBJECTIVES REVIEW

Refer students to the end of the unit for the Task checklist and Objectives review. Students complete the tables individually to reflect on their learning and identify areas for improvement.

WORDLIST

See Teaching tips page 10, section 6, for ideas about how to make the most of the Wordlist with your students.

REVIEW TEST

See pages 116–117 for the photocopiable Review test for this unit and page 107 for ideas about when and how to administer the Review test.

RESEARCH PROJECT

Research and explain festivals and celebrations

Divide the class into groups and work with them to produce some interview questions for people from different countries about festivals and celebrations. Students could interview people face-to-face or using a voice-over-IP service to interview people in other countries (e.g. students at a partner school). They will need to film / audio record the interview. Students should focus on the type of festival, customs, food, time and its function.

Each group will create a short video to explain the different festivals, using extracts from the interviews. Students will first need to create a script or storyboard. They will also have to think about who in the class will direct the video, who will work the camera, who will edit the video, and who will present or narrate the video. These will then be played to the class, who will vote for the most interesting festival. There are free online voting systems which allow you to do this. Search for 'voting software' to view some of these. Students could also use the forum on the Cambridge LMS to discuss the different festivals.

3 SCHOOL AND EDUCATION

Learning objectives

Before you start the Unlock your knowledge section, ask students to read the Learning objectives box so that they have a clear idea of what they are going to learn in this unit. Tell them that you will come back to these objectives at the end of the unit when they review what they have learned. Give them the opportunity to ask you any questions they might have.

UNLOCK YOUR KNOWLEDGE

Lead-in

Books closed. Ask students about the educational system in their country: 'At what age do children start school?' 'What is the name of the first school?' (e.g. primary or junior school) 'When do children move to their next school?' 'What is the name of that school?' (e.g. secondary or high school) 'At what age can they leave school?' 'When can they go to college or university?' 'What public exams do they take and when?'

👥 Tell students that they will be thinking about ways of learning, both inside and outside the classroom, and ask them to open their books at page 51. Ask them to work with a partner to discuss the questions. If appropriate, do question 1 with the whole class, referring to the photo. Allow about 4 minutes for this. Finish off by inviting feedback from some of the students and ask if other students agree or disagree where appropriate.

Optional activity

👤 Ask students individually to research on the internet new ways of learning. This is a follow-up to question 4 and will also help students with the Speaking task at the end of the unit. Either allow students to find a variety of new learning techniques or put students into groups and allocate a different learning technique to each group. Suggested new learning ideas can include: learning through mobile devices, e.g. smartphones and tablets; distance and online learning; using the internet in the classroom; blended learning (combining traditional learning in classrooms / lecture theatres with online/distance learning).

WATCH AND LISTEN

Video script

▶ This is morning in a primary school in China. The children are having assembly. This is when the teachers check that all the children are at school and call out the names of the children in their class. Each class has about 37 students.

This is Wushu City in China, a town that is famous for training in martial arts. There are schools like this all over the town, with thousands of students. The students live in very simple rooms with no heating. They get up at five in the morning and the training is very difficult. Children and teenagers travel here from all over China for one reason: to get a job. Getting a certificate from one of these schools can get them a job in the army, as a security guard, or in the police. All well-paid jobs for life, but they must work very hard to complete their education first.

This is a boarding school in India. The boys live, sleep and eat here. They take the same lessons as any other Indian school; from maths, to geography and languages. Without families, the boys make friends quickly. Anuj says he has exactly 106 friends! This school gives them hope for the future.

In this village in South Africa, children like Thobela Sohobese walk ten kilometres a day to school. Thobela is fourteen years old. Thobela's school doesn't have many text books. So the teacher uses newspapers. The teacher hopes that his students will get good jobs. Thobela wants to be the first person in her family to go to high school and university. She hopes to become a teacher. The school has a kitchen and feeds three hundred children each day. For many of them, it is their only hot meal. At home, Thobela and her brothers and sister eat together. After dinner Thobela does her homework. … She is studying for her end-of-year exams. It is the day of the exam results. Thobela has passed. She is very happy because she wants to find a good job when she is older and help her parents.

PREPARING TO WATCH

ACTIVATING YOUR KNOWLEDGE

Optional lead-in

Ask students: 'Do you think children all over the world have the same education as you had?' (no). Write the following numbers on the board: *10 million, 25 million, 70 million*. Tell students that many children in the world don't go to school at all. Ask: 'How many children do you think don't go to school?' Point to each number and ask for a show of hands (70 million). You could ask students: 'Why do you think this is?'

(poverty, some children have to work, countries where there is war, in some countries families don't like to send girls to school). And/Or you could ask students: 'What would your life be like if you hadn't been to school?' Point out that if children don't learn to read and write, then they can't easily become part of society. Move on to ask students: 'Do you know about any other education systems in other countries?' Encourage any contributions but if there are none, tell students that they are going to learn about education in some other countries.

1 👥 Tell students that they are going to watch a video about students in China, India and South Africa. Students work in pairs to choose the correct definition. If the class is strong, ask them to try first without their dictionaries. Allow about 4 minutes for this, before inviting feedback from the class. Tell students that *high school* is often referred to as a *secondary school* in the UK.

> **Answers**
> 1 b 2 a 3 b 4 a 5 b 6 b 7 a 8 a

2 👤👥 Students work individually to complete the sentences. Allow about 5 minutes for this. Ask students to check with a partner, before inviting feedback from the class.

> **Answers**
> 1 results 2 education 3 primary 4 feed 5 high school 6 pass 7 training 8 martial arts

3 👥 Students work with a partner to discuss if they agree with the sentences in Exercise 2, giving reasons for what they decide. Allow about 6 minutes for this. Circulate, monitor and give assistance where appropriate, before inviting feedback from the class.

> **Answers will vary.**

4 👥 Students work in pairs to predict whether schools in China, India and South Africa will be the same as or different from each other. Allow 2 minutes for this, before inviting feedback from the class. This could also be done as a whole-class debate. Write the students' predictions on the board. Do not check answers at this stage.

WHILE WATCHING

LISTENING FOR KEY INFORMATION

5 ▶ Ask students to watch the video and check their predictions from Exercise 4, which are on the board. Play the video. Were the students correct? Check all their ideas.

> **Answers will vary.**

6 👥 Students work with a partner to complete the sentences with the numbers. Allow about 3 minutes for this. Do not check answers at this stage.

7 ▶👤 Play the video again. Ask students to work individually to check their answers, before inviting feedback from the class.

> **Answers**
> 1 37 2 106 3 10 4 14 5 1st 6 300

DISCUSSION

8 👥 Students work with a partner to answer the questions. Allow about 3 minutes for this, before inviting feedback from the class. This activity can be extended by putting students into groups of four to share their ideas and see if they agree.

> **Optional activity**
>
> 👤👥 If your students are pre-university, ask them to research which courses they would like to do at university. In class, ask students which subjects they would like to study and put them into groups of the same subjects. Tell them to research which is the best university to do this course, what they will study on the course and what they think they will enjoy most about the course. If your students are in higher education, ask them to research the jobs they would like to do. In class, ask students what jobs they would like to do and put them into groups of the same/similar jobs. Ask them to find out what training they will need, what the job will involve and what they think they will like most about the job.

LISTENING 1

PREPARING TO LISTEN
UNDERSTANDING KEY VOCABULARY

Optional lead-in

Ask the class to think of some of the subjects that are studied at university, and accept six to eight subjects before moving on. Then ask students to think of the buildings of the university and what 'rooms' there are, and accept about four rooms. Ask students: 'Does anyone know the name of the place we walk down/ along to get to our classroom?' (to elicit *corridor*). Finally, ask students: 'What different types of people are there at a university?' to elicit *professor, student, lecturer, tutor*.

1 👥 Tell students that they are going to listen to some visitors on a tour of a university and in pairs ask them to write the words in the correct categories.

Answers

1 **subjects**: Biology, Physics, French, Chemistry, Geography, History, Art, Maths
2 **places**: classroom, computer room, laboratory, library, corridor, office, stairs
3 **people**: teacher, lecturer

PRONUNCIATION FOR LISTENING

2 👥 👥👥 Tell students to look at the first word *classroom* in the box in Exercise 1 and say it out loud for students to repeat. Ask them: 'Where is the stress?' (<u>class</u>room). Write it on the board and underline <u>class</u>. Ask students: 'How many syllables does *classroom* have?' (two). Then ask: 'Which column of the table will it go in?' (B). Then look at the example for *lecturer* and which column it is in. Students work with a partner and complete the table by saying the words out loud and deciding where the stress is. Allow 6 to 8 minutes for this, before inviting feedback from the class.

Answers

A	B	C	D
French (subject) Art (subject) Maths (subject) stairs (place)	classroom (place) Physics (subject) teacher (person) office (place)	lecturer (person) Chemistry (subject) Geography (subject) History (subject) library (place) corridor (place)	Biology (subject) computer room (place) laboratory (place)

3 👥👥 Students work in groups of 3 to discuss the questions. Allow about 5 minutes for this, before inviting feedback from the class.

Answers will vary.

4 👥 Read the Using visual clues box aloud while students follow. Then tell students that the map in their book on page 55 is of the university that they will hear about on a tour that they are going to listen to. Students work with a partner and answer the questions. Allow about 6 minutes for this, before inviting feedback from the class.

Possible answers

1 the library, the hall 2 borrow books; meet people, wait for people 3 a is opposite the stairs; b is next to room a / on the right of room a; c is to the left of room a; d (the library) is between rooms b and c / opposite room f; e is next to the library / down the corridor on the left; f is opposite room b

WHILE LISTENING

5 🔊 3.1 👥👥 Play the audio. Students work individually to complete the map with the places 1–7. Ask students to check their answers with a partner, before inviting feedback from the class.

Answers

2 canteen a 3 laboratories g 4 lecture theatre f
5 events office c 6 international office b
7 computer room e

Language note

In Exercise 2, point out that Josh is American and therefore uses the American English pronunciation for *laboratories* ('læb.rə.tɔːr.iz) whereas Ali uses the British English pronunciation *laboratories* (ləˈbɒr.ə.triz).

6 (◄)) 3.1 ▌▌ Play the audio again. Students work individually and match the places in Exercise 5 to what you can do there. After the audio, ask students to check their answers with a partner, before inviting feedback from the class.

> **Answers**
> 1 d 2 e 3 g 4 b 5 f 6 a 7 c

POST-LISTENING

7 ▌▌ Tell students that they are going to look at language to use when they want to explain purpose, i.e. the reason why something is done. Students work individually to match the sentence halves. Point out that *help* in this instance is being used as a noun. Allow about 2 minutes for this. If appropriate, ask students to check their answers with a partner, before inviting feedback from the class.

> **Answers**
> 1 a 2 c 3 b

8 ▌▌ Students work individually to write sentences of purpose, using the rules in Exercise 7. If appropriate, do one example for the first question with the whole class. Allow about 4 minutes for this. Ask students to check with a partner, before inviting feedback from the class.

> **Answers**
> 1 We go to a canteen for food / to eat. A canteen is a place where we can get food.
> 2 We go to a library for books / to read. A library is a place where you can read.
> 3 We go to a lecture to get information / to learn. A lecture theatre is a place where you can learn.

DISCUSSION

9 ▌▌ Students work with a partner to answer the questions. Allow about 4 to 5 minutes for this, before inviting feedback. For questions 1 and 3, ask students 'Why?' to encourage them to express purpose.

⊙ LANGUAGE DEVELOPMENT

COLLOCATIONS ABOUT LEARNING

> **Optional lead-in**
>
> Ask students if they remember what collocations are, to elicit *words that go together* or *word partnerships* or *words that like to be friends*, or any other explanation that fits. Tell them you are going to give them some nouns and ask them to call out the verb(s) that could go with them: school – go to, notes – take, fun – have, an exam – take / have.

1 Tell students that they are going to learn some collocations about learning and education. Ask them to look at the four verbs and subjects from the listening. Ask: 'Which verb is the odd one out and why?'

> **Answers**
> *teach* as all the others are things a student does

2 ▌▌ Students work with a partner to complete the sentences, using verbs from Exercise 1.

> **Answers**
> 1 study 2 learn 3 revise

3 ▌▌ Students work with a partner to discuss whether the sentences in Exercise 2 are true or false (for them for 1; generally for 2 and 3). Ask students to think of reasons for their answers and see if they agree or disagree with their partner. Allow about 4 minutes for this, before inviting feedback from the class. Encourage debate by asking students if they agree or disagree with the feedback from other students.

> **Answers will vary.**

REVIEW OF PREPOSITIONAL PHRASES

> **Language note**
>
> Explain that a prepositional phrase is made up of a preposition, its object and any of the object's modifiers, and they can modify nouns, verbs or complete phrases. The following section looks at prepositional phrases to define location. They answer the question 'where?'.

4 👥 Ask students to look at the example. Write *we* and *stairs* on the board and ask students: 'Where are we in relation to the stairs?' to elicit *in front of the stairs*. Write this on the board, underline it and tell students that this is a prepositional phrase which gives the relationship between two places. Students work with a partner to underline the prepositional phrases in the exercise.

> **Answers**
>
> 2 opposite the stairs 3 On the right, next to the canteen 4 to the left of the canteen 5 on the left 6 the second on the left 7 on the first floor

5 👥 Put students into small groups of 3 or 4 and ask them to look at the pairs of sentences to decide what the difference in meaning between them is. Ask them to draw diagrams to show the differences if possible.

> **Answers**
>
> 1 a If you go past the library and round the back of it, you come to the computer room. b If you stand in the doorway of the library, looking away from it, the computer room is on the other side of the corridor.
> 2 a She lives not far from the university. b She lives in a building beside the university, in the closest building to it.
> 3 a If you stand opposite the canteen, the lecture theatre is the room on the right. b If you walk past the canteen, there's a room on your right after it. Then there's another room – the lecture theatre.

BASIC VERB PATTERNS

> **Language note**
>
> There are a number of structures which can follow a verb and there are no simple rules for this. It is necessary to learn, for each verb, the structures that can follow it. Thus it is important to encourage students not just to learn the meaning of a verb but what structures follow it, and to put verbs, as with other vocabulary they learn, into example sentences.

6 👤👥 Ask students to work individually and underline the main verb in the sentence and look at the verb that follows it. If different coloured pens are available, students should underline the following verb in a different colour. Point out that the second verb may not come immediately after the first verb.

> **Answers**
>
> 1 want (to pass) 2 enjoyed (studying) 3 started (to apply) 4 began (talking) 5 didn't mind (helping) 6 apologized (for being) 7 planning (on going) 8 began (to learn) 9 started (getting) 10 agreed (to answer)

7 👥 If possible, show the table on the board, or copy it onto the board. Explain to students that when two verbs come together, they usually follow one of the patterns in the table. There is no rule for this and the vocabulary just has to be learned. Go through each example, matching the parts of the verb with the descriptions, for example, *is interested* (verb) *in* (preposition) *learning* (verb + *ing*). Students work in pairs to complete the rest of the table. Allow 5 to 6 minutes for this, before inviting feedback and writing the words on the board.

> **Answers**
>
> 1 apologize for 2 planning on 3 begin ('begin to learn Arabic …' and '… begin talking …') 4 start ('start to apply …' and 'start getting …') 5 want 6 agree 7 enjoy 8 mind

8 👤👥 Tell students that they are now going to practise these structures. Answer the first question with the class, eliciting that both infinitive and verb + *ing* are possible. Students work individually to complete the sentences. Allow about 5 minutes for this. Ask students to check their answers with a partner, before inviting feedback from the class.

> **Answers**
>
> 1 learning / to learn 2 reading 3 to speak 4 doing 5 working / to work 6 to help 7 talking about 8 to leave 9 driving 10 paying 11 discussing

LISTENING 2

PREPARING TO LISTEN

> **Optional lead-in**
>
> Books closed. Ask students who has a laptop at home. Do they use it to help them learn English? How? Then ask who has a smartphone. Do they use it to help them learn English? How? Finally, who has a tablet? Do they use it to help them learn English? How? If none of the students use this technology to help them learn English, you could suggest the following: **laptop:** using Word with a spell-checker on to improve their spelling, connection to the internet for specialist English-language websites; **smartphone:** there are apps that can help with learning English; **tablet:** apps and websites.

ACTIVATING YOUR KNOWLEDGE

1 Ask students to open their books at page 60 and look at the photographs to identify what kinds of technology the students are using.

> **Answers**
> Online learning on PCs, tablets and laptops

2 👥 Tell students that they are going to listen to some trainee teachers talking about using technology to learn. Students work with a partner to discuss if they think technology helps learning. Why / Why not? Allow 2–3 minutes for this, before inviting feedback from the class. Students will probably say it does help so suggest reasons why it might not, e.g. students don't actually do much, they just watch what is happening; the technology is very clever and students are impressed but there isn't any learning happening; it can break down or run out of power, which doesn't happen with books and boards. Encourage students to agree or disagree and give reasons. Alternatively, do this as a whole-class discussion, asking students if they think that technology helps learning and to give their reasons why or why not. Encourage students to agree or disagree and give their reasons.

PRONUNCIATION FOR LISTENING

3 Tell students to look at the sentence from Listening 2 and answer the question. Ask them how they can tell.

> **Answers**
> agreeing (because the words alone suggest agreement)

4 🔊 **3.2** 👤 Read the Understanding intonation box while the students follow. You could point out that people sometimes start by saying 'I agree' just to be polite, but the sound of their voice tells you they will add more and that they actually disagree. Tell students that in this section they will learn to understand the intonation, that is the sound patterns, we use when agreeing and disagreeing. Then play the audio which contains the sentence spoken twice; once to show agreement when the voice falls, and once to show disagreement when the voice falls and then rises. Ask

students to circle the correct response. After checking answers, drill the sentence, for both agreeing and disagreeing. Play the audio again and/or model the sentences yourself for students to repeat. Then just say 'agree' or 'disagree' for students to say the sentence with the correct intonation.

> **Answers**
> 1 agreeing 2 disagreeing

5 🔊 **3.3** 👤👥 Tell students that they are going to listen to more sentences from Listening 2. Students work individually to decide if the speaker is agreeing or disagreeing. Ask students to check their answers with a partner, before inviting feedback from the class.

> **Answers**
> 1 disagreeing 2 agreeing 3 disagreeing 4 disagreeing

WHILE LISTENING

LISTENING FOR DETAIL

6 🔊 **3.4** 👤 Tell students that they are now going to listen to the trainee teachers talking about different ways of learning and ask them to number the subjects in the order they hear them discussed.

> **Answers**
> 1 b 2 a 3 c 4 d

7 🔊 **3.4** 👤👥 Tell students that they are going to listen to the audio again and this time they have to match the people to the ideas. Point out that each idea may match more than one person. Play the audio. Students work individually to match the people to the ideas. Allow students to check their answers with a partner, before inviting feedback from the class.

> **Answers**
> 1 Sarah b, c, e 2 Nazlihan b, c, d, e 3 Peter a, e

POST-LISTENING

8 👥 Tell students that these sentences come from Listening 2. Do the first one with the class. Students work with a partner to decide if the sentences show agreement or disagreement. Highlight that one sentence shows both.

> **Answers**
>
> a 1, 3, 5
> b 2, 4 (although Peter is agreeing with Sarah's idea that it is convenient, he is disagreeing with her support for the small screen)

DISCUSSION

9 👤 Tell students that they are going to read some statements about learning. Students work individually and make notes about their reasons. Allow 2–3 minutes for this and circulate and monitor, offering help where required. If possible, make a note of which students are agreeing with which statements. Do not check answers at this stage.

10 👥 Put students into groups of 3, where possible ensuring that they do not all have the same responses. Students take it in turns to give their ideas and the rest of the group has to agree or disagree politely. Allow 5–6 minutes for this, before inviting feedback from the class. This activity can be extended by moving students into new groups to repeat the activity. Finish off by inviting groups to give feedback to the class. Encourage agreement or disagreement from the rest of the class.

CRITICAL THINKING

Students begin to think about the Speaking task that they will do at the end of the unit (*Hold a debate about whether students should choose how they learn. Explain if you agree or disagree with your classmates during the debate*). You could give some of the preparation work for this as homework.

UNDERSTAND

1 👤 Ask students to read the Holding a debate box on page 62. If necessary, explain that a debate is a formal discussion among a number of people, typically with one group arguing in favour of a statement and one against it.

Tell students to look at the Idea wheel. Students work individually and write the words from the box in the correct places on the wheel. Allow about 2 minutes for this. Ask students to check their answers with a partner, before inviting feedback from the class.

> **Answers**
>
> **people:** teacher, lecturer, student
> **places:** classroom, primary school, computer room, laboratory
> **ways of learning:** traditional, online, blended

2 👤 Give students a minute to read the debating topic and decide if they are 'for' or 'against' it.

3 👥 Students work with a partner to make notes in the diagram in Exercise 2 about whether the sentences are 'for' or 'against' the topic.

> **Answers**
>
> 'against': 1 5 7 8   'for': 2 3 4 6

4 👥 Students work with a partner (the same one as in Exercise 3 or a different one) to think of more arguments 'for' and 'against' the debating topic in Exercise 2 and to add them to the diagram.

5 👥 Tell students that this exercise is to practise the correct intonation for agreeing, disagreeing and giving reasons. Ask the students to work with a partner and to take it in turns to read out the debating topic from Exercise 2 and to agree or disagree with it using *Yes, I agree because …* or *Yes, but …* and giving one of the reasons from Exercise 3 or their own ideas. This activity can be extended by asking students to always respond by agreeing, then to always respond by disagreeing and/or asking students to swap roles so they are responding to the statements that they read out the first time. Do the first one with the class. Ask a student to read out a sentence for you to respond. Then allow 1 minute of silent thinking time to allow students to prepare their responses and perhaps write some one-word notes. Finish off by inviting feedback from some students and encouraging agreement or disagreement from the rest of the class.

> Answers will vary.

SPEAKING

PREPARATION FOR SPEAKING

> **Optional lead-in**
>
> Books closed. Tell students that although they have been thinking about school and learning, there are many things that people learn outside school. Ask: 'Can anyone think of any skills that we learn outside school?' If necessary, give them an example from your own life, such as driving lessons, a sport, cooking. Encourage students to be as creative and ambitious as possible.

1 👥 Ask students to open their books at page 64. Students work with a partner and look at the photographs and answer the questions. Allow 3–4 minutes for this, before inviting feedback from the class. It is likely that students won't know all the vocabulary so encourage them to describe the activities as best they can, e.g. *looking after a car*, and then you can write 'car maintenance' on the board.

> **Answers**
>
> 1 yoga, car maintenance, painting, scuba diving, gardening 2, 3, 4 Answers will vary.

2 👤👥 Tell students that later they are going to hold a debate about learning skills and that when preparing for a debate it is important to analyze the topic carefully and to plan your argument. Students work individually to underline the key words. Allow 1 minute for this. If appropriate, ask students to check their answers with a partner, before inviting feedback from the class.

> **Answers**
>
> skills, learn, life, more useful, skills, learn, school

3 👤 Students work on their own to think of 3 arguments 'for' and 'against' and add them to the chart in Exercise 2.

4 👥 Students work with a partner to compare notes and add at least two more arguments for and against the topic of the debate. If you think students need assistance with this, brainstorm ideas first. Tell them they can draw more boxes onto the chart to add their ideas.

Allow about 3 minutes for this, before inviting feedback from the class. Write the 'against' and 'for' arguments in the table on the board so that students have a reference for Exercise 6.

> **Answers will vary.**

5 👤👥 Tell students that in a debate they can use a number of phrases for agreeing and disagreeing as well as for giving opinions. Students work individually to complete the table with the phrases in the box. Allow about 6 minutes for this. If appropriate, ask students to check their answers with a partner, before inviting feedback from the class. If possible, put the table on the board to help with the speaking activity.

> **Answers**
>
> | giving your opinion | agreeing | disagreeing |
> | --- | --- | --- |
> | 1 I think
2 It seems to me
3 In my opinion
4 I feel | 5 I agree
6 I totally agree
7 That's true
8 Yes, that's right
9 Exactly!
10 You're right | 11 Yes, but
12 It's good but
13 I am not really sure
14 I don't think so
15 I don't agree with that
16 Yes, I see what you are saying but |

6 👥 Put students into groups of 3 and allocate each student A, B or C. If there is one student over, make a group of 4 with the extra student as A. If there are two students over, put them into a separate group and ask them both to tick phrases used during the activity. Tell students that they are going to discuss the statements in the flow chart on page 64, giving different opinions and using the phrases in the table in Exercise 5 to help. If possible, they should also give reasons. Remind students of the importance of using correct intonation. Seat the groups as far away from each other as possible. Allow 1 minute for silent thinking time before starting. Allow about 10 minutes for this and finish off by asking each group who had the best arguments. Ask Student Cs to feed back on how many phrases from Exercise 6 Student As and Bs used.

SPEAKING TASK

PREPARE

1 👤 Give students a minute to read the box and remind themselves of the Speaking task they are going to do. Students then work on their own to underline the key words in the debating topic in Exercise 1.

> **Answers**
> students choose how learn: class, online, studying home alone

PRACTISE

2 👥 Students work with a partner to decide if they generally agree or disagree with the debating topic and to give reasons. Allow about 2–3 minutes for this, before inviting feedback from the class. Write as many ideas/reasons as possible on the board.

> **Answers will vary.**

DISCUSS

3 👥 Put students into groups of 3, 5 or 7 and allocate the role of chairperson and members of both teams and whether each team agrees or disagrees with the statement. Allow students in their teams to make notes of their arguments on a flow chart like the one on page 64 (Exercise 2) and decide which team member is going to speak about which reason. Give them about 5 minutes for this. Circulate and monitor to make sure each student will be contributing to the debate. The way you manage the debates depends on the size of the class. For classes smaller than 11, it can be done as a whole-class activity. For larger classes, divide students into two groups and put the groups as far away as possible so that they do not disturb each other. Circulate and monitor so that each group has equal amounts of your time. Finish off by inviting feedback from each group as to which argument won.

ADDITIONAL SPEAKING TASK

See page 136 for the Additional speaking task (*Holding a debate*) and Model language for this unit.

Make a photocopy of page 136 for each student.

Tell students that they are going to hold a debate. Write on the board: 'Should schools and universities prepare young people for the world of work by training them to do jobs or should they focus only on academic skills?' Check the students understand this by asking which jobs usually require a university degree (e.g. doctor, lawyer, engineer). Then ask for some academic skills (e.g. languages, mathematics).

👥 Divide the class into two groups. Allocate one group the idea of education for jobs and the other group the idea of education for academic skills. Within each group put the students in pairs. Ask students to think of all reasons for and against their allocated idea. Allow about 10 minutes for this.

Put students in groups of four (two supporting education for jobs and two supporting education for academic skills). Ask students to take it in turns to give their opinion. The others should follow up by either agreeing or disagreeing. Allow about 10 minutes for this.

Finish off by inviting feedback from the class about which idea is the most popular.

TASK CHECKLIST AND OBJECTIVES REVIEW

Refer students to the end of the unit for the Task checklist and Objectives review. Students complete the tables individually to reflect on their learning and identify areas for improvement.

WORDLIST

See Teaching tips page 10, section 6, for ideas about how to make the most of the Wordlist with your students.

REVIEW TEST

See pages 118–119 for the photocopiable Review test for this unit and page 107 for ideas about when and how to administer the Review test.

RESEARCH PROJECT

Create a listening test for your classmates

Explain to your students that each group will create, administer and mark a listening test for the rest of the class. Each group will have to choose a different theme (which could be one from this or previous units), find information on that theme and write an intelligible text. They will then have to audio-record the text and create one or two tasks. They can use the Student's Book to look at some different task types.

Each group will then administer their test to the rest of the class. This could be done during class time, or the groups could upload their test to the Cambridge LMS (e.g. the forum: audio recordings should be saved as 128kb mp3 files) and students could complete the listening tasks for homework.

4 THE INTERNET AND TECHNOLOGY

Learning objectives

Before you start the Unlock your knowledge section, ask students to read the Learning objectives box so that they have a clear idea of what they are going to learn in this unit. Tell them that you will come back to these objectives at the end of the unit when they review what they have learned. Give them the opportunity to ask you any questions they might have.

UNLOCK YOUR KNOWLEDGE

Lead-in

Books closed. Write the word *technology* on the board. Ask students: 'What do you think of when you see this word?' Brainstorm ideas onto the board, and encourage students to be as creative and imaginative as possible.

👥 Tell students that this unit is about the world of technology and to open their books at page 69. Students work with a partner to look at and describe the photograph and answer the questions. Allow about 5 minutes for this, before inviting feedback from the class.

Answers

Answers will vary, but for 4, disadvantages could include: the dangers of using a mobile phone and not paying attention, e.g. driving, crossing roads, being mugged; spending too much time at a computer, e.g. could harm eyesight, posture; addiction to social media sites or online gaming; security issues.

Optional activity

Following on from question 4 above, ask students to do more research on the internet into some of the disadvantages of modern technology.

WATCH AND LISTEN

Video script

▶ Diving is a popular activity to do in your free time or on vacation, but it can be expensive. To dive, you need special clothes, tools and training and the best places to dive are often far away. But now, a team of scientists is using virtual reality so that everyone can go diving from their own home.

Usually, you have to wear a helmet to see virtual reality, but with this technology your whole body is used. The glasses can tell where you are standing, so it feels like what you are seeing is really there.

This technology means that people can swim with sharks safely, and without getting special training, inside a normal swimming pool.

The scientists will use this shark tank for testing. The team put a mini submarine and a camera in the shark pool. The cables send a picture of the sharks back to the screen. Happy that the camera works, they must next see if they can now project the image.

The team put a screen into a swimming pool. In the control room, they start the projector. Back at the shark tank, they get the camera ready. They cover the swimming pool and the first viewing starts. In the swimming pool the video from the shark tank can be seen clearly. It's amazing that with the right technology, you can now swim with sharks anywhere.

PREPARING TO WATCH

UNDERSTANDING KEY VOCABULARY

1 👥 Students work in pairs to match the words with their definitions. Allow 3–4 minutes for this, before inviting feedback from the class.

Answers

1 diving 2 helmet 3 tank 4 screen
5 projector 6 shark 7 virtual reality 8 submarine

2 👥 Students work in small groups to discuss the things they would like to do. Allow about 5 minutes for this before inviting feedback from the class. Encourage students to give their reasons.

| Answers will vary.

WHILE WATCHING

3 ▶️ 👤👥 Tell students they are going to watch a video about swimming with sharks using virtual reality. Play the video. Students work individually to choose the correct answer. Ask them to check their answers with a partner, before inviting feedback from the class.

| **Answers**
| 1 five 2 the world 3 laughing 4 under the tank 5 some
| 6 glass 7 dark 8 can

4 👤 Students work individually to fill in the gaps. Allow 3–4 minutes for this but do not check answers at this stage.

5 ▶️ Play the video again so that students can check their answers.

| **Answers**
| 1 expensive, far away 2 helmet, glasses 3 training
| 4 camera 5 sharks

DISCUSSION

6 👥 Students work in small groups to discuss the questions about the advertisement. Allow 4 minutes for this, before inviting feedback from the class.

| 1 Answers will vary. 2a swim with sharks and see them
| up close b you can't get hurt

7 👥 Allow 10 minutes for students to discuss any other virtual reality experience they would like to have and to create an advertisement for it. Circulate, monitor and give assistance where necessary.

8 👥 Give each group a maximum of 2 minutes to present their advertisement to the class. Then take a vote to find the most popular virtual reality experience.

LISTENING 1

PREPARING TO LISTEN

UNDERSTANDING KEY VOCABULARY

> **Optional lead-in**
>
> Books closed. Write the word *robot* on the board and elicit from students what they think a robot is and what it does. (A robot is a machine that is programmed to do mechanical tasks in the way of a human.) Encourage students to be as creative and imaginative as possible in their ideas about what robots can do.

1 👥 Ask students to open their books at page 72 and tell them that they are going to listen to a radio programme about robots. Students work with a partner to name some of the things they can see in the photographs. Allow about 2 minutes for this, but do not check answers at this stage as students will work with the photographs again in Exercise 2.

2 👥 Students work with a partner to match the words in the box to the pictures.

| **Answers**
| 1 fish 2 disabled person 3 a suit 4 water pollution
| 5 kitchen

PRONUNCIATION FOR LISTENING

3 👥 Write the three IPA symbols on the board: /s/ /ʃ/ /tʃ/ and use these words to model and then drill the sounds: /s/ <u>s</u>nake /ʃ/ <u>sh</u>ower /tʃ/ <u>ch</u>ess. Students work with a partner to say each word from Exercise 2 out loud and add it to the sound maps, according to the underlined letters. Allow 2 minutes for this, before inviting feedback from the class.

| **Answers**
| /s/ suit, disabled person /ʃ/ fish, water pollution
| /tʃ/ kitchen
| Note that the *s* in *person* also has the sound /s/.

4 👥 Students work with a partner to complete the sound maps with the words in the list.

| **Answers**
| /s/ sort, maths, face /ʃ/ nation, short, wish, ocean
| /tʃ/ which, match, cheap

5 👤 Students work individually to circle the correct word. Allow about 3 minutes for this, before inviting feedback from the class. Do not give the correct answer to the questions in 3 at this stage as students will listen and check their predictions in Exercise 7.

> **Answers**
>
> 1 sorts 2 cheap 3 b washing e sea

6 👥 Students work with a partner to predict the answers to the questions in Exercise 5. Allow 2 minutes for this, before inviting feedback from the class about their predictions. Is there any agreement in the class? Write the predictions on the board. Do not give definitive answers at this stage as students will check their predictions in Exercise 7.

WHILE LISTENING

LISTENING FOR MAIN IDEAS

7 🔊 **4.1** 👤 Tell students that they are going to listen to a radio programme about robots and to check their predictions from Exercise 5. Play the audio. Then check with the class which predictions written on the board were correct.

> **Answers**
>
> 1 yes 2 expensive but becoming cheaper 3 a, b, d, e

> **Background note**
>
> *Robotics* refers to the science of making and operating robots and the systems used for controlling them.
> A *disabled person* is one who lacks one or more of the physical or mental abilities that most people have.

8 🔊 **4.1** 👤👥 Write on the board *I passed my exam because I worked hard*. Ask students: 'Why did I pass my exam?' to elicit *Because I worked hard*. Underline this, write above it *reason*, circle it and draw an arrow to *passed my exam*. Tell students that *because* is one word we use to give reasons. Ask them to look at the Listening for reasons box and find out which other words we use, to elicit *as*, *because of* and *due to*. Write these on the board under the sentence and tell students that although they all mean the same, some of them have different word structures or grammar after them, but don't go into the differences at this stage. Tell students that you are going to play the audio again and ask them to work

individually to complete the reasons in the table. After the audio, ask students to check their answers with a partner, before inviting feedback from the class.

> **Answers**
>
> 1 expensive 2 (new types of) robots 3 age 4 robot fish

POST-LISTENING

9 👤 Students work individually to complete the sentences with the words in the box. Point out that in some cases more than one expression is possible, and tell students that *thanks to* is generally used for positive situations. Allow 2 minutes for this, before inviting feedback from the class.

> **Answers**
>
> 1 Thanks to 2 due to / because of 3 as
> 4 Due to / Because of

DISCUSSION

10 👥 👥👥 Students work with a partner to answer question 1. Either put pairs together to form groups of 4 to answer questions 2 and 3 or ask students to change partners to create new pairs. Allow about 4 minutes for this, before inviting feedback from the class. For question 3, encourage as many contributions as possible and follow up by asking what advantages and disadvantages they can think of.

⊙ LANGUAGE DEVELOPMENT

CAN / BE ABLE TO

1 👥 Tell students that they are going to look at the similarities and differences between *can* and *be able to*. Students work with a partner to look at the sentences from Listening 1 and then answer questions a–c below the box. Allow about 4 minutes for this, before inviting feedback from the class.

> **Answers**
>
> a now: 1 7 8 9 past: 2 3 4 5 6 b negatives: 3 4 6 7 8
> can→can't, could→couldn't, be able to→not be able to, e.g. isn't able to, wasn't able to c can/could

Language note

It is more common to use *can* than *be able to* to describe general ability. *Be able to* is used when it is grammatically impossible to use *can*, for example, for the infinitive form or for the past participle: *He must be able to relax in his own home. I might be able to come tomorrow. I haven't been able to concentrate since then.*

2 Tell students that the Explanation box contains the rules for when we use *can* and *be able to*. Students work with a partner, using the verb forms in Exercise 1 to fill in the gaps. Allow about 3 minutes for this, before inviting feedback from the class.

> **Answers**
>
> 1 can 2 can't 3 be able to 4 not be able to 5 could
> 6 couldn't 7 was able to 8 wasn't able to 9 couldn't

3 Tell students to work in pairs and circle the correct verb forms. Point out that more than one form is possible for most sentences. Allow about 3 minutes for this, before inviting feedback from the class.

> **Answers**
>
> 1 I can 2 could 3 was able to 4 couldn't / wasn't able to 5 couldn't / wasn't able to

4 Look at the examples in the grid and tell students to think of a different activity to write in each of the boxes. Point out that they need a verb and a noun that collocate and suggest that they can look through earlier units to get ideas. Circulate and monitor to ensure that the students are using correct collocations. Allow about 4 minutes for this.

> **Answers will vary.**

5 Students work in pairs and take turns to choose a number (1–9) from their partner's grid and be asked a question about it. They must not look at each other's grids. This could also be done as group work. Put students into small groups. Again they must not look at each other's grids. They take turns to choose a number and the student on the left of the person who chooses then asks the question, e.g. *Can you / Are you able to …?* about the activity in the appropriate box. Remind students to give reasons for their answer. Model this by asking a student to ask you the question in the box of the number you give them. Make sure you give good reasons.

Allow about 8 minutes for this. Circulate and monitor, looking for good examples which you can feed back to the class at the end. Finish off by asking if there were any students who could or couldn't do all the activities they were asked about.

> **Answers will vary.**

TECHNOLOGY

6 Tell students that they are going to look at some vocabulary related to technology. Students complete the sentences, using words in the word map. Allow about 5 minutes for this. Ask students to check with a partner, before inviting feedback from the class. Check that students understand the meaning of all the words.

> **Answers**
>
> 1 switch (it) on 2 keyboard; mouse 3 log on
> 4 wifi; go online 5 the cloud 6 shut down

7 Tell students that they are going to discuss some questions about how they use the internet. Students work with a partner to answer the questions. Allow about 4 minutes for this, before inviting feedback from the class. This activity can be extended by asking students to make notes about their first partner's answers. Then ask students to change partners and repeat the exercise, asking and answering questions about their first partner.

> **Answers will vary.**

8 Tell students that they are going to make another word map, using words related to smartphones and tablets. Students work individually to put the words in the box into the correct place. Allow about 3 minutes for this and, if appropriate, ask students to check their answers with a partner, before inviting feedback from the class. You could ask students to make example sentences with *text* as that is the word that can be both a noun and a verb, e.g. *I usually send about 20 texts a day to different friends. I'll text you later to let you know what time I'll arrive.*

> **Answers**
>
> **verbs:** surf, charge, text
> **nouns:** battery, apps, text, charger, keys

9 👥 Students work with a partner to complete the sentences, using the words from Exercise 8. Allow about 3 minutes for this, before inviting feedback from the class. Ensure students understand the meaning of the questions.

> **Answers**
> 1 keys 2 apps 3 surf 4 text 5 battery 6 charger; charge

10 👥 Put students into new pairs and ask them to ask and answer the questions. Answer the first one with the whole class and encourage students to tell you the advantages and disadvantages of touchscreens and keys. Allow about 5–6 minutes for students to discuss the questions. Circulate and monitor conversations for good language which you can feed back to the class at the end. Finish off by inviting feedback from the class.

LISTENING 2

PREPARING TO LISTEN

UNDERSTANDING KEY VOCABULARY

1 👥 Tell students that they are going to listen to a news report about how computers affect our memory and to open their books at page 78. Students work with a partner to match the words (1–7) to the meanings (a–g). Allow about 2 minutes for this, before inviting feedback from the class.

> **Answers**
> 1 b 2 f 3 a 4 c 5 g 6 e 7 d

PRONUNCIATION FOR LISTENING

2 👤 Tell students that we use linking words to add supporting examples or more details to key information. Allow a minute for students to work individually and underline the linking words. Then check the answers with the whole class.

> **Answers**
> 1 and 2 as well as

3 👥 Tell students to think about the sounds in the linking words. Model and then drill the sentences in Exercise 2, before asking students to work with a partner to answer the questions. Check that students understand *strong* and *weak* in this context and schwa /ə/. Drill the word *information*, which is in Exercise 2, and make sure students can identify the weak (schwa) sound: inf$\underline{o}$rmation. Point out that the 'd' in *and* is pronounced in the example sentence in Exercise 2 because it is followed by a vowel sound and give an example where *and* is followed by a consonant sound and the 'd' is therefore not pronounced: *fish and chips*. Allow about 2 minutes for this, before inviting feedback from the class.

> **Answers**
> 1 d 2 weak 3 weak

4 👥 Ask students to work with a partner to practise saying the sentences in Exercise 2 out loud, focusing on the correct pronunciation of the weak sounds. If appropriate, model and drill these again with the class.

WHILE LISTENING

LISTENING FOR SUPPORTING DETAILS

> **Language note**
>
> Tell students that when people give presentations or talks, they usually give the information in sections. The main information is usually at the start of each section (like the topic sentence is at the beginning of a paragraph). This main information is then followed by supporting details and examples. They should listen carefully as the speaker introduces each main point, and the supporting information will usually follow.

5 (◀)) **4.2** 👤👥 Tell students that they are going to listen to a report about how computers affect our memory. Students work individually to fill in the gaps in the first column of the table about the main information only. Play the audio. Ask students to check their answers with a partner, before inviting feedback from the class.

| Answers

2 difficult 3 websites 4 information 5 lazy

6 (◀)) **4.2** 👤👥 Play the audio again. Students work individually to complete the additional details in the second column. After the audio, ask students to check with a partner, before inviting feedback from the class.

| Answers

6 information 7 answer 8 how 9 put 10 facts
11 location 12 find

DISCUSSION

7 👤 Ask students: 'What types of information do you keep on your computer, smartphone or in the cloud?' Brainstorm a few ideas, asking for reasons, and then ask students to work individually and write down what information they keep in each place. Do not check answers at this stage.

8 👥 Students work with a partner to compare how they store their information. Ask them to see if they do exactly the same things or totally different things. Allow about 4 minutes for this, before inviting feedback from the class.

9 👥 Put students into different pairs and ask them to discuss the advantages and disadvantages of storing the information in the way they do. If appropriate, give students an example: losing photos stored on a laptop if the laptop is stolen. Allow about 3 minutes for this, before inviting feedback from the class. Is there agreement in the class or do students feel differently?

CRITICAL THINKING

Optional lead-in

Books closed. Ask students: 'Do you remember some of the advantages and disadvantages of other types of technology that we have discussed in this unit?' If necessary, prompt them with some of the technology from the unit (include the optional activities if they have done them).

Students begin to think about the Speaking task they will do at the end of the unit (*Present a report about technology, providing some information about a device. Look at advantages and disadvantages and give details to support the main ideas.*). Give them a minute to look at the box.

REMEMBER

1 👥 Ask students to open their books at page 80. You could do the first question with the whole class. Students then work with a partner to discuss questions 2 and 3. Allow about 3 minutes for this, before inviting feedback from the class.

| Answers will vary.

2 👤 Students work individually to decide if the sentences are advantages or disadvantages and complete the table.

| Answers

Answers will vary depending on the students' point of view but 1, 2 and 4 are definitely advantages. 3 and 5 are probably disadvantages, although not everyone will see them that way.

3 👥 Students work with a partner to compare their ideas and add more advantages and disadvantages to the table if they can. Circulate, monitor and give assistance with language or ideas if necessary. Make a note of any good language use or problems for feedback later. Allow 4 minutes for this, before inviting feedback from the class.

| Answers will vary

4 👥 Students work in pairs to complete the table at the top of page 81 with the main argument and some advantages and disadvantages. Allow 5 minutes for this but do not invite feedback at this stage.

5 👥 👥👥 Ask students to work with a different partner or put two pairs together to compare their ideas. Allow 5 minutes for this, before inviting feedback from the class. You could write the ideas on the board and see which are the most interesting ideas.

> **Answers will vary.**

SPEAKING

PREPARATION FOR SPEAKING

> **Optional lead-in**
>
> Books closed. Ask students: 'Can you remember any of the linking expressions we have used to introduce reasons?' (*because, because of, due to, thanks to, as*). Write them on the board. Ask students: 'Can you think of any more linking expressions?' (*and, as well as, but*). Write them on the board. Ask students: 'Do you think that the English we use in academic situations is the same as the English we use every day?' (*No, it's different, it's more formal*). Ask students: 'Which words on the board are the least academic?' (*and* and *but*). Ask students: 'Which words could we use instead to sound more academic?' (*as well as, however*).

1 👤 Ask students to open their books at page 81. Ask them how the linking words in the box are different from *and* and *as well as* in Listening 2, Pronunciation for listening (the ones here are to show contrast rather than additional information). Students work individually to put the correct linking words into the sentences. Highlight that sometimes more than one answer is possible. Allow about 3 minutes for this. Do not check answers at this stage.

2 🔊 **4.3** 👤 Play the audio and ask students to check their answers. Words in brackets show the other possible answers in Exercise 1, which aren't on the audio.

> **Answers**
>
> 1 However 2 whereas (but) 3 On the other hand (However) 4 but

3 👤 Students work individually to choose the correct option in the rule about what these words do. Allow a minute for this, before inviting feedback from the class.

> **Answers**
>
> link different information

4 Ask the class to look at the sentences and decide if the words in bold introduce different or additional information. If the students don't all agree, ask for a show of hands to decide the majority view, whether it is correct or not.

> **Answers**
>
> They all introduce additional information.

5 👥 Tell students that each of the sentences can be completed by both endings below but they must use the correct linking word. Tell them that in one case they will need to use two sentences. Do the first one with the class. Students work with a partner to complete the sentences. Allow about 3 minutes for this, before inviting feedback from the class. Check that students know that 3b has to be two sentences. (Robots assist people with difficult jobs. However, some people believe they are bad because people lose their jobs when robots are used.)

> **Answers**
>
> 1 a and b but 2 a whereas b and also 3 a as well as b However

6 👤 Give students a minute to read the instructions. Then ask them to look at the example paragraph at the foot of page 82 and call out the words that give reasons (*because*) and link ideas (*but, as well as, however*). Students then work individually to plan their short reports about the technology they thought about in Critical thinking Exercise 4 on page 80. Remind them to use linking words. Circulate, monitor and help as necessary.

7 👤 Students work individually to circle the correct option. Allow 2 minutes for this, before inviting feedback from the class.

> **Answers**
>
> finish

8 👤 Students work individually to add a conclusion to their reports. Allow 2 minutes for this but do not ask for feedback at this point.

9 👥 Students work in pairs to read their reports to each other. Allow 3 minutes for this before inviting feedback from the class. To finish off, you could ask how many pairs agreed with each other and how many did not.

| Answers will vary.

SPEAKING TASK

PREPARE

1 👤 Give students a minute to read the box and remind themselves of the Speaking task they are going to do. Students decide which piece of technology they want to present a report on. It should not be the one they chose in the Critical thinking section on page 80. If appropriate, allocate each student a device from the box. Alternative ideas can also be accepted.

2 👤 Students work individually to fill in the table with the advantages and disadvantages of the piece of technology they have chosen, using the steps from Preparation for speaking given in Exercises 6–8. They then write sentences using linking words. Do not do any feedback yet. This could be given for homework or if students have access to the internet in class, it can be researched in class.

3 👤 Students work individually and add a concluding sentence to their reports. Circulate, monitor and help as necessary. Allow 2 minutes for this. Do not do any feedback at this stage.

4 👤 Students work individually on the start of their reports. Circulate, monitor and help as necessary. Again do not do any feedback.

PRACTISE

5 👤 Students spend a few minutes silently rehearsing their reports, concentrating on the introduction, the advantages and disadvantages, linking words and the conclusion.

PRESENT

6 👥 Students work in pairs and present their reports to each other. Allow 4 minutes in total (2 minutes per student) before inviting feedback from the class. You could ask some of the more confident students to present their reports to the class or to tell the class what their partners said.

Optional activity

Alternatively, for Exercises 1–6, put students into groups and let them choose which piece of technology they would like to present a report about, or divide the class into 6 groups and allocate one piece of technology to each group.

👥 Ask students to work in their groups to write notes on their piece of technology using the table in Exercise 2. This can be given for homework so that they can research their piece of technology on the internet, or if they can use the internet in class, that will provide more interesting results. If they are researching in class, allow about 15 minutes for this. If they have done it for homework, put them back into their groups and allow them about 6 minutes to discuss and collate their ideas. Circulate, monitor and give assistance where appropriate.

👥 Put students into pairs from different groups. Ask students to present their reports to their partner. Allow about 6 minutes for this. The listener should make notes.

👥 Students go back to their original group and present the information they have received from their partner to the rest of the group. Allow about 2 minutes for each presentation, i.e. if there are 3 students in the group, allow 6 minutes for this. Finish off by inviting feedback from the class about the most interesting reports. If appropriate, take a vote.

ADDITIONAL SPEAKING TASK

See page 137 for the Additional speaking task (*A report on a piece of new technology*) and Model language for this unit.

Make a photocopy of page 137 for each student.

👥 Divide the class into 4 groups and allocate one of the ideas for new technology (1–4) to each group. Ask the groups to work together to think of as many positive features of their idea as they can. Allow about 7 minutes for this.

👥 Then tell students that each of them will present their idea to another group in the next part of the lesson. Ask them to work together to plan how they will present their report using the Model language to give additional and contrasting information, reasons and examples. Allow 5 minutes for this.

👥 Put students into new groups of four, one for each of the ideas. Students take turns to present their piece of technology and answer any questions the group has.

Finish off by getting some feedback from each group to decide which is the most useful new idea.

TASK CHECKLIST AND OBJECTIVES REVIEW

Refer students to the end of the unit for the Task checklist and Objectives review. Students complete the tables individually to reflect on their learning and identify areas for improvement.

WORDLIST

See Teaching tips page 10, section 6, for ideas about how to make the most of the Wordlist with your students.

REVIEW TEST

See pages 120–121 for the photocopiable Review test for this unit and page 107 for ideas about when and how to administer the Review test.

RESEARCH PROJECT

Research and explain cutting-edge technology

Divide the class into groups and assign each group a theme to do with technology, e.g. materials, computing, travel, space or food. Tell the class that they will be researching these different themes and then presenting them to the rest of the class. Each group will need to think about their theme as it is now and how it may be developed in the future. Students could use the tools on Cambridge LMS to share their initial research with the rest of the class.

Each group will then prepare a ten-minute presentation, including time for questions. Students could develop the wiki further with their final research and refer to this during their presentation, create slides using presentation software, or produce a leaflet to email to the rest of the class.

5 LANGUAGE AND COMMUNICATION

Learning objectives

Before you start the Unlock your knowledge section, ask students to read the Learning objectives box so that they have a clear idea of what they are going to learn in this unit. Tell them that you will come back to these objectives at the end of the unit when they review what they have learned. Give them the opportunity to ask you any questions they might have.

UNLOCK YOUR KNOWLEDGE

Lead-in

Books closed. Ask students: 'Why are you learning English?' Encourage as many students to respond as possible. Ask students: 'Do you really want to learn English or do you feel you have to?' 'Why / Why not?' Ask students: 'Do you think English will always be a world language?' 'Why / Why not?' Finally, ask students: 'Would you like [their language(s)] to be a world language?' 'Why / Why not?'

👥 Ask students to open their books at page 87 and look at the photograph. They work with a partner to answer the questions. Allow about 3 minutes for this, before inviting feedback from the class. Encourage as many ideas as possible.

WATCH AND LISTEN

Video script

▶ South America is one of the most interesting places in the world. It has 12 countries and nearly 400 million people. Some parts are very hot, other parts are cold and mountainous. There are rivers and lakes where people travel and work. There are places with few people and big cities where many people live.

Communicating in a place as big as South America is not easy. It reaches from the Equator to Antarctica. The Caribbean Sea is in the north. To the east is the Atlantic Ocean and the Pacific Ocean is in the west.

How do all the people in these different places talk to each other? The languages used most are Spanish and Portuguese but there are many other languages too.

Brazil is the biggest country in South America, famous for the city of Rio and its beautiful beaches. Almost all the people of Brazil speak Portuguese. But some also speak Guarani, a local language passed on from the people who lived in Brazil thousands of years ago.

Colombia is the second biggest country in South America and is home to cities like Bogotá. Most Colombians speak Spanish. But a few hundred people still speak a language called Uitoto. In fact Colombia once had 68 other languages but only a few of them remain.

Argentinians are also mostly Spanish speakers. A million and a half of the people speak Italian too. And, just like Brazil and Colombia, there are some local languages that have been spoken for thousands of years. Some, like Vilela, only have 15 or 20 speakers left.

But why is it that these old languages are not as popular as Spanish and Portuguese? Over 500 years ago, Europeans from Spain and Portugal arrived in South America just before 1500. They soon introduced their own languages. But before the Spanish and Portuguese came, there were many different people already living in South America, speaking hundreds of different languages.

Some people still live in the same way as their ancestors did hundreds of years ago. They still speak the same languages. The ancient cities and places where these languages started have mostly gone now. A few are left but they are not busy any more. They are places for tourists to visit, like Machu Picchu in The Andes Mountains. Many people hope that the same thing doesn't happen to the old languages of South America. They hope that people will continue to speak them.

PREPARING TO WATCH

UNDERSTANDING KEY VOCABULARY

Optional lead-in

If possible, show a map of the world on the board. Ask students what the main language spoken in their country is. Are there any other languages spoken? Ask them about the language of neighbouring countries.

1 👥 Students work in pairs. Give them 2 minutes to answer the questions, before eliciting feedback from the class. If possible, use a map of the world, point to South America and ask students: 'How many countries in South America do you know?' Write responses on the board (Brazil, Colombia, Argentina, Peru, Venezuela, Chile are the 6 largest in population of the 12 South American countries). Ask students: 'Do you know which languages they speak in these countries?' (Portuguese in Brazil, Spanish in the others).

2 👤 Students work individually to match the words to the definitions. Allow about 5 minutes for this, before inviting feedback from the class.

> **Answers**
>
> 1 c 2 e 3 f 4 b 5 g 6 d 7 a

3 👤 Students work individually to put the words from Exercise 1 into the sentences. Allow about 4 minutes for this, before inviting feedback from the class.

> **Answers**
>
> 1 Equator 2 beach 3 Antarctica 4 speakers 5 Many 6 ancestors 7 few

4 👥 Students work with a partner to discuss which sentences in Exercise 3 are true for them. Allow about 7 minutes for this, before inviting feedback from the class.

> **Answers will vary.**

WHILE WATCHING

5 👥 Students work in pairs to decide which are countries. Point out that countries have capital letters so that rules out three places, but so do continents and places of interest. Tell students that they will find out about all the places in the video. This could be done as a whole-class activity.

> **Answers**
>
> Argentina, Brazil, Colombia

6 ▶️👤👥 Remind students that all the words in Exercise 1 are places. Play the video from the beginning, including the introductory images before you see the video title. Students work individually to number the places in the order they see them.

> **Answers**
>
> 1 Machu Picchu 2 mountains 3 a river 4 South America 5 a market 6 Brazil 7 Colombia 8 Argentina

7 👤 Students work individually to decide if the sentences are true or false. Do not check answers at this stage.

8 ▶️👤👥 Play the video again. Students then work individually to check their answers. Students work with a partner to correct the false sentences. Allow about 3 minutes for this, before inviting feedback from the class.

> **Answers**
>
> 1F (400 million people) 2T 3F (Portuguese or Spanish) 4T 5F (a few hundred people) 6F (by 15 or 20 people now) 7T 8F (Machu Picchu is a place tourists visit)

> **Background note**
>
> Although many indigenous languages are spoken throughout Latin America, Portuguese (in Brazil) and Spanish (elsewhere) are official languages because Latin America was invaded and colonized by the Portuguese and Spanish.
>
> Machu Picchu /ˈmɑː.tʃuː ˈpiː.tʃuː/ is one of the most important sites of the Inca civilization. Located in Peru about 2,500 metres above sea level, it is also known as the 'Lost City of the Incas'.

DISCUSSION

9 👥 Students work with a partner to answer the questions. Allow about 4 minutes for this. Do not check answers at this stage.

10 👥 Put students into new pairs to share their ideas about learning English. Allow about 3 minutes for this, before inviting feedback from the class. Encourage students to share and discuss their ideas for learning. If appropriate, give your advice to the class.

> **Answers will vary.**

11 Ask students: 'Does anyone know what a documentary is?' Tell students to read the sentences and choose the correct option.

> **Answers**
>
> 1 a real person or event 2 formal

12 👥 Put students into groups of 3 or 4. Tell them that they are going to make a documentary about language(s) in their country. Allow about 5 minutes to discuss what information to include.

13 👥 Tell students to join with another group and compare their ideas and choose the best ones. Allow about 4 minutes for this, before inviting feedback from the class.

LISTENING 1

PREPARING TO LISTEN

USING YOUR KNOWLEDGE TO PREDICT CONTENT

1 Tell students that they are going to listen to some information about four different languages. Students work in pairs to answer the questions. Check students understand *official language* (the language recognized by government as the most important though not all countries have an official language). Allow about 2–3 minutes, before inviting feedback.

Answers

1 India is in South Asia, the USA is part of the American continent, Wales is part of the United Kingdom, Russia is in Northern Asia. If you have a map of the world, show which countries are close to these, e.g. India: Pakistan, Bangladesh, China; the USA: Canada, Mexico; Wales: England, Ireland; Russia: Poland, China.
2 India: Hindi; USA: English; Wales: Welsh and English; Russia: Russian

2 Tell students that when we are listening, other things, not just the words, can help us to understand. Students work in pairs to mark each statement S or O. Allow about 2 minutes for this, before inviting feedback from the class. Introduce other ideas about what can help understanding, such as the context of the conversation, or whether we know the speaker.

Answers

1 O 2 O 3 S 4 O

PRONUNCIATION FOR LISTENING

3 (◀) 5.1 Ask students to look back to question 2 in Exercise 2. Ask whether, if they hear someone speaking happily or enthusiastically, they think they sound positive or negative, to elicit *positive*. Tell them that they are going to listen to some phrases and to mark them P for positive and S for serious. Ask students: 'Does *serious* mean *negative*?' to elicit *no*. Then ask: 'What does *serious* mean?' to elicit *not laughing* or *important*, or similar. Play the audio for students to work individually and then check with a partner.

Answers

1 S 2 P 3 S

4 Ask the class: 'Which phrase might have come from an advertisement?' 'How do you know that?'

Answers

2 because it sounds positive, and also because it is more inviting/encouraging than the others

5 (◀) 5.2 Tell students that when we want to sound positive, our voices often go up at the end of the phrase, i.e. we use a rising intonation pattern. Illustrate this by saying the same thing in a positive and then a serious way and ask students to identify the difference. Students listen and repeat the sentences. Play the audio or model the sentences to drill with the students.

WHILE LISTENING

6 Read the Listening for genre box aloud as students read along. Ask students to look at the four genres in column A of the table. Ask: 'Which genre do you think will sound the most positive?' (radio advertisement). Give students 1 minute to look at the characteristics in column B. Students work in pairs to match the genres to the characteristics. Tell students to write the letters next to the appropriate genres. Allow about 3 minutes for this, before inviting feedback from the class.

Answers

Radio advertisement e h Telephone message f g Museum tour b c TV news report a d

7 (◀) 5.3 Play the audio. Students work individually to number the genres in the order they hear them.

Answers

Radio advertisement 4 Telephone message 2 Museum tour 3 TV news report 1

8 Ask students to look at the photograph of Boa. Ask students if they remember which country she was from and which language she spoke.

Answers

From the Indian Andaman Islands. She was the last person to speak Bo.

9 (◀) **5.3** 👤👥 Play the audio again. Students work individually to complete the table. Then, allow students to check with a partner, before inviting feedback from the class.

Answers

A genre	B country	C language
1 television news report	India	Bo
2 telephone message	the USA	Navajo
3 museum tour	Russia	Tuva
4 radio advertisement	Wales	Welsh

Background note

The Andaman Islands are a group of islands in the Bay of Bengal, between India and Burma.

The Navajo people are the largest Native American tribe of the USA, originating in the southwest.

Tuva is a Russian republic, located in southern Siberia.

Wales is one of the countries, along with England, Scotland and Northern Ireland, which make up the United Kingdom.

DISCUSSION

10 👤 Students work individually to write down their answers to the questions. Allow about 1 minute for this but do not do feedback at this stage.

11 Ask students to stand up and move around the classroom to talk to other students to find two others who have similar ideas to theirs. Allow about 5 minutes for this, before inviting feedback from the class.

Optional activity

👤👥 Ask students individually to research languages that are in danger, to find out the languages most at risk (apart from those referred to in Listening 1), how many people speak those languages and which countries they are in. Alternatively, put students into groups and ask each group to research one of the following languages: Askunu, Khwarshi, Manchu, Parenga, Arvanitika, Tunumiit. Askunu is spoken in parts of Afghanistan, Khwarshi in Dagestan, Manchu in northeast China, Parenga in India, Arvanitika in Greece, Tunumiit in Greenland.

👁 LANGUAGE DEVELOPMENT

IMPERATIVE CLAUSES

1 👤 Students work individually to match the sentences to the rules in the Explanation box. Allow 2 minutes for this, before inviting feedback from the class.

Answers
a1 b3 c3 d2

2 👤👥 Students work individually. Allow 2 minutes for this and then ask them to check their answers with a partner, before inviting feedback from the class.

Answers

1 ~~You~~ open your books. 2 Don't ~~to~~ be late. 3 Open ~~it~~ the window. 4 Come ~~you~~ back later. 5 Unlock~~ing~~ your screen, please.

3 👤 Students work individually. Allow 5 minutes, before inviting feedback from the class. Point out that *please* can go at the beginning or the end of a sentence.

Answers

1 [Please] listen to me [, please].
2 [Please} repeat your instructions [, please].
3 [Please] go back if you wouldn't mind [, please].
4 [Please] speak more loudly [, please].
5 [Please] start again if you wouldn't mind [, please].

VERB PATTERNS

Optional lead-in

Write on the board *She said it was very hot there.* and *She told me it was very hot there.* Ask students to identify what, apart from the main verb, is the difference between the two sentences (*me*). Point out that *me* is the direct object of the verb *tell* and that we can refer to *tell* as a *direct* verb. *Say* cannot have a direct object and we can refer to *say* as an *indirect* verb. (This is not related to direct and indirect speech.)

4 👤 Tell students to look at the rules in the Explanation box. Then check understanding, using simple examples: *He said this to me. He told me this. He spoke to me about this.* Draw students' attention to rule 4 and tell them that we can use *that* with both *say* and *tell* (but it isn't necessary to do so) but with *tell* there will be a direct object after the verb: *He said (that) he wasn't happy. He told his friend (that) he wasn't happy.* Look at the example for the first one with the class. Students work individually to cross out the incorrect sentences in each pair. Allow about 5 minutes for the exercise, before inviting feedback from the class.

Answers
Incorrect sentences apart from 1b are: 2 b 3 b 4 a 5 a 6 b 7 a

5 Ask students if they remember what a collocation is, to elicit *words that go together*. Students work with a partner to identify which word/phrase does not make a collocation with the verbs *say* and *tell*. Allow about 1 minute for this, before checking answers with the class.

Answers
1 the answer 2 me something

6 Students work individually to complete the sentences with the correct form of *say, tell, speak* or *ask*. Allow about 2 minutes for students to do this, before they check with a partner. Then invite feedback from the class.

Answers
1 tell 2 speak 3 tell 4 Tell 5 asked

LISTENING 2

PREPARING TO LISTEN

UNDERSTANDING KEY VOCABULARY

1 Tell students that they are going to listen to someone who uses sign language and to open their books at page 95. Students work with a partner to answer the question. Allow about 1 minute for this, before inviting feedback from the class.

Answers
Sign language is a language using hands and gesture to communicate or spell out words. It is used by deaf people or people who have hearing problems and/or people who work and communicate with deaf people.

2 Tell students that all the words in this exercise come from the listening they are about to hear. Students work individually to circle the words that are different and then check with a partner. Remind them to decide why the word is different. Allow about 2 minutes for this.

Answers
1 tall (the others are physical problems) 2 find (the others are words for learning) 3 head (the others are parts of the hand) 4 smell (the others are parts of the face) 5 speak (the others are movements of the hand)

3 Students work individually to complete the sentences with words from Exercise 2. Allow about 3 minutes for this, before inviting feedback from the class.

Answers
1 blind 2 pick up 3 palm 4 lip 5 pat

WHILE LISTENING

LISTENING FOR MAIN IDEAS

4 (◄) 5.4 Tell students that they are going to listen to someone who uses sign language. Allow students 1 minute of silent time to look at the questions and check understanding. Point out that we don't actually hear Lana, and that her signer is speaking as if she is Lana, i.e. not using reported speech. Play the audio and ask students to work individually to choose the correct option. After the audio, ask students to check their answers with a partner.

Answers
1 b 2 b 3 b 4 a 5 a

LISTENING FOR INSTRUCTIONS

5 (◄) 5.5 Tell students to look at the pictures and remember Lana's instructions for signing *happy* in Exercise 4. They then work individually to try to number the pictures in the correct order, before listening to the extract. Play the audio and ask students to check their order with a partner, before inviting feedback from the class.

Answers
Picture a 3; Picture b 2; Picture c 1

POST-LISTENING

6 👥 Students work in pairs to put together the elements of the sign to make one fluid movement, which they practise and help each other to get right.

7 👥 Students work with a different partner and do the signing to each other. Are their actions the same or different? Who is most accurate?

8 👥 Tell students to make the appropriate sign for *Hello!*, i.e. wave. They then work with a partner to think about how we can use gesture to communicate the other messages. Allow about 2 minutes for this, before inviting feedback from the class. Be careful that none of the gestures causes offence in the culture in which you are working or where your students are from.

> **Possible answers**
>
> 2 thumbs up 3 holding nose
> 4 rubbing fingers together 5 holding finger to lips

9 👥 Students work in pairs to think of two more signs. Allow 2–3 minutes, before inviting feedback from the class. Possible ideas are 'Come here!', 'Go away!'.

PRONUNCIATION FOR LISTENING

10 👥 Students work in pairs to say the words out loud to each other. Circulate and monitor. Alternatively, you can model the words and ask students to repeat after you.

11 👥 Tell the class that all these words have the letter *T* and then ask them what other letter they can see in all the words (*L*). Students work with a partner to say the words out loud again and decide if the *L* sounds the same in each word. Alternatively, do this as a whole-class activity.

> **Answers**
>
> L. It doesn't sound the same each time. In *tell* and *late*, you can hear it but in *told* it is almost silent (dark) and in *talk* it is silent.

12 👥 Tell students to look at the word map. Students work with a partner to find a route from column 1 to column 5 by finding words with a silent *L*. Tell them that they can go across or down but not diagonally.

If appropriate, do the first move with the whole class. Allow about 5 minutes for this. Circulate and monitor, providing help with pronunciation if required. If you think it is necessary, do a quick feedback with the whole class, modelling the words and asking students to repeat them.

> **Answers**
>
> 1a walk 1b could 2b calm 2c would 3c half 4c palm
> 4d should 5d talk

13 👥 Ask students to work with a partner and to take it in turns to think of a word and give the column and row to their partner, who will then say the word. Model once or twice with students before the rest of the class starts. Allow about 2 minutes for this. Finish off by asking students 'Which was the hardest word to say?'

> **Answers will vary.**

CRITICAL THINKING

Students begin to think about the Speaking task that they will do at the end of the unit (*Plan and give a set of instructions.*). Give them a minute to look at the box. Some preparation work could be given for homework.

REMEMBER

1 👥 Ask students to open their books at page 98 and work with a partner to fill in the gaps. Allow about 2 minutes for this, before inviting feedback from the class.

> **Answers**
>
> 1 put 2 put 3 thumb 4 chin 5 under 6 happy

2 👥 Students work in pairs to discuss the questions about the photograph. Allow 2 minutes for this, before inviting feedback from the class.

> **Answers**
>
> 1 It shows apps on a smartphone or tablet.
> 2 To see the time, set the time, set an alarm or perhaps see different time zones around the world.

APPLY

3 👥 Read aloud the Giving instructions box on page 98 while students follow. They then work with a partner to put the verbs in the flow chart. Allow up to 2 minutes for this, before inviting feedback from the class.

> **Answers**
> 1 pick 2 unlock 3 enter 4 select 5 save 6 press 7 put

4 👤 Students work individually to modify the instructions in the flow chart for their phones. Allow 2 minutes for this, before inviting feedback from the class.

5 👥 Students work with a partner and take it in turns to give the instructions in Exercise 3. If some of the students don't have mobiles, try to ensure that there is one for each pair. Allow about 3 minutes for this, before inviting feedback from the class.

EVALUATE

6 👥 Students work with a partner to discuss the ways of communicating instructions. Allow 4 minutes, before inviting feedback from the class. Remember to ask why when doing the feedback. You could take a vote on the most popular way of communicating.

SPEAKING

PREPARATION FOR SPEAKING

> **Optional lead-in**
> Brainstorm with students the easiest way for them to learn to do something new. Encourage as many ideas as possible. If appropriate, you could give them one idea to get them started, for example, someone could show another person how to do something.

1 🔊 **5.5** 👤 Ask students to think back to Listening 2 and how Lana used sequencing words to show when each thing happened. Tell students that we use sequencing words when we want to show the order in which things happen. Ask students to listen to the audio and work individually to number the words in the order in which Lana uses them.

> **Answers**
> 1 first of all 2 next 3 then

2 👥 Ask students why we use sequencing words, to elicit *to put things in the order they happen.* Then ask them to work in pairs to complete the table. Allow about 4 minutes for this, before inviting feedback from the class.

> **Answers**
> 1 firstly 2 to start with 3 after that 4 at the end 5 finally 6 to finish

3 👥 Tell students that they are going to prepare a set of instructions. Ask them to work with a partner to write the missing letters in the gaps to complete the rules about giving clear instructions. Allow about 4 minutes for this, before inviting feedback from the class.

> **Answers**
> 1 Think 2 Check 3 Make 4 explain 5 Use 6 Use

4 👤👥 Tell students that they will be looking at a process and then explaining that process to a partner. Nominate each student either A or B and ask Student As to stay on page 100 and Student Bs to go to page 197. Ask students to look at the pictures, to check the meaning of the words in the box and to work individually to complete the flowchart template. Allow about 10 minutes for this. Circulate and monitor, giving assistance where appropriate.

5 👥 Put students into pairs, As with As and Bs with Bs. Ask them to work through their instructions together and help each other to make improvements where possible. Allow about 5 minutes for this. Circulate and monitor, giving assistance where appropriate.

6 👥 Put students into new pairs, (As with Bs). Ask students to take turns to give each other their instructions. Allow 5 minutes for this, before inviting feedback from the class. Did the listeners understand the processes (preparing a photocopier for use and sending an instant message)?

Answers

Student A
1 Firstly, open the lid of the photocopier.
2 Put the paper face down on the glass.
3 Next open the paper tray.
4 Put the paper into the (paper) tray.
5 Straighten the paper.
6 Close the paper tray.
7 Finally, press the start button.

Student B
1 Firstly, press message/the message icon.
2 Select Create new message.
3 Choose the recipient from your address book.
4 Next type your message.
5 Select/Press send to … .
6 Finally, switch off your laptop/computer/tablet.

SPEAKING TASK

PREPARE

1 Give students a minute to read the box and remind themselves of the Speaking task they are going to do. Go through the list of tasks (1–5) with the class and brainstorm some more ideas. Write the new ideas on the board. Then allow 1 minute of thinking time for students to choose the task they would like to do.

2 👤 Students work individually to prepare their tasks by filling in the flow chart. Tell them that they may not need all the cells on page 101. Allow about 5 minutes for this. Circulate and monitor, giving assistance where appropriate.

PRESENT

3 👥 Put students into groups, with each member having worked on a different task. Ask each student to describe their task to the other members of their group without saying what the task is. Can the other students guess what it is? Allow about 2 minutes per student. Finish off by inviting feedback from students as to how many of them were able to identify the tasks.

ADDITIONAL SPEAKING TASK

See page 138 for the Additional speaking task (*Describing a process*) and Model language for this unit.

Make a photocopy of page 138 for each student but cut off the details about the 4 processes at the foot of the page. Cut up the details about the processes. Give each student a photocopy of the page without the processes.

👥 Divide the class into 4 groups and give each group a different process (1, 2, 3, or 4). Give the students about 10 minutes to work out together how to describe the process using the Model language. Circulate, monitor and give help as needed. Encourage students to talk about each step of their process,

👥 Put students into new groups of 4, one from each of the first groups (1–4). Ask students to take turns to describe their process without saying what it is. The other members of the group must guess what the process is.

Finish off by inviting feedback from the class about which were the best descriptions and, if appropriate, ask some of the students to describe their process to the whole class.

TASK CHECKLIST AND OBJECTIVES REVIEW

Refer students to the end of the unit for the Task checklist and Objectives review. Students complete the tables individually to reflect on their learning and identify areas for improvement.

WORDLIST

See Teaching tips page 10, section 6, for ideas about how to make the most of the Wordlist with your students.

REVIEW TEST

See pages 122–123 for the photocopiable Review test for this unit and page 107 for ideas about when and how to administer the Review test.

RESEARCH PROJECT

Create an audio library of languages

Ask students to think about different languages that are spoken in their country, or by people they are in contact with in different countries. They could use tools such as the forum on the Cambridge LMS to share ideas. Divide the class into groups and assign a different language to each group. Students have to find a person who speaks that language and ask for an audio recording. Each person should say this sentence in their language: 'My name is … and I am happy to be speaking [the language] to you today.' Students could record people face-to-face, using software that is compatible with a voice-over-IP service, or ask people to upload recordings to a social networking site.

Students could set up a website to upload the recordings and to give information such as country, history and culture of the language concerned. Alternatively, they could use the Cambridge LMS (audio recordings should be saved as 128kb mp3 files), or a media library application.

6 WEATHER AND CLIMATE

Learning objectives

Before you start the Unlock your knowledge section, ask students to read the Learning objectives box so that they have a clear idea of what they are going to learn in this unit. Tell them that you will come back to these objectives at the end of the unit when they review what they have learned. Give them the opportunity to ask you any questions they might have.

UNLOCK YOUR KNOWLEDGE

Lead-in

Books closed. Ask students: 'What's the weather like today?' Write the weather vocabulary they give on the board. Ask them: 'What's the weather like in [month]?' Then ask them if they know of any other different types of weather from different places in the world.

UNLOCK YOUR KNOWLEDGE

👥 Before asking students to open their books at page 105, ask them: 'Do you know what it is called when there is so much rain that there is water everywhere, in people's houses, shops etc.?' to elicit *flood*. Write the word on the board. Ask students: 'Do you know what it is called when there is not enough rain and not enough water?' to elicit *water shortage*. They will probably not know this. If any student comes up with *drought* first, accept it and explain that this is when there is no water at all for a long time; a water shortage comes before a drought. Tell students to look at the photograph and work with a partner to answer the questions. Allow 4–5 minutes for this, before inviting feedback from the class about the questions. To generate discussion, you could ask the following questions: 1 Is there any agreement about what type of weather people prefer? 2 Does everyone agree that the climate is changing or do some disagree? If so, how? 3 How many students do anything to help with preserving water? If so, what?

Optional activity

👤👥 Ask students individually to research the most dangerous forms of extreme weather in the world. Alternatively, put students into groups and allocate each group a specific type of extreme weather, e.g. floods, hurricanes, tornadoes, tsunamis, droughts, severe thunderstorms. Ask the groups to research exactly what kind of weather this is, what causes it, what the consequences of it are and what specific examples of it there are.

WATCH AND LISTEN

Video script

▶ Heat from the sun changes water from rivers, lakes and the sea to a gas. It goes up into the sky and then turns into a liquid to make clouds. The water in the clouds later falls as rain, ice or snow.

Most of that water goes back to the rivers, lakes and sea. This is called the water cycle and it is very important. 300 million litres of water fall from the sky every day.

However, in some places in the world, rain does not fall very often. But people need rain to grow food and to drink.

So now do we make rain when it doesn't rain? First, we need to think about how clouds become rain. Clouds are made up of small drops, or droplets, of water. When the droplets get bigger they fall as rain, ice or snow. However, droplets of rain can only fall if there is some dust in the air for the water droplet to join to. The dust makes the droplet heavy enough to fall from the sky.

In one part of Texas, in the United States, this hasn't happened for a long time. There has been no rain. Gary Walker is a pilot with a very special job. He makes rain.

Gary does something called 'cloud seeding'. This means that he puts a chemical into the clouds for water to join with to make rain. Gary attaches something called silver iodide on the plane. He flies 5,486 metres up in the air.

He shoots the silver iodide into the cloud. If everything goes well, rain should fall after 45 minutes. You can see more clouds in the sky. There has been 12 per cent more rain from the clouds that Gary has put silver iodide into. Gary will go back into the clouds, again and again, to try to make more rain.

PREPARING TO WATCH

UNDERSTANDING KEY VOCABULARY

1 👤 Tell students they are going to watch a video about rain and the water cycle. Students work individually to match the words to the definitions. Allow 3 minutes for this, before inviting feedback from the class.

> **Answers**
>
> 1 d 2 a 3 b 4 e 5 c

2 👤 Students work individually to decide if the sentences are true or false. Allow 3 minutes for this, before inviting feedback from the class. Ask students to correct the false sentences as you do feedback.

> **Answers**
>
> 1 T 2 F (oil rises to the top) 3 F (dust kicked up by vehicles travelling on roads may make up 33% of air pollution) 4 T 5 T

3 👥 Students work with a partner to discuss what they think happens in the water cycle. Allow 4 minutes for this, before inviting feedback from the class. Do not give the correct answer yet as this will be dealt with in the video.

WHILE WATCHING

MAKING INFERENCES

4 ▶ Tell students that you are going to play the first minute of the video with the sound turned off and they have to guess what the presenter is saying. Ask for feedback from the class but do not give the correct answer yet.

5 ▶ Play all of the video with the sound for students to check if their guesses were correct in Exercise 4. Discuss any problems that might have come up.

6 👤👥 Students work individually to match the numbers to the facts. Allow 2 minutes for this. Ask students to check their answers with a partner, before inviting feedback from the class. Do not give the correct answers yet as students will watch the video to check in Exercise 7.

7 ▶ Play the video again for students to check their answers.

> **Answers**
>
> 1 c 2 d 3 b 4 a

UNDERSTANDING DETAIL

8 👥 Students work with a partner to discuss the answers to the questions. Allow 3 minutes for this, before inviting feedback from the class. Do not give the correct answers yet as students will watch the video a final time to check in Exercise 9.

9 ▶ Play the video again for students to check their answers. Then invite feedback from the class.

> **Answers**
>
> 1 The sun 2 Snow 3 There hasn't been enough rain for a long time. 4 Gary puts silver iodide into the clouds (to join with the water in the clouds and make rain). 5 To make rain

POST-LISTENING

10 👤 Students work individually to match the types of weather to the climate words. Allow 4 minutes for this, before inviting feedback from the class.

> **Answers**
>
> 1 e 2 a 3 d 4 b 5 f 6 g 7 c

DISCUSSION

> **Background note**
>
> Climate change refers to changes in climate and weather conditions over a long period of time. There are many possible causes, one of which is considered to be pollution of the atmosphere, an effect which is often referred to as *global warming*.

11 👥 Students work with a partner to discuss the questions. Allow 5 minutes for this, before inviting feedback from the class. This activity can be extended by putting two pairs to work together to compare their answers. In the feedback you could ask them to tell the class what the pair they were working with had said.

LISTENING 1

PRONUNCIATION FOR LISTENING

Note: you can ask students to research climate change for homework in preparation for the Post-listening activity.

Optional lead-in

Books closed. Write the following on the board: /ɒ/ (clock) and /əʊ/ (phone). Underline the o in clock and phone and say the words and ask students to repeat. Ask students: 'In which word is the o short?' (clock) and then ask: 'How can you describe the o in phone?' (long). Say the words clock and phone again and ask students to repeat. Ask them: 'In which word does the shape of your mouth stay the same and not move for the letter o?' (clock). Then ask: 'What happens to your mouth when you say the o in phone?' (it closes a bit). Then point to the /ɒ/, say the sound and ask students to repeat, making sure it is short and the mouth doesn't change. Then point to the /əʊ/, say the sound and ask students to repeat, making sure that it is long and that their mouths close slightly from the beginning to end of the sound. If necessary, exaggerate this 'slide'. To drill these sounds, point to the words/sounds on the board, with the students saying the word or sound as clearly as possible. Increase the speed of your pointing while students try to keep up.

---

1 👥 Ask students to open their books at page 108 and look at the words in groups A and B. Students work with a partner to say the words out loud and decide which group of words goes with which sound – /ɒ/ (short o) or /əʊ/ (long o). Allow about 2 minutes for this, before inviting feedback from the class. Follow up by asking students if they can think of any other words with these sounds. Start by giving them stop, shop and stone, comb. When going through the answers, read out each word and ask the students to repeat it, more than once if necessary.

Answers
A /ɒ/ B /əʊ/

2 👥 Students work with a partner, using the words from Exercise 1 to complete the sentences. Allow about 4 minutes for this, before inviting feedback from the class.

Answers
1 don't 2 want 3 forest 4 known 5 cost

3 👥 Students work with a partner to decide if sentences 1–3 in Exercise 2 are true for them. Allow about 2 minutes for this, before inviting feedback from the class. You could drill each sentence, before discussing students' responses.

Answers will vary.

PREPARING TO LISTEN

UNDERSTANDING KEY VOCABULARY

1 Tell students that they are going to listen to a news report. Draw students' attention to the photograph and see if they can identify the animal it shows. Ask them if anyone has ever seen one before.

Answers
a purple frog. Answers will vary.

2 👤 Tell students to read the information about the Western Ghats rainforest. Students work individually to summarize the information into three key points, using note form. Allow about 6 minutes for this. Circulate and monitor, giving assistance where appropriate. Do not check answers at this stage.

3 👥 Put students into pairs, preferably not with the student they've been sitting next to. Ask students to compare their three key points with their partner. Did they choose the same points? Allow about 3 minutes for this, before inviting feedback from the class.

Answers
Answers will vary, but are likely to include: location of forest, climate or weather of forest, problems caused by climate change

4 👥 Tell students that in the listening they will hear the words that are underlined in the information about the Western Ghats rainforest in Exercise 2. Ask students to work with a partner to match the underlined words in the text to their definitions (1–5). Allow about 3 minutes for this, before inviting feedback from the class.

Answers
1 c 2 a 3 e 4 b 5 d

WHILE LISTENING

PREDICTING IDEAS FROM RESEARCH

5 👤👥👥 Read the information in the Predicting ideas from research box as students read along, and ask a couple of questions to check understanding, e.g. 'Why is it helpful to read some information in advance?' and 'What can you do as a result?' (predict the main ideas that you will hear). Students read the paragraph in Exercise 2 again and then work with a partner to tick the subjects on the list that they predict will be in the report. Allow about 4 minutes for this. Do not check answers at this stage.

6 (◀)) 6.1 👤👥👥 Play the audio and ask students to work individually to check their answers. Ask them to check with a partner, before inviting feedback from the class.

> **Answers**
> 2 3 5

7 (◀)) 6.1 👤👥👥 Tell students that they are going to listen to the audio again and work individually to choose the correct endings for the sentences. Alternatively, ask students to choose the endings from memory and then listen again to check. After the audio, allow students to check with a partner, before inviting feedback from the class.

> **Answers**
> 1 a 2 a 3 a 4 a 5 b

POST-LISTENING

If possible, ask students to research the subject of climate change in preparation for this class. Alternatively, if you have access to the internet, research climate change during the class.

8 👥 Students work with a partner to identify the problems caused by climate change that they can see in the photographs. Allow about 2 minutes for this, before inviting feedback from the class.

> **Answers**
> 1 water shortages / drought 2 damage to (rain)forests
> 3 flooding

9 👥 Students work with a partner to think about how the wildlife has been and will be affected in the places in the photographs in Exercise 8. If appropriate, do the first one with the class. Allow about 4 minutes for this. Circulate and monitor, giving assistance where appropriate.

> **Possible answers**
> 1 Wildlife won't find water to drink and plants won't grow well if at all, so there will be food shortages.
> 2 Damage to rainforests will cause wildlife to die or to move to new areas. 3 Wildlife will need to move to new areas to find dry land.

10 👥👥👥 Invite each pair to give feedback to the class on their ideas for Exercise 9. Depending on class size and time available, each pair could present their ideas for just one of the places. Is there general agreement or do students have different ideas? Alternatively, put students into groups of 4, splitting up the partners that worked together in Exercise 9. Allow 4 minutes for students to share their ideas and decide the best ones. Circulate and monitor, giving assistance where appropriate. Invite feedback from the class.

> **Answers will vary.**

◉ LANGUAGE DEVELOPMENT

VERB COLLOCATIONS

> **Optional lead-in**
>
> Books closed. Ask students if they remember what collocations are (words that go together / word partnerships). Write the following on the board: *go to, take, have* and ask students: 'Can you remember any of the collocations you learned in Unit 2?' Write all acceptable ones, whether from Unit 2 or elsewhere, on the board under the correct verb. From Unit 2: go to: a lecture, school, university, an exam; take: your time, notes, care, an exam, a picture, advice; have: a lecture, a problem, a nice time, a celebration, a party, an exam, fun.

1 👥 Tell students that they are going to learn about some more verb–noun collocations and ask them to open their books at page 111. Students work with a partner to match the verbs to the nouns to make collocations.

Remind students that sometimes more than one noun will collocate with the verb. Allow about 3 minutes for this, before inviting feedback from the class.

Answers

1 b / c / e 2 d 3 a 4 b / c 5 d

2 👥 Students work with a partner to complete the sentences, using the correct form of the verbs from Exercise 1. Allow about 3 minutes for this, before inviting feedback from the class.

Answers

1 protect 2 cut down 3 prevent 4 do 5 causes

REVIEW OF FUTURE FORMS

Language note

English has a number of different forms for talking about the future, and students can find this confusing. The series of exercises in this section focuses on the ways that will, going to and the Present continuous are used to talk about the future.

Optional lead-in

Ask students: 'When we make predictions, are we talking about the past, present or future?' (the future). Ask students: 'Can you think of some of the ways we use to talk about the future in English? to elicit will, going to and the Present continuous.

3 👥 Tell students that they will be reviewing the three main ways we use for talking about the future. Students work with a partner to circle the verb which refers to the future. Allow about 1 minute for this, before inviting feedback from the class.

Answers

1 will stop 2 won't be 3 is going to present
4 are meeting

4 Ask the class to find an example of the Present continuous in Exercise 3 and an example of the negative form of will.

Answers

1 are meeting (sentence 4) 2 won't be (sentence 2)

5 👥 Students work with a partner to complete the dialogue with the verbs and the future forms in brackets. If appropriate, do the first one with the class. Allow about 5 minutes for this. Circulate and monitor, giving assistance if required, before inviting feedback from the class.

Answers

What are you doing tonight?
I'll probably go home.
Are you doing something special?
I'm visiting Chile next month so I'm going to book a hotel.
I'll come with you!

6 👤👥 Tell students that the general rules for talking about decisions, plans and arrangements are in the Explanations box. Students work individually to complete the rules, using either will, going to or Present continuous. Allow about 2 minutes for this. Ask students to check with a partner, before inviting feedback from the class.

Answers

1 will 2 going to 3 Present continuous

7 👤👥 Students work individually or with a partner to complete the sentences, using the correct future forms of the verbs in brackets. Remind them that sometimes there could be more than one correct answer. Allow about 5 minutes for this, before inviting feedback from the class.

Answers

Decisions and plans: 1 am leaving 2 am going to do
3 am going; will come 4 is talking / is going to talk
Predictions: 1 are going to drop 2 will / am going to pass

8 👤 Tell students that they are going to think about their own futures. Ask them to work individually to write one or more ideas for each of the three sentences. Allow about 3 minutes for this. Circulate, monitor and give assistance where appropriate, in particular with correct use of the different future forms. Do not do feedback at this stage.

9 👥 👥👥 Ask students to work with a partner and tell each other about their ideas. Allow about 4 minutes for this, before inviting feedback from the class. This activity can be extended by moving students into new pairs and asking them to tell their new partner about their old partner's ideas and/or putting them into groups of 4 and asking them to tell their group about their ideas, and then each group decides who has the most interesting idea for each section. During feedback, encourage students to discuss which ideas they think are the most interesting.

> **Answers will vary.**

LISTENING 2

PRONUNCIATION FOR LISTENING

SOUNDING INTERESTED

> **Optional lead-in**
>
> Books closed. Ask four students to tell you one of their ideas from Exercise 8 in Language Development on page 112. For the first two, respond with an interested *really* and the second two with a bored *really*. Then ask the class: 'Do I think *all* those answers were interesting?' (no). Then ask the students: 'How do you know?' (because of the way you said *really*). Ask students: 'Do you think it's important to sound interested when you are listening to someone?' (yes). 'Why is it important?' (because it's polite and we want to encourage the speaker to continue speaking).

1 Tell students that they are going to learn how to sound interested when they are responding to someone. Ask students to open their books at page 113 and look at the words. Ask the class: 'What happens to our voice if we are interested or happy?'

> **Answers**
> It goes up at the end.

2 ◀) 6.2 👥👥 Tell students that they are going to listen to some short dialogues. Play the audio. Students work individually to mark the response I for interested or B for bored next to Speaker B. After the audio, ask students to check with a partner, before inviting feedback from the class.

> **Answers**
> 1 I 2 B 3 B 4 I 5 B

3 ◀) 6.2 👥👥 Rather than asking students to remember the intonation, you could play the audio again, stopping after each dialogue so that the students can repeat the sentences. Pay attention to the different intonation used by Speaker B. If appropriate, drill these dialogues with the class. Divide the class into two, one half As, the other Bs, and practise the dialogues. Then swap, so that all students have had a chance to practise the different intonation used by B. Students then work with a partner and read the dialogues out loud. This time B should change the intonation of their voice and A should guess if they are interested or bored. Finish off by asking students if they all guessed their partner's intonation correctly.

PREPARATION FOR LISTENING

UNDERSTANDING KEY VOCABULARY

4 👤 👥👥 Tell students that they are going to listen to a discussion between two students. Students work individually to match the pairs of opposite adjectives. Allow about 2 minutes for this. Ask students to check with a partner, before inviting feedback from the class. Check understanding of any of the adjectives students may not be clear about.

> **Answers**
> 1 e 2 f 3 a 4 g 5 h 6 b 7 d 8 c

5 Tell students that they are going to listen to two students discussing a survey on how the weather can change people's moods. Ask students to look at sentences 1 and 2 and decide which is the definition of *a survey*. Then ask: 'What is *mood*?' (the way we feel at a particular time).

> **Answers**
> 2

WHILE LISTENING

6 (♦) **6.3** 🎧 Read aloud the information in the Recognizing mood box as the students read along. Tell students that it is important for us to be able to recognize people's moods from the way they speak, whether they are happy, bored, upset or interested. Ask students to listen to the audio and decide who is more interested in the work, Sergio or Murat.

Answers

Murat

7 (♦) **6.3** 🎧🎧 Play the audio again and ask students to work individually to complete Sergio's notes on the ideas map. Ask students to check their answers with a partner, before inviting feedback from the class.

Answers

1 more upset 2 less tired 3 energetic 4 concentration
5 angry/angrier

8 🎧🎧 Ask students to try to remember what was said in the discussion and work with a partner to match the topics to the reasons for choosing or not choosing them. Allow about 2 minutes for this. Do not check answers at this stage.

9 🎧🎧 Tell students to go to the audioscript 6.3 on page 217 and work with a partner to check their answers. Allow about 2 minutes for this, before inviting feedback from the class.

Answers

1 c 2 a 3 d 4 b

10 (♦) **6.4** 🎧🎧🎧 Tell students that they are going to listen to the results of the survey in part 2 of the audio. Play the audio and ask students to work individually to choose the correct results. Ask students to check with a partner, before inviting feedback from the class.

Answers

1 14 2 13 3 light 4 more

DISCUSSION

11 🎧🎧 🎧🎧🎧 Before asking students to do this task, you could tell them about a time the weather changed your mood and if you have lived or are living in a different country, how the weather has affected you. Students work in pairs to discuss the questions. Allow about 2–3 minutes for this, before inviting feedback from the class. This activity can be extended by putting students into new pairs and asking them to discuss the ideas of their previous partner, or by putting students into groups of 4 to discuss the questions as a group to find out who has the most interesting responses. Do they all feel the same about living in a country with very different weather? Allow about 4 minutes for the group discussion, before inviting feedback from the class.

Answers will vary.

CRITICAL THINKING

Optional lead-in

Books closed. Ask students to suggest places they have been to where they have experienced really good weather. Encourage as many students as possible to nominate places and write these places on one half of the board. Then ask for suggestions of places where students have experienced really bad weather. You can give examples such as Vladivostok in Russia, where temperatures drop to −30 degrees Celsius, and Chicago, which is known as the windy city as it has very strong, cold winds. Again, write the names of the places on the board. Then ask students to think of as many weather collocations as they know, and write these on the other half of the board. If appropriate, allow students to open their books to search for collocations in this unit. Then ask students to match the places to the collocations.

Students begin to think about the Speaking task they will do at the end of the unit (*Create and complete a survey about the use of land and how it affects the climate. Present the results of the survey to your classmates.*). Give them a minute to look at the box and ask you any questions they might have. It might be useful to give some of the preparation work for the final task as homework.

REMEMBER

1 👥 Students work in pairs to make a list of how weather problems in Africa and the Arctic affect people, animals and the environment. Encourage students to use as much as possible of the new vocabulary that they have learned in the unit. Circulate, monitor and give help with vocabulary and collocations where necessary. Allow about 4 minutes for this but do not invite feedback at this stage as students will compare their ideas with those in Exercise 2.

2 👥 Students work in pairs and read the problems in the boxes to compare them with their lists from Exercise 1. Allow 5 minutes for this, before eliciting feedback from the class.

EVALUATE

3 👤 Students work individually to complete the table. Allow 2 minutes for this but do not check answers yet as students compare their answers in the next exercise.

4 👥 Students work in pairs to compare their answers to Exercise 3. Allow 2 minutes for this, before checking answers with the class. There are a number of possibilities for these so accept all logical answers.

> **Answers**
>
> **Africa** 2 drought – less food
> 3 less clean water – disease will spread
> **The Arctic** 4 ice will melt – sea levels rise
> 5 less sea ice for animals to hunt from – wildlife will begin to disappear

5 👥 Read aloud the Evaluating consequences box as students follow. Students then work in pairs to look at the consequence map for Africa and to create a consequence map for the Arctic using the ideas from Exercise 3.

6 👥 Students work with a new partner and take turns to explain their ideas using their consequence map. Allow 5 minutes for this, before inviting feedback from the class. If there is time, you could ask some students to present their ideas to the class.

> **Answers will vary.**

SPEAKING

PREPARATION FOR SPEAKING

PRONUNCIATION FOR SPEAKING

1 👥 Ask students to work with a partner to decide which one of each pair is the cause and which the consequence. Allow about 2 minutes for this, before inviting feedback from the class.

> **Answers**
>
> 1 a consequence b cause 2 a cause b consequence
> 3 a consequence b cause

2 🔊 6.5 👥 Students work individually to listen to the sentences and fill in the gaps. Ask students to check with a partner before inviting feedback from the class.

> **Answers**
>
> 1 so 2 Therefore 3 As a result

3 🔊 6.6 👤 Ask students to listen to the audio and repeat the words. Repeat and drill if necessary.

4 👥 Tell students to look at the example and ask them what happened, to elicit the cause (*the rainfall was too heavy*). Then ask them what happened because the rain was too heavy, to elicit *the village flooded*, and highlight that this is the consequence of the heavy rainfall. Ask students to work in pairs to think of a consequence for the things that happened in sentences 2–9. Encourage them to be as creative and imaginative as possible. Allow about 5 minutes for this, and circulate, monitor and give assistance where appropriate. When doing feedback with the class, accept all logical answers as there are a number of possibilities.

> **Possible answers**
>
> 2 The students didn't study much so they failed their exams.
> 3 A new factory was built in the city. As a result, more people had jobs.
> 4 Tigers are in danger of disappearing. Therefore we need to protect them.
> 5 Nowadays more people are interested in global warming so governments may feel they need to take more action.
> 6 New cars are very expensive. As a result, people keep their old ones for longer.
> 7 Rainforests are getting smaller. Therefore we need to protect them.
> 8 I've lost my passport so I need to apply for a new one.
> 9 Communication is much easier nowadays. As a result, we keep in touch with our friends.

5 Ask students to work in pairs to choose their four favourite sentences plus consequences from Exercise 4 and switch the order so that they focus on the causes, using *because of*, *because* and *due to*. Look at the example in Exercise 4 and relate it to the one in Exercise 5.

Possible answers

2 The students failed their exams because they didn't study much.
3 More people had jobs because of the new factory.
4 We need to protect tigers because they are in danger of disappearing.
5 Governments may feel they need to take more action on global warming because more people are interested in it.
6 People keep their old cars for longer due to the cost of new ones.
7 We need to protect rainforests because they are getting smaller.
8 I need to apply for a new passport because I've lost my old one.
9 We keep in touch with our friends due to easier communication.

6 Students work individually to look at pictures 1–6 and to try to understand how burning fossil fuels causes climate change. Allow 3 minutes for this and then move on to Exercise 7. Do not invite feedback at this stage.

7 Students work with a partner to create a consequence map to show the causes of climate change. Circulate, monitor and give assistance as appropriate. Allow 5–7 minutes for this but do not invite feedback at this stage.

8 Students could work with the same partner as in Exercise 7 or with a new partner to describe and compare their consequence maps. Allow 5 minutes for this, before eliciting feedback from the class. If there is time and it is appropriate, pairs could present their ideas to the class.

Possible answers

Homes, factories, cars and planes burn fossil fuels → [*so / as a result*] gases and smoke rise into the sky → [*so / as a result*] heat is trapped in the earth's atmosphere → [*therefore*] temperatures rise → [*so / as a result*] ice caps in the Arctic and Antarctic melt → [*so / as a result*] global warming/temperatures rise more

SPEAKING TASK

PREPARE

1 Give students a minute to read the box and remind themselves of the Speaking task they are going to do. Students work in groups of three of four to create two consequence maps for the two different uses of some land in the centre of their town. Encourage them to be as imaginative and creative as possible. Circulate, monitor and give assistance as appropriate. Allow 8–10 minutes for this but do not ask for class feedback at this stage.

2 Students go round the class and get answers to questions 1–5 from as many people as possible (at least 5). They must keep a note of all the answers.

3 Students go back into their groups and collate their answers. They should then draw conclusions from the information they have gathered and prepare a short summary to present to the class. Remind them to focus on causes and consequences. When they prepare to present their findings to the whole class, they could appoint one spokesperson for their group or they could divide up the summary and each person could present a different part of it.

PRESENT

4 The groups present their findings to the class. Note good uses of causes and consequences language for follow-up work. You could round off the class by having a vote on the various ideas for the land to see which is the most popular.

> ### ADDITIONAL SPEAKING TASK
>
> See page 139 for the Additional speaking task (*Discussing consequences and presenting a survey*) and Model language for this unit.
>
> Make a photocopy of page 139 for each student.
>
> Tell students they are going to discuss ideas about weather and climate and write survey questions.
>
> Before students write the survey questions, you could elicit some vocabulary related to the weather and mood that they met in the unit. Draw 3 ideas maps on the board. See Exercise 7 on page 114 in the Student's Book for how to draw the ideas maps. In the centre of one, write HOT WEATHER and draw a line coming from it with SUNNY written on the end of it. In the centre of the second, write COLD WEATHER and draw a line from it with DARK written on the end of it. In the centre of the third, write WET WEATHER and draw a line with FLOOD written on the end of it.

Ask students to call out words or phrases related to these three types of weather and add their ideas to the the ideas maps, adding more lines as necessary. Allow 5 minutes for this and then give each student a photocopy of page 139.

👥 Students work in pairs. Ask them to read questions 1–5 of the survey and then write 5 more questions. Leave the ideas maps on the board to help students. Circulate, monitor and give help as necessary and keep a list of good language as well as errors for the later feedback stage. but do not do any feedback at this point.

👥 Ask students to go round the class and ask and answer the 10 questions in their surveys. They should make notes of the answers so that they can present them to the class later. Allow 10–15 minutes for this stage, depending on the size of the class.

👥👥 Students could work with their partner again or you could put 2 pairs together to make a group of 4 to discuss and summarize the results of their surveys and plan their presentation for the class. Remind them to use the Model language on the photocopy. Allow 5 minutes for this.

Finish off by asking the groups to present the results of their surveys to the whole class and ask them which results are the most and least surprising.

TASK CHECKLIST AND OBJECTIVES REVIEW

Refer students to the end of the unit for the Task checklist and Objectives review. Students complete the tables individually to reflect on their learning and identify areas for improvement.

WORDLIST

See Teaching tips page 10, section 6, for ideas about how to make the most of the Wordlist with your students.

REVIEW TEST

See pages 124–125 for the photocopiable Review test for this unit and page 107 for ideas about when and how to administer the Review test.

RESEARCH PROJECT

Create a website to explain weather phenomena to children

Divide the class into groups and assign each group a weather phenomenon such as rain, hale, wind, cloud, fog, snow and dust storms or even tornadoes, hurricanes, cyclones or typhoons. Each group will need to find out how and why these phenomena occur and collect relevant video, audio and images. Students could use tools on the Cambridge LMS to share ideas.

Students then use this information to create a website or eBook explaining the weather phenomena in a simple way to children. You can find guides and eBook software by searching for 'create eBook'. The website/eBook could include the media collected by each group and quizzes for the children.

The class can then find ways to publicize their creation to local schools as a resource.

7 SPORTS AND COMPETITION

Learning objectives

Before you start the Unlock your knowledge section, ask students to read the Learning objectives box so that they have a clear idea of what they are going to learn in this unit. Tell them that you will come back to these objectives at the end of the unit when they review what they have learned. Give them the opportunity to ask you any questions they might have.

UNLOCK YOUR KNOWLEDGE

Lead-in

Books closed. Ask students: 'What do we call it when I ask you to do something in groups and the person/group that finishes first is the winner?' to elicit *race*.

Write *race* on the board. Ask students if they can think of different sports races, to elicit ideas such as running, horse, camel, bicycle/bike/cycle, Formula 1. Accept any reasonable suggestions. Point out that apart from *running*, these collocate with *race*.

👥 Students work in pairs to answer the questions. Encourage students to give reasons for their responses to the questions and to 3 in particular. Allow about 3 minutes for this, before inviting feedback from the class.

Answers

1 The BMX event at the London 2012 Olympic Games. BMX is a type of off-road racing, individually or in teams.
2 and 3 Answers will vary.

WATCH AND LISTEN

Video script

▶ Siena is in Tuscany in the northwest of Italy. The city is well known for its beautiful old buildings and its main square. It is also famous for the Palio di Siena: the most famous horse race in Italy, which takes place on the 2nd of July and the 16th of August each year.

Alberto is an Italian jockey. He practises all year for the race. The race is only 3 laps and takes 90 seconds. Only ten jockeys are able to ride in the race. Each year 50 jockeys from all over Italy fight to be one of the ten.

Each jockey races for a different neighbourhood in the city. The winning neighbourhood receives the Palio: a banner which the race is named after.

One horse is chosen for each neighbourhood, using a lottery. It is only after the lottery that the neighbourhood will decide which jockey they will use in the race. Will Alberto ride in the Palio?

Alberto gets a phone call. The small neighbourhood of Lupa wants him to ride for them. Alberto is very happy because Lupa is where he was born.

The day of the race has come. Everyone is going to the main square. Many of them wear the colours of their neighbourhood. 60,000 people fill the square.

The jockeys enter the square. Alberto Ricceri's horse is called Zodiac. Alberto has won the Palio before. Can he win it now for his neighbourhood?

The Palio is a very dangerous race. The crowd is excited, but also worried.

On the second lap a jockey falls in front of Alberto's horse. There is nothing Alberto can do. He falls too.

The race is won by the Bruco neighbourhood. Winning the Palio is everything.

Alberto wasn't hurt in the fall. Zodiac is also OK. Everyone in his Lupa neighbourhood is very sad that they didn't win. But tomorrow, the people of Siena will start making plans for the next Palio.

PREPARING TO WATCH

USING YOUR KNOWLEDGE TO PREDICT CONTENT

Optional lead-in

Write the word *horseracing* on the board. Ask the class if anyone knows anything about horseracing. Accept any reasonable suggestions. Write the following on the board: *Dubai, Japan, Arabia*. Ask students: 'Where is the race with the biggest prize in the world?' (Dubai, Dubai World Cup, with a prize of 10 million US dollars). 'Which country has the most horse races?' (Japan, with 21,000). 'Where do the best racehorses come from?' (Arabia).

1 👥 Ask students to work with a partner to answer the questions. Allow 1 minute for this, before inviting feedback from the class.

   Answers will vary.

2 Ask the class to make a list of the things they expect to see in the video. Allow 2 minutes for this, before inviting feedback. Write their suggestions on the board, e.g. *horses, riders/jockeys, people watching, racetrack, advertisements*. These suggestions will be checked in Exercise 7.

UNDERSTANDING KEY VOCABULARY

3 👤👥 Students work individually to match the words to the photographs. Allow about a minute for this. Ask students to check with a partner, before inviting feedback from the class.

> **Answers**
>
> 1 a 2 d 3 b 4 c

4 👥 Students work with a partner to match the words to the definitions. Allow about 5 minutes for this, before inviting feedback from the class.

> **Answers**
>
> 1 g 2 d 3 c 4 e 5 f 6 a 7 b

5 👤👥 Students work individually to complete the sentences with words from Exercise 4. Allow about 3 minutes for this. Ask students to check with a partner, before inviting feedback from the class.

> **Answers**
>
> 1 worried 2 disappointed 3 neighbourhood 4 excited 5 dangerous 6 lap 7 fall

6 👥 Students work with a partner to discuss whether sentences 1–4 in Exercise 5 are true for them. Allow about 3 minutes for this, before inviting feedback from the class.

> **Answers will vary.**

WHILE WATCHING

LISTENING FOR KEY INFORMATION

7 ▶️👤👥 Tell students to look at the words in the list and check that they understand all the meanings. Play only the first two minutes of the video and ask students to work individually and tick the things they see. After the video, allow students to check with a partner, before inviting feedback from the class. Compare these results with students' answers for Exercise 2.

> **Answers**
>
> 1 horses 4 drums 5 banners 6 people running 8 a town square 10 a racetrack

8 ▶️👤👥 Tell students that they are now going to watch the whole of the video. Give students a minute to look at the questions and check that they understand them all. Play the video. Students work individually to answer the questions. After the video, ask students to check with a partner, before inviting feedback from the class.

> **Answers**
>
> 1 a famous horse race 2 3 3 10 4 He was born in the neighbourhood of Lupa. 5 His horse falls and he doesn't win the race.

> **Background note**
>
> The jockeys in the Palio di Siena ride bareback (with no saddle), so it is not surprising that they can easily be thrown from their horses.

DISCUSSION

> **Language note**
>
> Tell students that one skill that will help them improve their English is to 'guess the meaning of a word from its context'. We call this *inferencing*, as we infer the meaning from the context. Often, although we do not understand every word in a text, we can guess the meaning from the words around it.

9 👤 Ask students to look at the underlined word in the sentence from the video and guess what it means by looking at the words around it and what they can remember from the video. Allow 1 minute for this, before eliciting feedback from the class.

> **Answers**
>
> famous

10 👥 Ask students to work in pairs and discuss the famous places in their town or city. Include the whole of their country if this will help the discussion. Allow about 2 minutes for this, before inviting feedback from the class.

Optional activity

👤👥 Ask students individually to research some well-known places related to sport. Alternatively, put students into groups and ask them to research a specific place related to sporting events. Places could include: Siena; Dubai, the richest horse race in the world; Barcelona, the Camp Nou football stadium; Wimbledon, tennis; Monaco, F1 Grand Prix; Lambeau Field, USA, American football, home of the Green Bay Packers.

LISTENING 1

PREPARING TO LISTEN

UNDERSTANDING KEY VOCABULARY

Optional lead-in

Ask students: 'Can you think of any special clothes or equipment people use when they are playing sports?' Encourage ideas by thinking of different sports: horseracing – safety helmet, gloves; football – boots, ball, etc.

1 👤👥 Ask students to look at the photograph and ask: 'Does anyone know what type of sport this is?' (a martial art, but unless a student suggests it, don't tell them that it's taekwondo). Students work individually to label the photograph with the words in the box. Allow 1 minute for this. Ask students to check with a partner, before inviting feedback from the class.

Answers
a gloves b helmet c vest d competitor

2 👤👥 Students read the paragraph individually. Allow about 2 minutes for this. Students could then work with a partner to match the underlined words in the text to the definitions (a–e) below. Allow about 2 minutes for this, before inviting feedback from the class. Check understanding of the text and ask if anyone knows any examples of football players scoring with their hands (Diego Maradona scored a goal for Argentina with his hand against England in the World Cup in 1986).

Answers
1 c 2 e 3 d 4 a 5 b

3 👥 Write taekwondo on the board and ask students if they know what this is. Refer them to the photograph above and explain that taekwondo is a martial art similar to kung fu, but that it comes from Korea. Students work in pairs to look at the underlined words in Exercise 2 and decide which of them might apply to taekwondo. Look at the example first and then allow about 2 minutes for this, before inviting feedback from the class.

Possible answers
All of the words (there is a referee who keeps the score; it is a competitive sport; you kick the other person; you try to hit each other).

4 👥 Tell students that they are going to listen to a panel discussion about taekwondo. Students work with a partner to decide the correct definition of panel discussion. After confirming the answer, ask for or give examples of TV panel discussion shows in the country you are in. You could ask if students know what the other definitions are of (1 a speech/lecture 3 a debate).

Answers
2

Optional lead-in

Books closed. The listening aim here is to understand the bias of speakers. To illustrate this, divide the board into three columns: in the first column, write jockey and footballer. In the second column, write very interesting and not interesting. In the third column, write horseracing and football. Point to jockey and horseracing and ask students: 'What will the jockey probably say about horseracing?' (very interesting). Ask the students: 'What will the footballer probably say about football?' (very interesting). Then ask students: 'What will the jockey probably say about football?' (not very interesting). Finally, ask the students: 'What will the footballer probably say about horseracing?' (not very interesting). Ask the students why this is (because it is their job, or similar). Write the words bias (noun), biased (adjective) on the board and explain that this refers to someone having a special reason to say something positive or negative about something, or to agree or disagree with something. When we listen, it is important to think about who is speaking and why, as they may be biased. Concept-check by asking students: 'Why is it important to think about who is speaking and why?' (because they may have a special reason for their opinion and they may be biased).

5 👤👥 Tell students to open their books at page 127 and to read the information in the Understanding bias box. Answer any questions they may still have. Then ask students to work in pairs to match the speaker to the statements. Allow about 2 minutes for this, before inviting feedback from the class.

> **Answers**
> 1 c 2 a 3 b

WHILE LISTENING

LISTENING FOR BIAS

6 👥 Write the word *sensor (noun)* on the board and ask students if anyone knows what a sensor does (it senses things). If no student responds, hold up your hand with your fingers and thumb extended to show *five* and ask the students what the five senses are (seeing, hearing, smelling, tasting, feeling/touching), counting them off on your fingers. Point back to the word *sensor* and repeat the question: 'What does a sensor do?' (it senses things). Hold up your hand and tell students to imagine that it is a computer sensor. Bring a pointed finger from your other hand to the 'computer sensor' and just as it's about to touch, ask the students: 'What will happen when my finger touches the computer sensor?' (make a sound, make a light flash or any other alternative which indicates registering the touch).

Tell students that they are going to listen to a panel discussion about a plan to use a computer sensor (repeat the motion of your finger touching your palm) in a taekwondo vest (put the hand that represents the computer sensor in the middle of your chest). Ask students: 'Who normally does the scoring in a sports competition?' (the referee). Tell students that this computer sensor could help the referee with scoring. Concept-check this by asking students if the computer sensor will help the referee, to elicit *yes, it will.* Tell students to think about bias and to work in pairs to read the details of the three members of the panel discussion and decide what they will feel about the new plan. Allow about 2 minutes for this, before inviting feedback from the class.

> **Possible answers**
> It is likely that the director of the company will like the system as his company will benefit. The taekwondo champion might welcome it if he thinks it will be good for the sport. The head of the Referees' Association may not like it if he or she feels it will take away the work/authority of referees.

7 🔊 **7.1** 👤👥 Ask students to listen to the audio and work individually to match the names of the speakers to the jobs in Exercise 6 and to decide who agrees with the use of computer sensors and who disagrees. After the audio, ask students to check their answers with a partner, before inviting feedback from the class.

> **Answers**
> a (Nam Ki Gam, former international taekwondo champion) and c (Sunan Wattana, Managing Director of Sports Technology Ltd) agree, though Nam Ki doesn't think it should be used exclusively, without a referee. b (Raina Akintola, Head of the Referees' Association) disagrees.

8 🔊 **7.1** 👤👥 Ask students to listen again and work individually to mark each statement with the name of the speaker. After the audio, ask students to check with a partner. Do not check answers at this stage.

9 👥 Ask students to work in the same pairs and check their answers to Exercise 8 in the audioscript on page 218.

> **Answers**
> 1 S 2 S 3 R 4 R 5 N 6 N

DISCUSSION

10 👥 Students work in pairs to discuss the questions. Allow 5 minutes for this, before inviting feedback from the class.

> **Background note**
> Technology is used increasingly in sport and will probably be used more and more as it becomes more reliable. It helps referees to make the right decisions, for example by allowing them to watch video replays. However, there are those who feel it can be too slow and it takes away from the excitement.

⊙ LANGUAGE DEVELOPMENT

REVIEW OF THE PRESENT PERFECT

> **Optional lead-in**
>
> Books closed. Tell students that you've lost your keys. Write *I've lost my keys.* on the board. Ask students: 'When did I lose my keys?' (we don't know, it doesn't matter). 'Do I know where my keys are now?' (no). 'Are my keys important to me now?' (yes). 'What tense is the sentence on the board?' (the Present perfect).

1 👥 Ask students to open their books at page 128 and to work with a partner to put the words in the correct order to make sentences. Make sure that the students are writing the sentences in full in their notebooks and not just numbering the words in their course books. Allow about 6 minutes for this. Circulate and monitor, giving assistance where appropriate, before inviting feedback from the class.

> **Answers**
>
> 1 I've brought one here to show you. 2 In recent years the scores have caused arguments. 3 The scoring has worked well compared to other sports. 4 Has the scoring caused problems before? 5 Competitors have tried to confuse them. 6 The vest hasn't been tested enough.

2 👥 Students work with a partner and underline the Present perfect verb forms. Allow about 2 minutes for this, before inviting feedback from the class. Ask students: 'Does the Present perfect connect the present with the future or with the past?'

> **Answers**
>
> 1 've brought 2 have caused 3 has worked
> 4 Has … caused 5 have tried 6 hasn't been tested
> It connects the present with the past.

3 👤 Students work individually and look at sentences 4 and 6 in Exercise 1 and answer the questions. Allow about 1 minute for this, before inviting feedback from the class.

> **Answers**
>
> 1 have 2 after

4 👥 Tell students that the Present perfect can be used in three ways. Ask students to work with a partner to match the uses to the time lines. Allow about 2 minutes for this, before inviting feedback from the class. Point out that with all three situations, the main idea is that the action was at an unknown time in the past but that it links to now. Focus on each part of the time lines and concept-check, using the example sentences to establish meaning. For example, with line b, example 2, concept-check by asking: 'When did someone break the glass – now or in the past?' (sometime in the past). 'Do we know when the glass was broken?' (no). 'Does it matter that we don't know?' (no, it's not important). 'Is it broken now?' (yes).

> **Answers**
>
> 1 b 2 c 3 a

5 👤👥 Students work individually to complete the sentences with the Present perfect form of the verb in brackets. Look at question 1 and the Present perfect example with the class and then elicit the verb form for question 2 if you think students need additional help. Allow about 7 minutes for this. Circulate, monitor and give feedback where appropriate, before inviting feedback from the class.

> **Answers**
>
> 2 Have … used 3 has had 4 has … changed
> 5 have … taken 6 has opened 7 have visited
> 8 haven't met 9 have … done 10 Have … worked
> 11 haven't done

6 👤👥 Students work individually to match the sentences in Exercise 5 to the uses 1–3 in the Explanation box in Exercise 4. Allow 2 minutes for this. Then ask students to work with a partner to compare answers. Allow 2 minutes for this, before eliciting feeback from the class.

> **Answers**
>
> 1 Use 1 2 Use 3 3 Use 2 4 Use 1 5 Use 3 6 Use 1
> 7 Use 3 8 Use 3 9 Use 1 10 Use 2 11 Use 1

ADVERBS: *EVER* / *JUST* / *ALREADY* / *YET*

7 Write the adverbs *ever*, *just*, *already* and *yet* on the board and tell students that these adverbs are frequently used with the Present perfect. Ask them to look at sentences 1, 2, 4, 9 and 11 in Exercise 5 and underline the adverbs. Allow 2 minutes for this, before inviting feedback from the class.

Answers
1 already 2 ever 4 just 9 already 11 yet

8 👤👥 Ask students to work individually to match the adverbs with their definitions. Allow about 1 minute for this. Ask students to check with a partner, before inviting feedback from the class.

Answers
1 c 2 a 3 b 4 d

9 👥 Students work with a partner to choose the correct adverb to complete the sentences. Allow about 3 minutes for this, before inviting feedback from the class.

Answers
1 ever 2 yet 3 already 4 just 5 just 6 already

10 👤 Students work on their own to think of ideas. Allow about 1 minute of silent thinking time and encourage students to make notes.

11 👥 Students work with a partner and tell each other their ideas. Allow about 5 minutes for this. Circulate and monitor, giving assistance where appropriate, before inviting feedback from the class. Find out which are the most interesting ideas. This activity can be extended by asking students to change partners and tell each other about their ideas and the ideas of their first partner. Find out which are the most interesting ideas. Allow about 6 minutes for this, before inviting feedback from the class.

Answers will vary.

LISTENING 2

PRONUNCIATION FOR LISTENING

> **Optional lead-in**
>
> Books closed. Say to students: 'OK, we're going to have a test tomorrow … oh, sorry, I mean on **the day after tomorrow**.' Make sure you clearly emphasize the correct day. Ask students: 'What did I do there?' (gave the wrong information). Tell students that when people speak, they sometimes make mistakes and correct themselves. If they correct themselves, they often emphasize the correct version. They do this with intonation and stress to make sure the people listening hear the change clearly.

1 👥 Say: 'Open your books at page 135 … no, that's wrong … page 130.' Tell students to look at the sentences, which all contain corrections. Students work with a partner to underline the correct information in each sentence. Answer the first question with the class. Allow about 3 minutes for this, before inviting feedback from the class.

Answers
1 Rosson 2 golf 3 thirty 4 sport 5 Azerbaijan

2 🔊 7.2 👤 Ask students to listen to the sentences in Exercise 1 and to notice which word the speaker stresses and whether the intonation goes up or down.

Answers
The correct information is stressed and the intonation goes up slightly.

3 👥 Students work with a partner to change the underlined words to make them true or true for them. Allow about 3 minutes for this, before inviting feedback from the class. Encourage students to stress the new information and make sure their intonation goes up.

Answers will vary.

PREPARING TO LISTEN

UNDERSTANDING KEY VOCABULARY

4 👥 Students work with a partner to match the sports with the equipment and the place. Do the first one with the class. Allow about 3 minutes for this, before inviting feedback from the class.

| **Answers**
| 1 e iii 2 d v 3 b ii 4 a iv 5 c i

> **Optional activity**
>
> Brainstorm with the class any more sports, equipment and places they can think of, e.g. tennis, racket, court.

WHILE LISTENING

LISTENING FOR CORRECTIONS

5 🔊 7.3 👥👥 Tell students that they are going to listen to a sports science student giving a presentation about a project. Ask them to work individually to number the photographs in the order she talks about them. After the audio, ask students to check with a partner, before inviting feedback from the class.

| **Answers**
| d 1 a 2 b 3 c 4

6 🔊 7.3 👥👥 Play the audio again. Students work individually and circle the mistakes that Yasmin makes and write the correct word. After the audio, ask students to check with a partner, before inviting feedback from the class.

| **Answers**
| 1 boxing–chess 2 golf ball–soft/tennis ball
| 3 a week–six days 4 Indonesia–Malaysia

POST-LISTENING

7 👥 Students work with a partner to complete Yasmin's sentences with the phrases in the box. Do the first sentence with the class. Allow about 2 minutes for this, before inviting feedback from the class.

| **Answers**
| 1 sorry, I mean 2 well actually 3 or rather 4 no, not

3 👤 Students work individually to think of a sport and to write one sentence about it with a mistake. If there is time and/or if this is a strong class, ask students to write two or three different sentences, each with a mistake.

9 👥👥 Students work with a partner to read out their sentences, correcting them using a phrase from Exercise 7. Ask a stronger student to read the example and make sure they use good stress and intonation for the correction. Some students may argue that a goalkeeper is a player, but not an outfield player. If so, tell them to correct the example, using good stress and intonation (– … or rather, ten *outfield* players and a goalkeeper).

> **Optional activity**
>
> 👥👥👥 👥👥 As an alternative to Exercises 8 and 9, put students into groups of 4 and give each group a familiar sport. Ask them to think of as many facts as they can about the sport. Allow about 2 minutes for this. Then put students into pairs, each pair from a different group, and ask them to tell their partner about the sport they have chosen. Remind them that if they make a mistake, they should correct it, using the phrases from Exercise 7 and the correct stress and intonation. Allow about 4 minutes for this, before inviting feedback from the class about the sports they chose.

DISCUSSION

10 👥👥👥 Ask students to name as many sports as they can and write all reasonable suggestions on the board. Include the sports from Listening 2. Put students into groups of 4 and ask them to discuss whether they would like to watch or try any of the sports on the board. If they have tried/watched any of them, ask them to say if they have enjoyed them, encouraging use of the Present perfect. Remind them that they should give reasons. Allow about 5 minutes for this, before inviting feedback from the class. Encourage students to give their reasons.

CRITICAL THINKING

Students begin to think about the Speaking task that they will do at the end of the unit (*Have a panel discussion about sport and money. Talk about advantages and disadvantages.*). Give them a minute to look at the box and ask you any questions they might have. You could give some of the preparation for this as homework.

REMEMBER

1 👥👥 Students work in pairs to answer the questions. Allow 4 minutes for this, before inviting feedback from the class.

| Answers will vary.

APPLY

2 👥👥 Students work in pairs to decide which sentences give the advantages and which the disadvantages of urban golf. Allow 2 minutes for this, before inviting feedback from the class.

Answers

Advantages: 1, 3, 4 Disadvantages: 2, 5, 6

3 👥👥 Read the information in the Using ideas rakes box while students follow. Direct their attention to the rake at the foot of the page. Students then work with a partner to write the advantages of urban golf onto the ideas rake. Ask them to think of two more advantages. Allow about 2 minutes for this, before inviting feedback from the class.

Answers

Answers will vary, but could include: easy to get to, you don't need a lot of players

4 👥👥 Students work with a partner to write the disadvantages of urban golf on the ideas rake and add another two ideas of their own. Allow about 3 minutes for this, before inviting feedback from the class.

Answers

Answers will vary, but could include: you don't get as much exercise as on a full-size golf course, a car could run you over

5 👤 Students work individually and choose one of the sports from Listening 2 on page 131 (or allocate the sports if you think everyone might choose the same one). Ask them to make two ideas rakes, one for the advantages and one for the disadvantages of the sport they have chosen. Tell them that they can use the audioscript 7.3 on page 129 to help them. Allow about 5 minutes for this. Circulate, monitor and provide assistance where appropriate. Don't invite feedback at this stage as the information in the rakes will be used in Preparation for speaking.

SPEAKING

PREPARATION FOR SPEAKING

1 👤👥👥 Tell students that these are all sentences from Yasmin's presentation when she was talking about the advantages of different sports. Ask students to work individually to complete the sentences with the words in the box. Allow about 2 minutes for this. Ask students to check their answers with a partner, before inviting feedback from the class.

Answers

1 benefit 2 advantage 3 best 4 thing

2 👥👥 Students work with a partner to match the phrases about disadvantages (a–d) to the phrases in Exercise 1 about advantages. Allow about 1 minute for this, before inviting feedback from the class.

Answers

a 3 b 4 c 2 d 1

3 (🔊 7.4) 🧑👥 Tell students that they are now going to listen to the phrases from Exercises 1 and 2. Students work individually to underline the word that is stressed. After the audio, ask students to check with a partner, before inviting feedback from the class.

| **Answers**

1 advantage 2 disadvantage 3 benefit 4 problem 5 best 6 worst 7 good 8 bad

4 (🔊 7.4) Play the audio again or drill for students to repeat using the correct stress.

5 🧑 Students work individually and use the ideas rakes that they completed on pages 133 and 134 to complete the sentences in Exercise 3.

6 👥 Students work with a partner who chose the same sport for Exercise 5 on page 134. Ask students to compare ideas to see if they have the same ideas or different ones, before inviting feedback from the class.

7 👥 Students work with a partner to answer the questions. Allow 1 minute for this, before inviting feedback from the class.

| **Answers will vary.**

8 👥 Students work with a partner to put the sentences in the correct order. Ask them to start by locating the first sentence, with the example 1. Allow about 3 minutes for this, before inviting feedback from the class.

| **Answers**

2 b 3 d 4 e 5 a 6 c

Optional activity

👥 As an alternative to Exercise 8, photocopy the exercise and cut it into individual sentences. Put students into groups and give each group one set of sentences. Ask them to find the first sentence (f). Ask students to put the sentences in order to make a conversation. The first group to do this successfully is the winner. Circulate, monitor and give assistance where appropriate.

---

9 👥 Tell students to look at the words in italics in Exercise 8. These show ways of asking people for explanations. Students work with a partner to think of other ways we can ask people to explain things. Allow about 3 minutes for this, before inviting feedback from the class. Write all acceptable answers on the board.

| **Answers**

Answers will vary, but could include: Can you clarify ...? What does ... mean? Could you tell me more about ...?

10 🧑👥 Ask students to work individually to mark the phrases either *DU* (I don't understand) or *EM* (I want you to explain more). Answer the first question with the class. Allow about 2 minutes for this and ask students to check with a partner, before inviting feedback from the class.

| **Answers**

1 DU 2 EM 3 DU 4 DU 5 EM

11 👥 Check that students know what a *sports centre* is (a large place where different sports are played) and tell them that they are going to plan a sports competition to encourage people to use one. Put students into groups of 3 and ask them to follow steps 1–4. Allow about 8 minutes for this. Circulate and monitor, giving assistance and helping with vocabulary where appropriate.

12 👥 Put students into pairs, each one from a different group. Ask them to explain their competitions to each other. They should ask for more information if they don't understand. They choose the competition they think will be more successful. Allow about 4 minutes for this. Circulate, monitor and give assistance where appropriate, before inviting feedback from the class. Finish off by deciding which is the best competition. This activity can be extended by putting pairs into groups of 4 and discussing the two best competitions and deciding which of those is the best.

SPEAKING TASK

PREPARE

1 👥 Give students a minute to read the box and remind themselves of the Speaking task they are going to do. Put students into pairs and ask them to work with their partner to think of three advantages and disadvantages of sportsmen and women getting paid a lot of money. Ask them to think about it from the point of view of sportspeople themselves, of people who work with poor people and of journalists. You may wish to write these on the board and discuss with the students how these people would feel generally about the issue.

2 👥 Ask students to work with a partner to complete the two ideas rakes for the advantages and disadvantages of sportsmen and women earning a lot of money. Allow about 3 minutes for this. Circulate, monitor and give assistance where appropriate, but do not invite feedback from the whole class at this stage.

3 Assign roles to students. Student A (footballer) should go to page 195, Student B (charity worker) should go to page 197 and Students C (journalist) and D (moderator) should go to page 198 to prepare their roles. Students could work in pairs (2 As, 2 Bs etc.) to prepare their roles. Allow students about 5 minutes to work out their arguments. Circulate, monitor and give assistance where necessary, but again do not do feedback with the class.

DISCUSS

4 👥 Put students into groups for their panel discussion, with each group containing only one D (moderator) and one (or more) A, B and C. Student D should start the discussion by introducing the topic. Remind students to talk about the advantages and disadvantages and to ask for clarification and more information. Allow about 10 minutes for this. Circulate and monitor for good language. Give assistance where appropriate. Finish off by inviting feedback from the groups about which panel members had the best arguments.

ADDITIONAL SPEAKING TASK

See page 140 for the Additional speaking task (*A panel discussion about whether sport in schools should be compulsory*) and Model language for this unit.

Make a photocopy of page 140 for each student.

Write on the board 'Sport in schools should be compulsory'. Check that students understand *compulsory* by asking them to give you an example of something that they have to do.

👥 Divide the class into 2 groups of 4-5 students each and give each student a photocopy. Tell one group that they agree with the statement about sports in schools and the other group that they disagree with it. If you have a large class, make 4 groups (2 agreeing and 2 disagreeing). Allow 10 minutes for students to think of all the advantages of their position with reasons to support them, using the Model language. Ask them also to think of the disadvantages and how they will respond to the other group's questions about the disadvantages. Ask them to fill in the table on their photocopies with the advantages of their position, the disadvantages and their responses to the disadvantages.

👥 Then put the students into groups of 4, with 2 students from each side. Students take turns to explain the advantages of their position. Encourage the other 2 students to ask questions to clarify the advantages and disadvantages. Allow about 10 minutes for this. Finish off by inviting feedback from the class about which side had the strongest arguments.

TASK CHECKLIST AND OBJECTIVES REVIEW

Refer students to the end of the unit for the Task checklist and Objectives review. Students complete the tables individually to reflect on their learning and identify areas for improvement.

WORDLIST

See Teaching tips page 10, section 6, for ideas about how to make the most of the Wordlist with your students.

REVIEW TEST

See pages 126–127 for the photocopiable Review test for this unit and page 107 for ideas about when and how to administer the Review test.

RESEARCH PROJECT

Become a sports commentator

Find videos of sports commentators on a video-sharing website. When you have found one or two clips, show them to your students so that they can get an idea of the genre of sports commentary. Divide the class into groups and ask students to think about sports played in their own country. This could be a homework task, with students sharing ideas using the tools on the Cambridge LMS. Assign each group one of these sports and then ask them to find an example of the sport. Students could search a video-sharing website, visit and film a sports event, or arrange and film their own sports event.

Each group will create a short video including sports commentary and clips of the event they attended, or an audio-recorded commentary to accompany an online sports video. Students could be spontaneous with their commentary, but they will probably feel more comfortable creating and reading from a script. For videos, each group will have to think about who will work the camera during filming, who will edit the video, and who will provide the commentary.

8 BUSINESS

Learning objectives

Before you start the Unlock your knowledge section, ask students to read the Learning objectives box so that they have a clear idea of what they are going to learn in this unit. Tell them that you will come back to these objectives at the end of the unit when they review what they have learned. Give them the opportunity to ask you any questions they might have.

UNLOCK YOUR KNOWLEDGE

Lead-in

Books closed. Ask students: 'How do you go to work?' or 'How do your parents go to work?' Write up all answers on the board. Then ask students: 'How far do you / your parents have to travel?' Find out who lives nearest to their work and who lives furthest away. Then ask: 'How long does it take you / your parents to get to work?' Find out who has the shortest and the longest journey times. Ask students: 'Do you / your parents like making this journey every day?' 'Why / Why not?'

👥 Tell students to open their books at page 141 and to look at the photograph. Ask students to work with a partner to answer the questions. Allow about 4 minutes for this, before inviting feedback from the class. Encourage as much response as possible to questions 3 and 4, and ask students to think of reasons for their choice in 3. If you are planning to do the Optional activity below, write the jobs given in 3 on the board.

Answers

She is working in an office, probably doing an administrative job.

Optional activity

👥👥 Ask students to research the jobs they suggested in question 3. Put students into small groups and ask them to choose one of the jobs written on the board in response to question 3. Alternatively, give each group a different job, making sure no group has the same job. Ask students to research these jobs. What skills are needed? Where can the jobs be done? Is any special equipment required? Do they pay well? Who employs these types of people?

WATCH AND LISTEN

Video script

▶ This is South Africa's cape peninsula – the Cape of Good Hope. The weather here is dangerous, and changes quickly. Storms and the dangerous sea in this area have caused a lot of ships to sink.

David fishes here and understands these dangers very well. His father went missing when he was fishing. David never saw him again. David knows the dangers better than most people, but these waters are also a way for him to earn money.

The waters around the Cape are rich in small plants and animals and are home to 2,000 different types of fish. David fishes for one of these: the Snoek, a food that is very popular in the area. The problem is that they are very difficult to find.

This is because Snoek look for food and don't stay in the same place for long.

David has a modern fishing boat but he still catches Snoek in the old way, with hand-held fishing lines. Sometimes David can wait many months before he finds any fish.

But then his luck changes! Snoek are dangerous and can bite a man. So David teaches his sons what he learned from his father: how to catch Snoek. He says this helps to make the family strong because everyone works together. Today they find lots of Snoek. They catch over 300 fish – it's a good day!

PREPARING TO WATCH

ACTIVATING YOUR KNOWLEDGE

Optional lead-in

Books closed. Ask students: 'Can you think of any jobs where people work outside?' Accept all reasonable answers. If students haven't suggested any jobs linked to food, ask students: 'Can you think of any jobs outside that involve food?' to elicit farming, fruit picking, etc. Then ask students: 'Can you think of any jobs that are outside, are involved with food and are on/in water?' to elicit fishing. Write the word fisherman on the board. Ask students: 'Do you think this is a good job?' 'Why / Why not?'

1 👤👥 Tell students that they are going to watch a video about fishermen in South Africa. Students work in pairs to answer the questions. Allow 5 minutes for this, before inviting feedback from the class.

Possible answers

1 It's the south of South Africa.
2 It changes a lot.
3 In photograph 1, the sea is very high. In 2 a man is driving a boat on the sea. In 3 the sun is shining and the sea is calm. In 4 a fisherman is holding a big fish.
4 He goes out in his boat to try to catch fish.
5 Nothing about a fisherman's job is easy! The weather can be very bad, the sea rough and the fish are hard to find.

UNDERSTANDING KEY VOCABULARY

2 👤👥 Ask students to work individually to complete the sentences using words from the box. Allow about 3 minutes for this. Ask students to check with a partner, before inviting feedback from the class.

Answers

1 popular 2 line 3 catch 4 dangerous 5 Fishermen

3 👥 Ask students to get into groups of 3 or 4 to discuss the sentences in Exercise 2, giving reasons for their opinions. Allow about 4 minutes for this, before inviting feedback from the class.

Answers

Answers will vary.

WHILE WATCHING

UNDERSTANDING DETAIL

4 ▶👤👥 Tell students that they are going to work individually to choose the correct words to complete some notes. Allow about 1 minute for students to read the notes. Draw attention to *Snoek* and ask students what they think this is, to elicit *a kind of fish*. Play the video for students to choose the correct words. After the video, ask students to check with a partner, before inviting feedback from the class.

Answers

1 storms 2 father 3 understands dangers 4 fish 5 food 6 family 7 sons 8 together

5 ▶👥 Students work with a partner to match the sentence halves. Allow about 3 minutes for this, before playing the video again for students to check their answers, and then invite feedback from the class.

Answers

1 e 2 b 3 d 4 f 5 a 6 c

Background note

A cape is a large headland which extends into water, usually the sea. Although the Cape of Good Hope is not exactly the southernmost point of Africa (that's a little further east), it is generally thought of as the dividing point between the Atlantic Ocean and the Indian Ocean.

The Snoek is a large predatory fish belonging to the snake mackerel family. It is found throughout warmer waters in the southern hemisphere and is one of the most well-known fish in South Africa.

DISCUSSION

6 👥 Students work with a partner to discuss the questions. Encourage them to think of reasons for their answers. Allow about 3 minutes for this, before inviting feedback from the class. If appropriate, suggest jobs such as *ship's captain, sailor, port worker*. This discussion can be extended by including some of the advantages of working outside (healthy, no commuting, not office hours) and disadvantages (dangerous, long hours, not much money).

LISTENING 1

PREPARING TO LISTEN

UNDERSTANDING KEY VOCABULARY

1 👥 Students work with a partner and choose the correct word or phrase which shows the meaning of the word in bold. Allow about 2 minutes for this, before inviting feedback from the class.

Answers

1 working 2 we work with 3 use time doing it 4 use time badly 5 piece of planned work

PRONUNCIATION FOR LISTENING

2 👥 Tell students that they are going to listen to a business student speaking about a project which includes different numbers and words related to numbers. Write % on the board and ask students: 'What does this mean?' (percent,

a number out of a hundred). Ask students to work with a partner to decide how to say the numbers. Allow about 2 minutes for this. Do not check answers at this stage.

3 (◀) 8.1 Play the audio once to allow students to listen. Play it again, stopping after each number for them to repeat. Tell students that it is possible to say some of these numbers differently and elicit *a/one* for fractions (*a/one quarter of the population*) and *a/one* with hundred and thousand (*a/one thousand years*). For further practice, write similar numbers on the board and point to them at random for students to say them, using alternatives as appropriate.

Answers

1 forty-eight percent 2 a half 3 one-third
4 thirty-one point five 5 one hundred and three (or a hundred and three) 6 one thousand five hundred and forty 7 six thousand and one

4 👥 Students work with a partner to answer the questions on how we say numbers. Allow about 2 minutes for this, before inviting feedback from the class. For further practice, put similar numbers on the board. Focus on the use of *and* and where we pause in long numbers and telephone numbers. Pausing is very important when saying numbers. Also note the use of *double* in phone numbers, e.g. *07742 305723 – oh double seven four two, [pause] three oh five [pause] seven two three.* Point out that people now sometimes say *zero* in phone numbers.

Answers

1 usually after hundreds, but only after thousands if the number has thousands and then a single unit with no hundred in between, e.g. *six thousand **and** one* but *six thousand one hundred and one* 2 fifty percent 3 yes 4 usually we say *nought* 5 usually we say *oh*, especially for phone numbers, or *zero*; occasionally we say *nought* but not in a phone number.

WHILE LISTENING

5 (◀) 8.2 👤👥 Tell students to read the information in the Understanding numbers box or read it aloud as students follow in their books. Write on the board *percent* and *point* and ask students if they can think of any other words that go with numbers to elicit *and*, words like *sixth* that make up fractions,

approximately, etc. Tell students that they are going to listen to a conversation between a university professor and a student. Play the audio. Students work individually to decide if the sentences are true or false. After playing the audio, allow students to check with a partner, before inviting feedback from the class. Follow up by asking students to correct the false sentences.

Answers

1F (she hasn't finished yet) 2T
3F (she looked at how people spend time at work) 4T
5F (people wasted time because they weren't happy with their job)

RECOGNIZING NUMBERS

6 (◀) 8.2 👥 Tell students to look at the charts to see what kind of information they need in order to complete them (facts, not numbers). Play the audio. Students work with a partner to complete the chart. If necessary, play the audio again. After the audio, allow about 1 minute for students to check their work, before inviting feedback from the class. Follow up by highlighting the phrases *just under half* and *approximately half* from the listening and point out that in these cases *a* is not used with *half*.

Answers

Time wasted at work
5% texting, making plans for after work; 15% taking longer coffee and lunch breaks than they should; 31.5% talking to colleagues; 48% surfing the internet or writing personal emails
Reasons for wasting time
35% didn't work as hard as they should because they thought they weren't paid enough; 45% weren't happy with their jobs; 20% said they were working too many hours

DISCUSSION

7 👥 Tell students that they are managers of a company and that they are worried about the amount of time being wasted at work. Ask students to work with a partner and choose the two best ideas that they think will stop people wasting time at work. Remind students to give reasons for their answers. Allow about 3 minutes for this, before inviting feedback from the class. Did all the students agree? Take a vote to find the two best methods. Alternatively,

after pairs of students have chosen their two favourite ideas, put them into different pairs and ask them to discuss which ideas they have chosen and why, and to decide on a final two.

8 ▌ Students work individually to decide if they agree or disagree with the sentences. Remind them to think of reasons for their answers. Ask students to make notes as they will have to discuss their answers with a partner. Allow about 3 minutes for this. Circulate, monitor and assist where appropriate. Do not check answers at this stage.

9 ▌ Ask students to work with a partner to discuss their answers to the questions in Exercise 8. Ask them to find out how many they agree on. Allow about 6 minutes for this. Circulate, monitor and assist where appropriate, before inviting feedback from the class.

Optional activity

▌ As an alternative to Exercises 8 and 9, put students into small groups of 3 or 4. Ask them to decide together which statements they agree or disagree with. Ask them to give their reasons and make notes of their decisions. Allow about 6 minutes for this. Circulate, monitor and give assistance where appropriate. Put students into pairs, each student from a different group, and ask them to discuss which ones they agreed on and why. Do they agree on the same ones or different ones? Allow about 6 minutes for this, before inviting feedback from the class. Is there general agreement in the class or do groups have different views?

◉ LANGUAGE DEVELOPMENT

REVIEW OF COMPARATIVES

Optional lead-in

Books closed. Ask students to think back to the beginning of this unit when you were talking about how they, or their parents, got to work. Ask: 'Which were the ways that people travelled to work?' Write the different ways on the board. If everyone (students and/or their parents) travels by car, ask if they drive on their own, take other people to work, etc. Elicit the following categories and write them on the board: *by car (alone or with others), by bus, by train, by tram, on the underground / metro, by (motor)bike, on foot.* Once you have all the categories on the board, point to each category and ask students to raise their hands if they / their parents use this type of transport to get to work and write the numbers on the board. Ask students: 'Which way do most people use?' 'Which way do fewest people use?' 'Do more people use X than Y?'

1 ▌ Tell students that they are going to review the language of comparatives and to open their books at page 146. Start by asking: 'What does *compare* mean?' to elicit *looking at two or more things to see the similarities and differences.* Ask students to work with a partner to put the words in bold on the correct place on the line in the box. Allow about 1 minute for this, before asking for feedback from the class.

Answers

0% the least → less → more → the most 100%

2 ▌ Students work with a partner to complete the sentences, using the information in the table. Allow about 2 minutes for this, before inviting feedback from the class.

Answers

1 on the phone 2 in meetings 3 working at a desk
4 having breaks

3 ▌ Tell students to work individually to write sentences using the words in bold in Exercise 2 and the information in the table. Check understanding of all the ideas in the table. Allow about 3 minutes for this. Circulate, monitor and give assistance where appropriate, before inviting feedback from the class.

Possible answers

The most time is spent helping someone else finish their work. More time is spent waiting for someone to finish their part of the project than going to meetings. The least time is spent filling in papers and forms. Less time is spent going to meetings than waiting for someone to finish their part of a project.

4 ▌ Tell students to use the sentences to help them complete the rules in the Explanation box. Look at the example sentences with students and check understanding. Students work with a partner to complete the rules. Allow about 4 minutes for this, before inviting feedback from the class. Point out that when two things are not the same, we use *not as … as.*

Answers

2 -er 3 more 5 as … as 6 the most exciting; the least experienced; the longest; the best (any two)
7 -est 8 most 9 best

5 👤👥 Students work individually to complete the sentences, using the correct comparative or superlative form of the word in brackets. Do the first one with the class and check understanding. Allow about 3 minutes for this. Ask students to check with a partner, before inviting feedback from the class.

> **Answers**
> 1 more important than 2 better than 3 worse than 4 faster than 5 the neatest 6 the most exciting

6 👥 Students work with a partner and ask and answer the questions in Exercise 5. Allow about 5 minutes for this. Then move students into new pairs and repeat the activity. Allow about 4 minutes for this. Finally, put students into new pairs and repeat the activity, this time allowing only 3 minutes. Ask students to return to their own desks, before inviting feedback from the class.

> **Optional activity**
> Ask students to write 4–6 sentences using comparatives and superlatives. Start by writing some examples from the class feedback above on the board, e.g. *Lina can type faster than Noor. Most people prefer to do a job inside.* Circulate, monitor and give assistance where appropriate.

MULTI-WORD VERBS

7 👤👥 Write *multi-word verbs* on the board and ask students if they can give you examples, e.g. *pick up* (Unit 5), *switch off/on* (Unit 4). Tell students that a multi-word verb can also be known as a *phrasal verb* and is made up of a verb and a particle (or two particles). Label the verbs and the particles in the multi-word verbs that you have written on the board. Tell students that there are a lot of multi-word verbs in English and that they usually mean something different from the verb and the particle separately. Give an example: write *pick up* on the board and ask students what it means, miming reaching down to the floor and picking up a pen. Then ask 'Does anyone know what else this means?' to elicit *collect someone in your car from somewhere.* Write the following on the board as an example: *Don't take a taxi, I'll come and pick you up from the station.* Tell students that it is often hard to work out the meanings from the two

words, though as with *pick up* there may be some logic to it, and that they have to learn them as separate items of vocabulary. When they are learning multi-word verbs, they should always write an example sentence, like the one on the board, to help them remember the meaning. Ask students to look at the example sentence and check understanding. They then work individually to underline the multi-word verbs in the sentences. Allow about 2 minutes for this. Ask students to check with a partner, before inviting feedback from the class.

> **Answers**
> 2 ran out 3 noted down 4 took part in 5 found out 6 found ... out 7 looked at 8 get on with 9 get by

8 👤 Students work individually to write the infinitive form of the multi-word verbs in Exercise 7 next to their definition in the table. Allow about 3 minutes for this, before inviting feedback from the class.

> **Answers**
> 1 run out (of) 2 get on with 3 find out 4 get by 5 note down 6 take part in 7 look at

9 👥 Explain to students that multi-word verbs can have different patterns. Read the Explanation box aloud while students follow in their books. Make sure they understand what a particle is by asking 'Which words in the blue sentences in the box are particles?' Students then work in pairs to fill in the gaps (1–6) in the Explanation box with sentences from Exercise 7. Circulate, monitor and give help as appropriate and while students are working, make three columns on the board, headed *1 verb + object + particle or verb + particle + object, 2 verb + particle + object, 3 verb + no object.* After 5 minutes, invite feedback from the class and write the sentences in the correct columns.

> **Answers**
> **verb + object + particle:** 1 I found a lot of information out.
> **verb + particle + object:** 2 I noted down the key information. 3 I found out a lot of information.
> **verb + particle + object (inseparable):** 4 I took part in the discussion on this. 5 I looked at how people spend time at work. 6 ... the reasons they didn't get on with their work.

10 👤👥 Tell students to look at the sentences. Each sentence contains a multi-word verb. Students work individually to match these multi-word verbs to rules 1–3 in the Explanation box. Allow about 2 minutes for this. Ask students to check with a partner, before inviting feedback from the class.

> **Answers**
>
> 1 look after = rule 2
> 2 take up = rule 1
> 3 carry on = rule 3

11 👥 Students work with a partner to match the sentence halves. Allow about 5 minutes for this, before inviting feedback from the class.

> **Answers**
>
> 1a 2c 3d 4f 5e 6b

12 👥 Check understanding of all the multi-word verbs in Exercise 11. You could do this by writing some example sentences on the board with the multi-word verbs missing and ask students to complete them, e.g. *We need to _____ our parents as they get older.* (look after). Ask students to work with a partner to ask and answer the questions in Exercise 11. Tell them to use the multi-word verbs in their answers as well as in their questions. Allow about 8 minutes for this. Circulate, monitor and give assistance as required, especially with the correct use of the multi-word verbs, before inviting feedback from the class. This activity could be extended by asking students to work with a new partner and to ask and answer the questions about their first partners.

LISTENING 2

PREPARING TO LISTEN

UNDERSTANDING KEY VOCABULARY

> **Optional lead-in**
>
> Books closed. Write the word *interview* on the board. Ask students: 'When do people have interviews?' (for jobs, for university, for a newspaper/radio/television/ blog article). Ask students: 'Are interviews for jobs and university important?' (yes). Then ask: 'Why are interviews important?' to elicit *you can get a good job or a place at university if you do well in one, interviewers need to be sure of getting the right person,* etc. Ask students: 'Has anyone had an

interview recently?' Follow up with a few questions such as: 'What was it for?' 'How did it go' 'Can you remember any of the questions they asked you?' You could also tell students about an interview you had at some time, especially if something funny happened during it.

1 👥 Tell students that they are going to listen to someone giving advice to a student about interviews and to open their books at page 150. Students work with a partner to match the words with their opposites. Suggest that they do the ones they know first and then try to guess the rest before using their dictionaries. Allow about 3 minutes for this, before inviting feedback from the class.

> **Answers**
>
> 1 d 2 a 3 f 4 e 5 g 6 c 7 b 8 h

2 👥 Ask students to work with a partner to answer the questions, giving each other as much information as possible. Allow about 8 minutes for this. Circulate, monitor and give assistance where appropriate, before inviting feedback from the class.

> **Answers will vary.**

3 👥 Write *mentor* on the board and tell students that they are going to listen to a mentor talking to Sami. Ask students if they know what a mentor is (an older or more experienced person who helps a younger or less experienced person). Students work with a partner to discuss the questions. Allow about 3 minutes for this, before inviting feedback from the class. Is there general agreement about any of the answers?

> **Answers will vary.**

WHILE LISTENING

LISTENING FOR REACTION

4 🔊 8.3 👤👥 Tell students they are going to listen to Sami getting advice from his mentor. Ask students to work individually to tick the advice he received. After the audio, ask students to check with a partner, before inviting feedback from the class.

> **Answers**
>
> 1 3 4 6 7 8

5 (◀) 8.4 Play the first part of the audio again. Students work individually to mark the phrases in the order they hear them. After the audio, ask students to check with a partner, before inviting feedback from the class.

Answers

1 c 2 b 3 e 4 a 5 d

6 Students work with a partner to decide which of the phrases in Exercise 5 look like statements and which look like questions. Emphasize *look like* and tell students not to worry about how they were spoken on the audio. Allow about 2 minutes for this, before inviting feedback from the class.

Answers

Statements b, d, e Questions a, c

7 (◀) 8.5 Play sentence e in Exercise 5 again. Ask students: 'Does this sound like a statement or could it be a question?' (question). 'How can we tell it's a question?' (because the speaker's voice goes up at the end).

8 (◀) 8.6 Play the audio, or drill the phrases, for students to repeat.

POST-LISTENING

9 Ask students to work with a partner to put the words in the correct order to make the questions Sami was asked. Allow about 8 minutes for this. Circulate, monitor and give assistance where appropriate, before inviting feedback from the class. You could get students to check their questions by looking at the audioscript 8.3 on page 220.

Answers

1 Why would you like to work with us? 2 What are your strengths and weaknesses? 3 Why should we give you the job? 4 What do you want to do long term? 5 Are you always on time? 6 Are you good at working in a team? 7 What kind of qualifications have you got? 8 When did you last solve a difficult problem?

Optional activity

Exercise 9 would work well as a 'sentence race'. Photocopy the sentences and cut them up into words. Put the words for each sentence in a separate envelope and number each envelope 1–8. Put students into groups and place yourself in the middle of the groups. A student from each group comes and collects an envelope and takes it back to their group. Together they write out the correct sentence and bring it to you to check. If it is correct, exchange the first envelope with a second one. If it is not correct, the group must try again. You will need to keep a note of which groups have had which sentences. The winning group is the one which is first to correctly write out all the sentences.

DISCUSSION

10 Students work with a partner to discuss the questions, giving reasons for their answers. Allow about 2 minutes for this, before inviting feedback from the class, asking students to say whether their partner's assessment of himself/herself is accurate or not.

CRITICAL THINKING

Students begin to think about the Speaking task that they will do at the end of the unit (*Think of some solutions to a work or study problem and give advice to someone.*). Give them a minute to look at the box. It might be useful to give some of the preparation for this task as homework.

REMEMBER

Optional lead-in

Remind students that they discussed the fact that interviews are very important. Ask students: 'Do you think that interviews are the only way to choose a person for a job?' (no). Elicit ideas for alternatives, e.g. questionnaires, writing about yourself, spending some time at the job. Ask students to think of any advantages and disadvantages of these ideas. At the end of this, ask students: 'Although interviews are not the perfect way of choosing people for a job, do you think they are the best way?'

1 Tell students that in this section they will be looking further at job interviews. Ask students to work with a partner and remember some of the interview dos and don'ts Sami was given in Listening 2. Allow about 1 minute for this, before inviting feedback from the class. Students could check answers in the audioscript 8.3 on page 220, e.g. *be calm, don't look nervous*.

2 👥 Ask students to work with a partner to complete the interview questions. Make sure they don't look at the previous page or the audioscript when they do this. Allow about 4 minutes for this, before inviting feedback from the class.

> **Answers**
> 1 work 2 strengths 3 give 4 long term 5 did 6 at 7 on 8 have 9 person

APPLY

3 👤 Ask students to work individually to write down one job for each question. Allow about 4 minutes for this, before inviting feedback from the class. Encourage as many answers for each question as possible.

> **Answers**
> Answers will vary, but could include: 1 doctor 2 farmer 3 office worker 4 accountant 5 firefighter 6 waiter/waitress 7 translator 8 travel guide 9 mechanic 10 teacher

4 👥 Put students into groups of 3 and ask them to work together to match the questions to the jobs they thought of for Exercise 3. Look at the example together first and check understanding. There may be more than one possible answer. Allow about 6 minutes for this. Do not check answers at this stage.

5 👥 Put two groups together to form a group of 6 and ask students to compare their answers. Are they the same or different? Look at the example and then allow about 5 minutes for the exercise, before inviting feedback from the class.

> **Possible answers**
> b 9 c 3 d 5 e 2 f 1 g 10 h 4 i 7 j 8

ANALYZE

6 👤 Ask students to read the Using cluster diagrams box. They then work individually and write a job title in the middle of the cluster diagram. Remind them they can choose a job from Exercise 3 or any other job they can think of.

> **Answers will vary.**

7 👥 Students work with a partner to complete each category in their cluster diagrams. Allow about 4 minutes for this. Circulate, monitor and give assistance where appropriate.

> **Answers will vary.**

CREATE

8 👤 Tell students that they are going to write the questions for an interview and remind them to look at the questions in Exercises 2 and 4 to help them. They should write their questions next to the appropriate headings in the table. Allow about 5 minutes for this. Circulate, monitor and give assistance where appropriate. Alternatively, put students who have chosen the same job into a group so that they can work together to write the questions.

EVALUATE

9 👥 Tell students that they are going to interview each other. Students work in pairs and imagine that their partner wants the job they have written about. They use their questions to interview their partner and make notes of their answers. Allow about 10 minutes for both students to be interviewed.

10 👤 Students work individually to think about the responses they got to the interview questions and if the candidate took the advice from Listening 2. Ask them to decide if they would give their partner the job and to think of reasons why / why not. Allow about 1 minute of silent thinking time for this, before inviting feedback from the class.

SPEAKING

PREPARATION FOR SPEAKING

> **Optional lead-in**
>
> Ask students: 'Has anyone ever given advice to someone?' Ask some follow-up questions such as: 'Who did you give advice to?' 'What was the problem?' 'Did they take your advice?' 'What happened?'

1 👤 Tell students to work individually to match the sentence to its function. Allow about 1 minute for this, before inviting feedback from the class.

Answers

c

2 👥 Students work with a partner to identify other phrases that we use to give advice. Allow about 1 minute for this, before inviting feedback from the class. Ask them: 'Which is the most direct way of giving advice?' (*Be careful not to …*) 'Which is the most polite?' (*Why don't you …?*)

Answers

2 3 6

3 👥 Tell students to look at the picture of JP and work with a partner to explain why he can't find a job. Allow about 2 minutes for this, before inviting feedback from the class. Write all reasonable suggestions on the board.

Answers

Answers will vary, but could include: he is untidy; he hasn't got any qualifications / experience; he doesn't look interested; he doesn't look hardworking.

4 👥 Ask students to work in pairs to give five pieces of advice to JP, using the sentence beginnings to help them. Allow about 5 minutes for this. Circulate, monitor and give assistance where appropriate, before inviting feedback from the class.

Answers

Answers will vary, but could include: 1 If I were you, I would dress smartly. 2 I think you should take your exams again. 3 If you want to do better, you should sleep more. 4 Be careful not to look bored. 5 You should try to get some experience.

5 👤👥 Tell students to read the conversation and work individually to underline the advice JP is given. Allow about 2 minutes for this. Ask students to check with a partner, before inviting feedback from the class.

Answers

I think you should try to work a bit harder. If you want to do better, you need to complete more project work.

6 👥 Tell students that they are now going to give each other some advice. Put students into pairs and nominate each one A or B. Tell Student As to go to page 195 and Student Bs to page 197. Allow 1 minute of silent reading time, before asking students to work with their partner to discuss their problems and offer advice. Allow about 6 minutes. Circulate, monitor and give assistance where appropriate, before inviting feedback from the class.

7 👥👥 Put students into groups of 3. Students work together to make a list of ten dos and don'ts about the best ways to find a job and succeed at an interview. Note that it doesn't have to be five dos and five don'ts – any combination is fine. Allow about 8 minutes for this. Circulate, monitor and give assistance where appropriate. Do not invite feedback at this stage.

8 👥 Put students into pairs from different groups. Ask students to take it in turns to give advice to their partner. Encourage the partner to ask questions about why this is good advice. Ask students to work together to find the best five pieces of advice. Allow about 8 minutes for this, before inviting feedback from the class. Take a vote on the best five pieces of advice.

SPEAKING TASK

PREPARE

1 👥 Give students a minute to read the box and remind themselves of the Speaking task they are going to do. Ask students to work with a partner and think of 2 or 3 solutions to each of the problems 1–5 below the word box. Tell them that they can use the words and phrases in the box to help them but that they can also think of their own ideas. Ask students to do as much as they can without dictionaries and then allow them to use dictionaries as appropriate. Allow about 6 minutes for this. Circulate, monitor and give assistance where appropriate.

2 👤 Students work individually and choose two problems from Exercise 1. They do not tell anyone what they have chosen.

DISCUSS

3 👥 Students work with at least three different partners and take turns to tell each other the problem they chose in Exercise 2 so that their partners can give advice, using the language they have learned in the unit. Tell students to listen to the advice that their partners give them and perhaps make a note of it. Allow about 12 minutes for this. Then ask students to go back and sit in their usual places. Allow 1 minute of silent thinking time for them to analyze the advice they received from their partners. Did each partner give them the same advice? Which of the three partners gave them the best advice? Finish off by inviting feedback from the class on each of the problems. What do students think is the best advice for that problem? Who gave the best advice of all?

ADDITIONAL SPEAKING TASK

See page 141 for the Additional speaking task (*Give solutions to problems to do with work and studying*) and Model language for this unit.

Make a photocopy of page 141 for each student.

Additionally, prepare further copies of the 'problems' for the next stage by photocopying and cutting up as many as needed so that there is one problem for each student in the class. Fold these up and put them in a bag or envelope.

👥👥 Put students in groups of three or four and ask them to think of as many solutions as they can to each problem on the list. Tell students to make notes in the table because they are going to have to remember the solutions to the problems to help their classmates. Allow about 15 minutes for this.

Each student then selects a problem from the envelope / bag. They do not show it to their classmates.

Students go round the class and find three to five students, depending on the class size and what time you have available, who were not in their group, and take turns to tell each other about their problem and to offer solutions. Allow about 10 to 15 minutes for this.

Finish off by asking which were the best solutions to each problem.

If time is short, put students into six groups and give each group one of the problems. Allow five minutes for the students to think of good solutions to this one problem.

Then give each student one problem that is different from the one they have been working on. Students then mingle, looking for a solution to their problem. If they ask a student who does not have a solution to this problem, then the response is: 'Sorry, I can't help you with that.'

TASK CHECKLIST AND OBJECTIVES REVIEW

Refer students to the end of the unit for the Task checklist and the Objectives review. Students complete the tables individually to reflect on their learning and identify areas for improvement.

WORDLIST

See Teaching tips page 10, section 6, for ideas about how to make the most of the Wordlist with your students.

REVIEW TEST

See pages 128–129 for the photocopiable Review test for this unit and page 107 for ideas about when and how to administer the Review test.

RESEARCH PROJECT

Design the perfect workplace

Ask students to search the internet for information on different designs for workplaces, e.g. by searching 'creating an office for work and play' or 'creative office'. Students could share the ideas that they find using the forum or blog on the Cambridge LMS.

Divide the class into groups and ask each group to design a workplace which will motivate and engage employees to produce high-quality work. Students could create an image collage, a floor plan (you can find free software by searching 'draw floor plan') or a 3D model. Each group will present their design to the class and then students can vote on which work environment is the best. There are free online voting systems which allow you to do this. Search 'voting software' to view some of these.

9 PEOPLE

Learning objectives

Before you start the Unlock your knowledge section, ask students to read the Learning objectives box so that they have a clear idea of what they are going to learn in this unit. Tell them that you will come back to these objectives at the end of the unit when they review what they have learned. Give them the opportunity to ask you any questions they might have.

UNLOCK YOUR KNOWLEDGE

Lead-in

Books closed. Put students in small groups and ask them to make a list of three very unusual or very dangerous jobs and why they think they are unusual or dangerous. Give them 3 minutes to make the list, before inviting one person from each group to read out their list to the class and write the jobs on the board. Take a vote on which is the most unusual or dangerous job of all.

WATCH AND LISTEN

Video script

▶ The internet has become part of our daily lives. We use it for work, to talk with friends, to buy things and to find out information. But, do you ever think about who invented the world wide web and who started the websites that you use every day?

They all came from one person's good idea. The British computer scientist Sir Tim Berners-Lee invented the world wide web in 1989. He wanted it to be free for everyone to use. He didn't want it to be a place for big businesses. The web is now a place where we can all speak and be listened to.

In the past, big book, film and music companies decided what we read, watched and listened to. We often had to spend a lot of money to get what we wanted. But that has changed. Websites like Craigslist™ and Wikipedia™ show what can be done for free.

In the old days you had to pay to put advertisements in the newspaper. On Craigslist™, you don't have to pay a thing. You can find jobs and houses, sell a computer or buy a car. All for free. Craig Newmark started Craigslist™ in 1996 and runs it from a small office in San Francisco. It is now a free online noticeboard in 50 countries around the world.

Craig Newmark is not the only one building an online community. Jimmy Wales started Wikipedia™. Wikipedia™ is an encyclopaedia that anyone can write for.

It was started in 2001 and is available in 285 languages. It has 100 times more information than old, paper encyclopaedias, but anyone can change pages on the site. It means that new information is added as soon as things happen.

So, next time you talk to your friends, buy or sell something online, think about how one good idea can change people's daily lives.

PREPARING TO WATCH

USING YOUR KNOWLEDGE TO PREDICT CONTENT

1 👥👥👥 Tell students to open their books at page 160. Students work in groups to come up with as many famous websites as they can. You could make it into a race. Then invite feedback from the groups. You could write the names of the websites on the board and see which are the most popular.

> **Answers will vary.**

2 👥👥👥 Students work in groups again to answer the questions. Allow 3 minutes for this, before inviting feedback.

> **Answers**
>
> 1 and 2 Answers will vary. 3 Possible answers: from people, letters, books, newspapers, the radio, TV. 4 Possible answers: people can be in touch with their friends more easily and frequently than in the past. They can get information whenever they want to.

UNDERSTANDING KEY VOCABULARY

3 👥👥 Students work in pairs to answer the questions. Allow 3 minutes for this, before inviting feedback.

> **Answers**
>
> 1 A company is the business not the owner.
> 2 Inventing something means making or designing something new for the first time.
> 3 A group of people with similar interests.
> 4 Encyclopaedias are usually organized alphabetically.
> 5 You can see advertisements in newspapers, magazines, in the street, on public transport (buses, trains etc.), on TV, at the cinema, on websites. They try to persuade you to buy things.

WHILE WATCHING

UNDERSTANDING MAIN IDEAS

4 ▶ Before you play the video ask the students to listen for all the websites mentioned on the video. They can make a list of the sites while they listen or give them a few minutes afterwards. Invite feedback from the class and add any new sites to your list on the board from Exercise 1.

5 👤 Students work individually to answer the questions. Do not check answers at this stage.

6 ▶ Play the video again for students to check their answers. Then invite feedback from the class.

> **Answers**
> 1 b 2 a

UNDERSTANDING DETAILS

7 ▶ Before you play the video again ask students to look at the table and make sure they understand what information they have to add to it. Then play the video again. Allow 2 minutes for students to fill in the gaps but do not check answers at this stage.

8 👤 Students read the videoscript on pages 220–221 to check their answers. Then invite feedback from the class.

> **Answers**
> 1 advertise 2 Craig Newmark 3 1996
> 4 50 (countries) 5 encylopaedia 6 Jimmy Wales
> 7 2001 8 285 (languages)

DISCUSSION

9 You could do this exercise as a whole class discussion.

> **Answers will vary.**

10 👥 Read the Saying dates box aloud while students follow in their books. Students then work in pairs to say the dates. Allow 2 minutes for this, before inviting feedback from the class.

> **Answers**
> 1 fourteen hundred 2 fifteen fifty
> 3 two thousand and five 4 twenty ten
> 5 twenty twenty-four

11 👥 Students work in pairs to answer the questions. Encourage them to ask each other follow up questions to find out more details. Allow 3 minutes for this, before inviting feedback from the pairs. You could ask one person in each pair to talk about the other.

> **Answers will vary.**

LISTENING 1

PREPARING TO LISTEN

PREDICTING CONTENT USING VISUALS

> **Optional lead-in**
>
> Books closed. Ask students: 'Who is the most interesting person you know or know about?' Ask follow-up questions like: 'Why do you think they are interesting?' 'How do you know about them?'

1 👥 Tell students that they are going to find out about some interesting people and to open their books at page 162. Students work with a partner to discuss the questions about the photograph. Check students understand the meaning of *emperor* (the ruler of an empire, which is a group of countries). Write the following on the board to help them think about Joshua Abraham Norton's life: *rich/ poor? intelligent? country? brothers/sisters?* Allow about 2 minutes for this, before inviting feedback from the class.

> **Answers will vary.**

UNDERSTANDING KEY VOCABULARY

2 👤👥 Tell students to read the sentences individually and allow 1 minute of silent time for this. Check that they understand the words not in bold and that they know who Einstein (a theoretical physicist) and Napoleon (a French emperor, as the sentence says) were. Students work with a partner and discuss the meanings of the words in bold. Allow about 3 minutes for this, but do not do feedback at this stage. Definitions are given in Exercise 3.

3 Students work individually to match the words in bold from Exercise 2 to the definitions. Allow about 2 minutes for this, before inviting feedback from the class.

> **Answers**
>
> a 3 b 4 c 2 d 5 e 1 f 6

WHILE LISTENING

LISTENING FOR ATTITUDE

4 (◀) 9.1   Ask students to read the information in the Recognizing attitude box or read it aloud as students follow in their books. Explain to students that people often like to be polite and positive even when they want to say something negative, and that this is part of British culture. Tell students that they are going to listen to two students talking about their work. Play the audio. Ask students to work individually to answer the questions, and then to check with a partner. Invite feedback from the class.

> **Answers**
>
> 1 write a history essay on a remarkable person from the past 2 Yasmin

5 Ask students to work with a partner and write down three facts about each man. If appropriate, play the audio again. Allow about 3 minutes for this. Circulate and monitor, giving assistance where appropriate, before inviting feedback from the class. If students find it difficult to remember facts about the men, they could look at the audioscript on page 221 and make notes from that. As well as the key vocabulary that students have just worked with, there is other vocabulary in the listening that may be challenging for students. Invite students to ask you about any other words that they don't know or are not sure about. If appropriate, allow some time for students to use their dictionaries to find out about new words and feed back to the rest of the class.

Possible answers

(any three for each man, note form of the following):
Joshua Abraham Norton: He had a company in South Africa but went to the USA in 1849. He was quite successful but lost all his money in 1853. He became homeless and started living in the streets. In 1859, he declared to everyone in San Francisco that he was the President of America. He walked around the streets in a uniform with a big hat and a sword. The people around him called him 'emperor' and when the police tried to arrest him people were very angry and he was let free again. He issued his own paper money and the shops let him use it. When he died in 1880 he was still homeless but thirty thousand people came to his funeral.
Joseph Conrad: He was Polish. He was a writer. He wrote in English. He was a sailor before he became a writer.

6 (◀) 9.1   Play the audio again. Students work individually to decide which person said the sentences. After the audio, ask students to check with a partner, before inviting feedback from the class.

> **Answers**
>
> 1 S 2 Y 3 Y 4 Y 5 S 6 S

7 Tell students to look at the information in the Recognizing attitude box again. Ask them to work individually and match the sentences in Exercise 6 to the two ways of sounding more positive. Allow about 2 minutes for this, before inviting feedback from the class.

> **Answers**
>
> Sentences 1, 2, 5 and 6 use a positive adjective but a negative (not). Sentences 3 and 4 use a bit and that to weaken the negative.

8 Students work individually to choose the correct word which shows what Sam really thinks. Allow 3 minutes for this. Then ask them to check their answers with a partner, but don't check answers at this stage.

9 (◀) 9.1   Play the audio again. Students work individually to complete the sentences. Allow 2 minutes for this, before inviting feedback from the class on Exercise 8 as well as this one.

> **Answers**
>
> Exercise 8
> 1 bad 2 hasn't done 3 bad 4 doesn't know
> Exercise 9
> 1 not that 2 all of it 3 not very good 4 a lot about

PRONUNCIATION FOR LISTENING

10 👥 Students work with a partner to decide who they think said which sentences. Allow about 1 minute for this. Do not check answers at this stage.

11 🔊 9.2 👤 Play the audio. Allow students to work individually to check their answers, before checking with the class.

> **Answers**
>
> 1 Y 2 Y 3 S 4 S

12 🔊 9.2 👤 Ask students if they remember (from Unit 5 Listening 1, Sounding positive) what happens with our voice when we are positive or enthusiastic about something (our voice tends to go up). Play the audio again and ask students to work individually to mark the sentences in Exercise 9 in which the speaker sounds enthusiastic. Invite feedback from the class.

> **Answers**
>
> 2, 3

13 👥 Model the first phrase using a very bored / negative tone and then a very enthusiastic tone so that students can hear the difference. Students work with a partner to practise saying the phrases in either an enthusiastic or bored way. Can the student listening tell the difference? Allow about 2 minutes for this. If appropriate, drill all the phrases with the class for both enthusiastic and bored tones.

DISCUSSION

14 👥 Put students into groups of 3 or 4 to discuss people they know, from either their country or somewhere else in the world, in the past or in the present, who have done amazing things. Allow about 3 minutes for this, before inviting feedback from the class.

> **Optional activity**
>
> 👤👥 Ask students individually to research people who have done something remarkable. Alternatively, put students into small groups and let them choose one of the people they thought of in Exercise 14 and ask them to research their lives. If they would prefer to research different people, they could select, or you could nominate, one from the following list: Leonardo da Vinci, William Shakespeare, Abraham Lincoln, Saladin (Salah Al-Din), Omar Khayyam.

👁 LANGUAGE DEVELOPMENT

-ED AND -ING ADJECTIVES

> **Optional lead-in**
>
> Books closed. Write -ing on the board and ask students: 'Can you remember any adjectives ending in -ing from the previous section?' (interesting, fascinating, amazing). Write these on the board. Ask students: 'Can you remember what kinds of things these adjectives were describing?' (people, facts). On the board, underline the root of each of the adjectives: interesting, fascinating, amazing. Ask students: 'Do you know of any other adjectives that look similar to these?' to elicit interested, fascinated, amazed. Ask students: 'Why do you think there are two different ways of saying the same adjective?' Listen to what suggestions the students may have but don't explain the difference at this stage.

1 👤👥 Tell students that they are going to learn when to use adjectives ending in -ed and ones ending in -ing and to open their books at page 164. Students work with a partner to underline the adjectives in the sentences. Allow about 1 minute for this, before inviting feedback from the class.

> **Answers**
>
> 1 amazing 2 interested 3 fascinating 4 bored

2 👥 Students work with a partner to underline the words that the adjective is describing in each sentence. Look at the first item with the class. Allow about 3 minutes for this, before inviting feedback from the class.

> **Answers**
>
> 2 a I b She 3 a He b His idea 4 a The man b story 5 a The walk b I 6 a picture b My friend

3 👤 Students work individually to complete the rules in the Explanation box. Allow 1 minute for this, before inviting feedback from the class. Concept-check by relating the rules to some of the sentences in Exercise 2.

> **Answers**
>
> 1 -ing 2 -ed

4 👥 Ask students to work with a partner to discuss examples of the ideas. If appropriate, tell the class about one of them yourself, using examples of -ed and -ing adjectives. Allow about 4 minutes for this. Circulate, monitor and give assistance where appropriate, before inviting feedback from the class.

| Answers will vary.

SUFFIXES

5 👤👥 Ask students to work individually to choose the correct option to complete the rules in the Explanation box. Ask students to check with a partner, before inviting feedback from the class. Ask students if they know the term for the opposite of *suffix* (prefix) and give some examples: return, review (*re-* means *back* or *again*); prepare, preview (*pre-* means *before*).

| **Answers**
| 1 end 2 adjectives

6 👥 Tell students that we can turn both verbs and nouns into adjectives. Point out the adjective suffixes for the verbs and nouns in the tables and look at the example with the class. Draw students' attention to the fact that some of the spellings of the root need to change and that not all the suffixes can be used for each verb / noun. Ask students to work in pairs to complete the tables, changing the verbs and nouns in column A into adjectives, using the correct suffixes. Allow about 5 minutes for this. Circulate, monitor and give assistance where appropriate, before inviting feedback from the class.

Answers

A	Adjectives			
Verbs	*-ing*	*-ed*	*-able*	*-ful*
surprise	surprising	surprised	–	–
believe	–	–	believable	–
succeed	–	–	–	successful
comfort	comforting	comforted	comfortable	–
relax	relaxing	relaxed	–	–
shock	shocking	shocked	shockable	–

Nouns	*-ive*	*-e*	*-y*
expense	expensive	–	–
happiness	–	–	happy
politeness	–	polite	–

7 👤 Students work with a partner and use the words in the tables to help them to answer the questions. Allow about 2 minutes for this, before inviting feedback from the class.

| **Answers**
| 1 excite, surprise, believe, expense
| 2 the e is dropped and a different ending is added
| 3 the i is replaced with a y.

8 👤👥 Tell students that this text is about Joseph Conrad, the man they learned a little about in the Listening 1. Students work individually to read the text and answer the questions. Encourage students to ask you if there is any vocabulary they don't understand. Emphasize that they can answer the questions without knowing the words in the gaps, which contain adjectives. Allow about 3 minutes for this. Ask students to check with a partner, before inviting feedback from the class.

| **Answers**
| He was a writer. He only became a writer when he retired from being a sailor. He was born in Ukraine and spent his childhood in Russia, but he wrote books in English. He rejected an expensive schooling in order to go to sea.

9 👥 Ask students to work with a partner to complete the text, using the correct form of the words in brackets. Allow about 3 minutes for this, before inviting feedback from the class and writing answers on the board.

| **Answers**
| 1 fascinated 2 happy 3 surprising 4 expensive
| 5 interesting 6 successful 7 believable

LISTENING 2

PREPARING TO LISTEN

UNDERSTANDING KEY VOCABULARY

1 👥 Tell students to open their books at page 167 and to work with a partner to match the shapes to the nouns in the box. Allow about 2 minutes for this, before inviting feedback from the class.

> **Answers**
>
> 1 diamond 2 square 3 oval 4 circle 5 triangle
> 6 rectangle 7 semicircle

2 👥 Students work with a partner to say the words out loud and decide where the main stress is. Do the first one with the class. Allow about 2 minutes for this, before inviting feedback from the class. Drill the pronunciation of these words with the class.

> **Answers**
>
> circle diamond oval rectangle semicircle square triangle

3 👤👥 Students work individually to underline all the nouns and circle all the adjectives related to shapes. Allow about 2 minutes for this. Ask students to check with a partner, before inviting feedback from the class.

> **Answers**
>
> **nouns:** question 2 semicircles question 3 triangles question 5 halves;
> **adjectives:** question 1 round, rectangular, triangular, oval, square question 4 circular, square, diamond-shaped

4 👥 Students work in pairs to answer the question.

> **Answers**
>
> Circle, rectangle, semicircle, triangle all lose the -e or -le and add -ular to make the adjective form. Diamond, square and oval are the exceptions because the adjectives are diamond-shaped, square-shaped and oval.

5 👥 Ask students to look at all the adjectives of more than one syllable that they circled in Exercise 3 (rectangular, triangular, oval, circular, diamond-shaped). Write them on the board. Ask students where the stress is on rectangular and underline the syllable on the board. Students then work with a partner to identify where the stress is in each of the other adjectives. Allow about 1 minute for this, before inviting feedback from the class. Deal with semicircular when you talk about circular. Then ask what the equivalent nouns are (rectangle, triangle, oval, circle, semicircle, diamond) and ask if the stress is the same for these. Go through them with the class, asking students to say each one out loud, paying attention to the stress.

> **Answers**
>
> rectangular, triangular, oval, circular, diamond-shaped, semicircular
> Some of the stresses change – with the -angular ending adjectives, the stress is on the second syllable, whereas it is on the first syllable for the noun.

6 👥 Ask students to work with a partner to answer the questions in Exercise 3. Allow about 5 minutes for this, before inviting feedback from the class.

> **Answers**
>
> Answers will vary, but could include: 1 **round**: cake, pizza, coin; **rectangular**: book, tablet, smartphone, football pitch; **triangular**: sides of the Pyramids, slice of cake / pizza; **oval**: egg, watermelon; **square**: a box with four equal sides, a town square with four equal sides 2 a circle 3 a diamond, a square, a rectangle 4 Answers will vary.

WHILE LISTENING

LISTENING FOR DETAIL

7 (◄) 9.3 ﹡ ﹡﹡ Tell students that they are going to listen to part of a seminar about design engineering. Write the word *invention* on the board and ask students if they remember what it means (something new, designed or created for the very first time). Play the audio and ask students to work individually to write the names of the inventions and the inventors under the correct photographs. After the audio, ask students to check with a partner, before inviting feedback from the class.

> **Answers**
>
> 1 a 2 c 3 a 4 b
> From left to right the pictures are:
> a hand-dryer; a wheelbarrow; a climbing car;
> an egg chair

8 (◄) 9.3 ﹡ ﹡﹡ Play the audio again and ask students to work individually to complete the notes. After the audio, ask students to check with a partner, before inviting feedback from the class.

> **Answers**
>
> 1 (kind of) round 2 colours 3 comfortable 4 two
> 5 square 6 easily 7 expensive 8 rectangular 9 quickly
> 10 oval 11 space 12 building

> **Background note**
>
> Roman Mistiuk: American industrial designer, born 1980
>
> Sir James Dyson: British inventor and industrial designer, born 1947, probably best known for the invention of the bagless vacuum cleaner
>
> Arne Jacobsen: Danish architect and designer, 1902–1971

DISCUSSION

9 ﹡﹡﹡ Put students into small groups to discuss the questions. Encourage them to give reasons for their answers. Allow about 5 minutes for this. Circulate, monitor and give assistance where appropriate, before inviting feedback from the class. This activity can be extended by putting students into pairs from different groups to share answers from their first groups. Allow another 5 minutes for this. Circulate, monitor and give assistance where appropriate, before inviting feedback from the class.

> **Answers**
>
> Answers will vary, but could include the wheelbarrow for question 3.

CRITICAL THINKING

> **Optional lead-in**
>
> Books closed. Ask students: 'What recent inventions can you think of that use electricity?' Encourage as many ideas as possible. Then ask: 'Do you know that there are many people in the world who do not have electricity?' 'What do you think that would be like?' Encourage as many comments as possible from the students and ask follow-up questions.

Students begin to think about the Speaking task that they will do at the end of the unit (*Describe an object. Talk about what it looks like and its functions. Consider its advantages and disadvantages.*). Give them a minute to read the box.

1 ﹡﹡ Students work with a partner and answer the questions. Allow 3 minutes for this, before inviting feedback from the class.

> **Answers will vary.**

2 ﹡ ﹡﹡ Read the Description wheel box aloud while students follow in their books and ask them to look at the one at the foot of the page. Check that they understand all the sections. Ask: 'Where will you put what something is made of?', to elicit *materials*. 'Where will you put what something does?', to elicit *functions*. Students then work individually to write words from the box in the wheel. They could draw a larger wheel in their notebooks. Allow 4 minutes for this and then ask them to check their answers with a partner, before inviting feedback from the class. Draw the wheel on the board and either ask students to come up and fill in the parts or you write in what they tell you.

> **Answers**
>
> **functions:** 1 to provide entertainment 2 to provide information; **colour:** 3 black; **shape:** 4 flat 5 rectangular; **size:** 6 large 7 1 metre wide; **features:** 8 internet display 9 high definition; **weight:** 10 heavy; **price:** 11 expensive; **materials:** 12 plastic 13 glass

3 Ask the class the question.

> **Answers**
> The object is a TV.

REMEMBER

4 👤 Students work individually to correct the words in the description of the torch. Allow 3 minutes for this, before inviting feedback from the class.

> **Answers**
> 1 two 2 round 3 circular 4 long

5 👥 Ask students to work with a partner to fill in the description wheel for the mechanical torch. Allow 5 minutes for this, before inviting feedback from the class, or ask students to raise their hands when they have finished.

> **Answers**
> **colour:** pale blue, black; **shape:** round; **size:** small; **feautures:** easy to carry, good for the environment; **weight:** light; **price:** not given but possibly cheap; **materials:** plastic, glass; **functions:** to provide / give light, there is a handle to wind up to give power

EVALUATE

6 👥 Students work with a partner to complete the table about the mechanical torch, using the ideas in the list to help them. Allow about 3 minutes for this, before inviting feedback from the class.

> **Possible answers**
>
> | invention | |
> |---|---|
> | advantages | disadvantages |
> | does not need electricity, small, easy to take with you, e.g. on journeys in a car, can use anywhere | you have to wind it up to start it so it may not give light immediately so not good if you are tired |

APPLY

7 👥 Put students into pairs. Tell Student As to go to page 195 and Student Bs to page 198 and look at the photographs. Make sure that students do not look at their partner's photographs. Tell students that they have to describe the photograph that is labelled so that their partner can label their photograph of the same object. Allow 1 minute of silent thinking time so students can prepare their descriptions. Allow about 4 minutes for this, 2 minutes for each student, before asking students to compare their labelled photographs with the correctly labelled ones. Invite feedback from the class to find out which students were able to label the most parts correctly.

SPEAKING

PREPARATION FOR SPEAKING

> **Optional lead-in**
>
> Ask students: 'When you describe something, what information do you have to give?' (name, what it's made of, different parts, what it's used for, advantages and disadvantages).

1 👥 Remind students that at the end of this unit, they are going to describe an object and give its advantages and disadvantages. Students work with a partner to match the headings in A to the information in B. Allow about 2 minutes for this, before inviting feedback from the class.

> **Answers**
> 1 a 2 c 3 f 4 b 5 e 6 d

2 👥 Tell students to look at the language notes a–f. Ask students to work with a partner to complete the description of the radio in the diagram, using the grammatical information a–f to help them. Allow about 3 minutes for this, before inviting feedback from the class.

> **Answers**
> 1 main 2 made 3 for 4 for 5 lets 6 to

3 👤👥 Students work individually to answer the questions, using the text. Allow about 2 minutes for this and then ask students to check with a partner, before inviting feedback from the class.

Answers

1 plastic and metal 2 it's shaped like a rectangle (it's rectangular) and has a handle 3 for listening to radio programmes where there is no electricity 4 The antenna lets people receive different radio channels 5 to get energy from the sun

PRONUNCIATION FOR SPEAKING

4 👥 Ask students to work with a partner to decide what happens to the pronunciation of the words in bold in the answers (bs). Do question 1 with the class as an example, asking students to identify the difference in the phonemic script between a and b (the vowels have a strong form in a and a weak form in b). Allow about 3 minutes for this, before inviting feedback from the class.

Answers

The final sounds are strong in a, when they are the final sound in the sentence or question, but weak /ə/ in b, when they come within the sentence.

5 (🔊 9.4) Play the audio for students to repeat. Stop the audio after each question and answer, and drill if appropriate. You could give further practice by calling out e.g. 4a for students to say the sentence, focusing on the strong and weak forms.

6 👥 Ask students to work in pairs to write down the name of the objects in the photographs, some of which they may remember from Listening 2. Allow students to look at the audioscript 9.3 on page 221 to help them with the answers, and / or to use their dictionaries. Allow about 5 minutes for this, before inviting feedback from the class.

Answers

1 a match 2 a table lamp 3 a rucksack 4 a bucket 5 a mug 6 a comb 7 a ruler 8 a broom 9 headphones 10 a belt

7 👥 Put students into groups of 3 and nominate each student A, B or C. Starting with A, students choose one of the objects but do not tell the group. Look at the example conversation and check understanding. The group ask the 3 questions and try to guess the object. Allow about 10 minutes for this. Alternatively, photocopy the pictures of the objects and cut them up to make a set of ten object cards. Put students into groups of 3 and give each group a set of object cards, which should be placed face down in the centre of the group. Student A picks up the top card and does not show it to the group. Other members of the group ask questions from Exercise 3 until they guess the object correctly. Whoever guesses correctly keeps the object card. The student with the most object cards at the end is the winner. Allow about 15 minutes for this.

SPEAKING TASK

PREPARE

1 👥 Give students a minute to read the box and remind themselves of the Speaking task they are going to do. Students work with a partner and choose an object, preferably not one from Exercise 6 on page 173. Students complete the table with notes about their object. Allow about 8 minutes for this. Circulate, monitor and give assistance where appropriate but do not do class feedback.

DISCUSS

2 👥 Put students into different pairs. Ask students to take turns to describe their object to their partner without giving its name. Remind students that they can ask their partner questions to help them identify the object. Allow about 4 minutes for this. This activity can be extended by putting students into new pairs to repeat the activity. Finish off by inviting feedback from students about what objects were chosen and if they were able to guess them.

ADDITIONAL SPEAKING TASK

See page 142 for the Additional speaking task (*Describe an object and others guess what it is*) and Model language for this unit.

Make a photocopy of page 142 for each student.

Start by ensuring that students know what all the objects in the table are. Students could work in pairs and use their dictionaries or you could check with the whole class either by showing the objects or pictures of the objects or by drawing them on the board.

Students work with a partner. Allocate each pair one of the objects in the table. This can be done by cutting up a photocopy of the table and giving students one of the objects. Tell students that they will take it in turns to come to the front of the class in pairs and describe the object and what it does, but that they must not say what it is. Allow students about 5 minutes to prepare for this by using the Model language. Circulate, monitor and give help where appropriate. Make sure that both students in the pair will speak.

Each pair comes up and describes their object while other students try to guess what it is.

Finish off by inviting feedback from the class about which pair gave the best description.

TASK CHECKLIST AND OBJECTIVES REVIEW

Refer students to the end of the unit for the Task checklist and Objectives review. Students complete the tables individually to reflect on their learning and identify areas for improvement.

WORDLIST

See Teaching tips page 10, section 6, for ideas about how to make the most of the Wordlist with your students.

REVIEW TEST

See pages 130–131 for the photocopiable Review test for this unit and page 107 for ideas about when and how to administer the Review test.

RESEARCH PROJECT

Create a vox pop about interesting people

Ask students to think about someone they find particularly interesting and why that person is interesting. This could be a sports person, inventor, actor, friend or family member. Tell them they are going to use these opinions to create a class vox pop. You can find examples of these on video-sharing websites (select these carefully in advance), and there are guides on how to create them online (search 'radio vox pop').

Each student will audio-record themselves responding to the prompt: 'Tell me about an interesting person'. You could ask students to record other people as well and upload the recordings to the Cambridge LMS (these should be saved as 128kb mp3 files). Select two or three students to edit the audio recordings into a vox pop (students can find editing software by searching for 'free audio editing software/apps'). Each contribution will need to be edited so that it is short and only includes the most important information, before all contributions are edited into a single file.

10 SPACE AND THE UNIVERSE

Learning objectives

Before you start the Unlock your knowledge section, ask students to read the Learning objectives box so that they have a clear idea of what they are going to learn in this unit. Tell them that you will come back to these objectives at the end of the unit when they review what they have learned. Give them the opportunity to ask you any questions they might have.

UNLOCK YOUR KNOWLEDGE

Lead-in

Books closed. Write *space* on the board. If necessary, indicate, through the window, pointing towards the sky, that space is 'out there'. Ask students: 'What do you know about space?' to elicit ideas such as *space travel, satellites that are used for TV, GPS systems*. Write all the ideas on the board, and encourage students to think about as many different ideas as they can which lead from the main ideas above.

👥 Tell students to open their books at page 177 and work with a partner to answer the questions. Allow about 3 minutes for this, before inviting feedback from the class.

> #### Answers
>
> The photograph shows satellite dishes which are round aerials that receive television and radio signals broadcast from communication satellites in space. They work by sending and receiving microwaves. Answers to 2 and 3 will vary.

WATCH AND LISTEN

Video script

▶ People have already been to the moon. Will we one day go to Mars? Mars was one of the first planets that was seen through a telescope. A spacecraft was sent to take pictures of Mars in 1964. Before this, some astronomers believed that there might be life on the planet. They were wrong. But NASA didn't stop looking.

Spacecraft sent to Mars since 2000 have found that there might be ice on the planet. In 2002 the Odyssey spacecraft took pictures of Mars using a special instrument that could see the details of the light from space. It found that there could be ice on Mars.

Other pictures show us that there might have been old lakes and rivers. Was there once life on Mars? On August 4th, 2007 the Phoenix Mars Lander was sent into space. It finally arrived on Mars on May 25th, 2008. Phoenix's job was to study the history of water on the planet. Phoenix was digging the soil on Mars. It found ice about 1 metre down. The ice that Odyssey had shown was there.

Phoenix spent five months sending important information to NASA. It was the first spacecraft sent to Mars that found water on the planet. Phoenix last sent a message to NASA in November 2008, but that was not the end.

The Curiosity Rover arrived on Mars on August 6th, 2012. It is looking for life. Curiosity has enough batteries to look at Mars for ten years. What will it find?

PREPARING TO WATCH

USING VISUALS TO PREDICT CONTENT

Optional lead-in

Ask students: 'Which planets do you know?' to elicit *Mercury, Venus, Mars, Earth, Jupiter, Saturn, Uranus, Neptune* (NB Pluto has been declassified as a planet). There are other smaller dwarf planets too. Follow up by asking: 'What else is there in space?' to elicit *the sun, the moon, stars*.

1 👥 Tell students that they are going to watch a video about space and astronomy. Give them a minute to choose the correct definition of astronomy, before eliciting the answer from the class.

> #### Answers
> a

2 👥 Tell students to look at the photograph of Mars and the caption. They then work in pairs to answer the question. Allow about 2 minutes for this, before inviting feedback from the class.

> #### Possible answers
> Perhaps the lines in the rocks were once rivers.

UNDERSTANDING KEY VOCABULARY

3 👥 Students work with a partner to divide the words in the box into the three groups given. Ask students to draw a table like the one below and complete it. Allow about 2 minutes for this, before inviting feedback from the class.

Answers

a equipment	b places	c people
telescope	solar system	astronaut
spacecraft	Mars	scientist
spacesuit	planets	astronomer

4 👤👥 Students work individually to complete the sentences, using words from Exercise 3. Allow about 5 minutes for this. Ask students to check with a partner, before inviting feedback from the class.

Answers

1 astronaut 2 spacesuit 3 scientist 4 astronomer
5 solar system 6 planets; Mars 7 telescope 8 spacecraft

5 👥 Students work with a partner to answer the questions. Allow about 2 minutes for this, before inviting feedback from the class.

Answers will vary.

Optional activity

👤👥 Ask students individually to research the planets in our solar system. Alternatively, put students into small groups and give each group a planet – Mercury, Venus, Mars, Jupiter, Saturn, Uranus, Neptune – and ask them to find out some information about that planet, e.g. size, distance from the sun, what it could be made of.

WHILE WATCHING

6 ▶👤👥 Tell students that they are going to watch a video about space. Before playing the video, give students a minute to read the events and check that they understand them. Highlight words that will help them put the events in order, e.g. *1964* and *now*. Play the video. Ask students to work individually and number the events in the order that they happened. Then ask students to check with a partner, before inviting feedback from the class.

Answers

1 d 2 a 3 c 4 e 5 b

7 ▶👤👥 Ask students to look at the dates and elicit the correct way of saying them. Remind them about the way we say dates beginning *20…*: *two thousand and …* generally for dates up to 2009, but *twenty …* for dates after that. Play the video again and ask students to work individually to make notes about why the dates are important. After the video, ask students to check with a partner, before inviting feedback from the class.

Answers

1 Spacecraft have been going to Mars since 2000.
2 Odyssey took photos of Mars in 2002.
3 Phoenix Mars Lander was sent into space in 2007.
4 Phoenix landed on Mars in 2008.
5 Curiosity Rover landed on Mars in 2012.

Background note

NASA is the National Aeronautics and Space Administration, the United States' civilian space agency.

DISCUSSION

8 👥 Ask students to work with a partner to answer the questions. Allow about 3 minutes for this, before inviting feedback from the class.

9 👤👥 Ask students to work individually to match the words in italics to the definitions. Allow about 2 minutes for this. Ask students to check with a partner, before inviting feedback from the class. Point out that running water is fresh water that we can drink, but that in many places in the world fresh water isn't available in people's houses and they have to go to a well, a pump or a tap to get fresh water for drinking or cooking.

Answers

1 b 2 c 3 a

10 👥 Ask students to work in pairs and answer the questions. Allow about 5 minutes for this, before inviting feedback from the class. Encourage a debate as a follow-up to question 3.

LISTENING 1

PRONUNCIATION FOR LISTENING

Optional lead-in

Books closed. Write *sea* and *see* on the board and ask students to say them out loud. Ask students: 'Do they sound the same or different?' to elicit *the same*. Then write *two* on the board and ask: 'Can you think of any other words that sound the same as this?' to elicit *to* and *too*. Write these on the board to show the different spellings. Ask students if they can think of other examples, e.g. *there, their* and *they're, here* and *hear, right* and *write*. Tell students that there are many words in English that sound the same, but are spelled differently and have different meanings, but we know which one to use because of the context. If appropriate, you can tell the class that these are called *homophones*.

1 10.1 Tell students to open their books at page 180. Tell them that they are going to listen to some sentences and to work individually to underline the two words in each sentence that sound the same. You could ask students to look through the sentences before listening to see if they can spot the words that sound the same, and then listen to check. After the audio, ask students to check with a partner, before inviting feedback from the class. Highlight the other pronunciation of *read* /riːd/ when it is in the present tense.

Answers

1 sun/son 2 read/red 3 whether/weather 4 ate/eight
5 There/their 6 our/hour

2 Ask students to work with a partner and to say the words out loud. Ask them to notice the spelling and the sounds. Allow about 2 minutes for this, before inviting feedback from the class. If appropriate, drill the words. Highlight that *to* and *for* have their strong sounds here but that in sentences they often have weak sounds /tə/ and /fə/. Check the meanings of the words in 6 *sent/scent* and 8 *mined/mind*.

Answers

The words have the same pronunciation but different spellings and meanings.

3 10.2 Tell students that they are going to hear some sentences and they should write them down. If they ask if this is a dictation, you can say that it is, but remind students to take particular care over which target word from Exercise 2 is being said and therefore what the spelling is. Stop the audio after each sentence. You may have to play the audio a few times to allow students to complete their writing. After the audio, ask students to check with a partner, before inviting feedback from the class. Alternatively, students could check by looking at the audioscript on page 222.

Answers

1 It is very nice weather today.
2 I waited for an hour.
3 Are you going there later?
4 I read the book yesterday.
5 We ate our dinner.
6 I don't mind.

PREPARING TO LISTEN

UNDERSTANDING KEY VOCABULARY

4 Tell students that they are going to listen to a radio programme about space travel. Ask them to work with a partner to discuss the meanings of the words in bold. Allow about 2 minutes for this, before inviting feedback from the class.

Answers

Answers will vary, but could include: 1 places, like Earth, in our solar system 2 precious stones
3 two of something
4 something we do at college or work
5 when people go to a new place

5 Put students into different pairs and ask them to work with their partner to answer the questions in Exercise 4. Allow about 3 minutes for this, before inviting feedback from the class.

Answers

Answers will vary, but could include: 1 Mars, Jupiter, Venus, etc., as in Optional lead-in on page 97 above, and any relevant information 2 for jewellery; for cutting things 3 usually; husband and wife 4 carefully planned 5 somewhere new to them

WHILE LISTENING

USING CONTEXT TO GUESS WORDS

6 (10.3) 👤👥 Tell students that they are going to listen to part of a radio programme called *Astronomy Today*. Play the audio. Students work individually to complete the sentences. After the audio, ask students to check with a partner, before inviting feedback from the class. Do not write or spell the words at this stage.

Answers

1 whether 2 our 3 sun 4 Red 5 to; two 6 four

7 👥 Tell students to read the information in the Recognizing words with easily confused sounds box, and remind them of pairs of words already discussed. Ask students to read again the sentences in Exercise 6 and check their spelling. They could compare their spelling of the words they wrote with the spelling of the words in Exercise 2. Does their spelling of the words here fit the context? Allow 2 minutes for this, before inviting feedback from the class.

8 (10.4) 👤👥 Tell students that they are now going to listen to the second part of the programme. Play the audio. Students work individually to decide if the sentences are true or false. After the audio, ask students to check with a partner. Follow up by asking them to correct the false sentences.

Answers

1F (they want a couple as they will help each other) 2T 3T 4F (they are all outside our solar system) 5F (it is 8 times heavier than Earth) 6F (one year passes in 18 hours)

9 (10.4) 👤👥 Tell students that they need to listen out for more information about Inspiration Mars and the planet Lucy. After playing the audio again, ask students to check with a partner, before inviting feedback from the class.

Answers

Other information about Inspiration Mars can include: the journey will take 501 days; the spacecraft won't land on Mars, it will just circle Mars. Lucy: it was created by heat; it is 4,000 km across; there are more diamonds there than all the ones found on Earth through history; it is very hot (3,500 degrees Centigrade/Celsius)

DISCUSSION

10 👥 Tell students that they are space explorers and that they have found a new planet. Students work with a partner and decide on the name of the new planet and what they will find on the planet to make it a good place to live. Allow about 4 minutes for this. Do not invite feedback at this stage.

11 👥👥 Put two pairs together to make groups of 4. Ask students to share their ideas and decide which of the planets they like best. Allow about 4 minutes for this, before inviting feedback from the class. Encourage as many students as possible to share their ideas. To finish off, have a vote on the best planet or decide with the class which are the top five things they would like to see on the planet.

Optional activity

👤👥👥 Ask students individually to do more research into the ideas for their planets. Alternatively, put students into groups and ask them to decide which of the planet ideas they liked best. Ask them to research their ideas to create more information about their planet. Ask them to consider things like climate, geographical features, sea and land, what there is to eat and drink, what houses can be built of, etc.

⊙ LANGUAGE DEVELOPMENT

TRAVEL VERBS AND NOUNS WITH SIMILAR MEANINGS

Optional lead-in

Write the word *travel* on the board. Ask students: 'Can you think of any words that are associated with travel?' to elicit ideas like *holiday, journey, trip, aeroplane/plane, explore.* Tell students about a journey you made that was either very interesting or a disaster. Ask students about their last holiday journey, to elicit some stories about journeys and travel.

1 👥 Tell students to work with a partner to complete the table on page 183 with the words in italics in sentences 1–5 in the box. Allow about 2 minutes for this, before inviting feedback from the class.

> **Answers**
> 1/2/3 travel 4 journey 5 trip 6 voyage

2 👤👥 Students work individually to complete the sentences, using words from column A of the table. Allow about 4 minutes for this. Ask students to check with a partner, before inviting feedback from the class.

> **Answers**
> 1 journey 2 travel 3 cruise / voyage 4 flight 5 trip
> 6 voyage 7 trip 8 voyage

3 👥 Students work with a partner and answer the questions. Allow about 4 minutes for this, before inviting feedback from the class. This activity can be extended by putting students into new pairs and asking them to talk about what their first partner told them.

> **Answers will vary**

CONDITIONALS

4 👥 Ask students what two-letter word is used in most conditional sentences (*if*). Students work with a partner and match the sentence halves. Allow about 2 minutes for this, before inviting feedback from the class.

> **Answers**
> 1 b 2 a

5 👤👥 Students work individually to match the complete sentences in Exercise 4 to the functions. Allow about 2 minutes for this. Ask students to check with a partner, before inviting feedback from the class.

> **Answers**
> 1 i 2 i

Language note

(This should only be used if students ask about it.) Although it is very common to use the Present simple in the condition (*if*) clause of the first conditional, a variety of present tense forms can be used. Present continuous and Present perfect are often found in these types of structures. Similarly, the second conditional uses a range of past tense forms, including Past continuous.

6 👤👥 Students work individually to write the sentences into the table. Allow about 2 minutes for this. Ask students to check with a partner, before inviting feedback from the class.

> **Answers**
>
> | condition clause | result clause |
> | --- | --- |
> | *If + present tense* | *will / going to* |
> | If they can find a married couple, | they believe the couple will be able to help each other. |
> | *If + past tense* | *would/could* |
> | If the planet Lucy were mined, | there would be more diamonds than on Earth. |

7 👥 Ask students to work with a partner to choose the correct form of the verb. This will depend on whether they think the situations are possible or probably won't happen. Allow about 3 minutes for this, before inviting feedback from the class. This activity can be extended by asking students to write sentences 1–5 with the result clause first.

> **Answers**
> 1 i meet; will 2 ii met; wouldn't 3 ii spoke; would
> 4 i lose; will (ii *lost; would* is also acceptable – if you feel that you probably won't lose your phone)
> 5 i is; will 6 ii could; had

8 👥 Ask students to work with a partner to discuss whether their answers in Exercise 7 are true for them. Allow about 3 minutes for this, before inviting feedback from the class. This activity can be extended by putting students into new pairs and asking them to talk about what their first partner said. Allow about 3 minutes for this, before inviting feedback from the class.

> Answers will vary.

LISTENING 2

PREPARING TO LISTEN

UNDERSTANDING KEY VOCABULARY

> **Optional lead-in**
>
> Write *travel* on the board and ask students if it is a noun or a verb (both). Ask them what the word is for the person who performs the action of travelling, to elicit *traveller*.

1 👥 Students work with a partner to complete the table, using the same root for the verb, person and noun for each row. Tell them that they can look back through the unit to help them and also use their dictionaries. If appropriate, do the first row with the class, pointing out that the number of missing letters will help them find the right word. Allow about 5 minutes for this, before inviting feedback from the class.

> **Answers**
>
> | verb | person | noun |
> |------|--------|------|
> | 1 explore | 2 explorer | exploration |
> | 3 research | researcher | 4 research |
> | work | 5 worker | 6 work |
> | **travel** | 7 traveller | travel |
> | present | 8 presenter | 9 presentation |
> | **think** | 10 thinker | thought |

PRONUNCIATION FOR LISTENING

2 👥 Ask students to work with a partner and say the words in bold in Exercise 1 (*travel, think*) out loud. Does the *t* in each word sound the same or different? Allow about 1 minute for this, before inviting feedback from the class. Write the IPA symbols /t/ and /ɵ/ on the board and point to the /t/ when saying *travel* and to the /ɵ/ when saying *think*.

> **Answers**
>
> The *t* sounds different in the two words. It is /t/ in *travel* but /ɵ/ in *think*.

3 👥 Students work with a partner and practise saying the words, using the correct pronunciation. Allow about 2 minutes for this.

4 (◀) 10.5 👤 Play the audio for students to check and repeat. Write the words on the board. Point to one word for students to say it out loud. Point to other words in a random order for students to say them out loud, and make sure that students use the correct pronunciation. Increase the speed of your pointing so that students have to say the words faster.

5 👥 Students work with a partner to underline the two sounds in the sentences. Allow about 1 minute for this, before inviting feedback from the class. If appropriate, model and drill the sentences with the class. Point out that the *th* in *the* and *whether* are voiced sounds and that this is a different phoneme (/ð/). The *t* in *about* may not sound clearly because it is elided with the following *th*.

> **Answers**
>
> 1 We'll think about the type … 2 … and whether it is worth it.

WHILE LISTENING

LISTENING TO AN INTRODUCTION

6 👥 Tell students that they are going to listen to a discussion about the International Space Station. Ask students to work with a partner, look at the photograph and answer the questions. Allow about 1 minute for this, before inviting feedback from the class.

Answers

Answers will vary, but could include for question 2: research, testing space equipment, experiments in astronomy, biology, etc.

7 (◀)10.6) 👤👥 Before playing part one of the audio, explain to students that the person who is controlling a discussion often gives an introduction at the beginning. They use key words so you know what to listen for in the rest of the discussion. Play the audio. Students work individually to complete the sentences. After the audio, ask students to check their answers with a partner, before inviting feedback from the class.

Answers

1 exploration 2 work; money; future

8 👥 Students work with a partner to decide the reason for the discussion. Tell them to use what they heard in the introduction to help them choose the right option. Allow about 1 minute for this, before inviting feedback from the class. Ask students to give reasons for their answers. Do not give the answer at this stage. Students will check when listening in Exercise 10.

9 👥 Ask students to work with the same partner and predict the topics that will be included in the discussion. Allow about 2 minutes for this, before inviting feedback from the class. Do not give the answers at this stage. Students will check when listening in Exercise 10.

10 (◀)10.7) 👤👥 Tell students that they are now going to listen to part two of the discussion. Students work individually to check their answers to Exercises 8 and 9. After the audio, ask students to check with the partner they worked with before.

Answers

Exercise 8 2 Exercise 9 2 and 4

11 (◀)10.7) 👤👥 Play the audio again. Ask students to work individually and match the people to their opinion. After the audio, ask students to check with a partner.

Answers

1 c 2 a 3 b

Background note

The International Space Station (ISS) is an artificial satellite located in space. Scientists from many different countries, including Japan, Russia, the USA and Canada, have lived and studied there since the 1990s.

Optional activity

👥 Introduce this by reminding / asking students what collocations are (words that go together, word partnerships) and that they have studied several collocations throughout this course. Tell students that you are going to look at some more verb–noun collocations. Write the following words on the board: *research, experiments, information, money, about the Earth*. Students work in groups of 3 or 4 to find the verb that goes with these nouns. If the class is strong, ask them to do it without reference to the book. If students need some assistance, write the verbs on the board and ask students to match the verbs to the nouns. Verbs: *get, learn, do, spend, do*. Allow about 2 minutes for this, before inviting feedback from the class. Answers are: *do research, do experiments, get information, spend money, learn about the Earth*

DISCUSSION

12 👥 Put students into small groups of 3 or 4. Ask them to look at the photograph and discuss the questions. Allow about 5 minutes for this. Circulate, monitor and give assistance where appropriate, before inviting feedback from the class. This activity can be extended by putting students into pairs, each from a different group, to discuss the questions again with their new partner.

Answers will vary.

CRITICAL THINKING

Students begin to think about the Speaking task that they will do at the end of the unit (*Plan a conference about space exploration. Discuss and find solutions to any possible problems.*). Give them a minute to look at the box and ask you any questions they might have.

APPLY

1 Tell students that they are going to start an astronomy club to help students at their school / college / workplace. Students work with a partner to think about the problems that can happen when you are planning a new club or event and make notes about ideas 1–3. Circulate, monitor and give assistance where appropriate. Allow about 6 minutes for this, before doing some feedback with the class. Keep feedback relatively light as students will continue to work on this topic in Exercises 2 and 3.

Answers

Answers will vary but could include the following:
time: there is no time in the day when everyone is free so some won't be able to come; the school / company can only provide rooms after the end of the working day when people will want to go home
place: the school / company won't allow the club to use its rooms; the only rooms available have no windows
people coming regularly: people have a lot of commitments outside school / work; people won't come when there are big football matches or other sporting events

ANALYZE

2 Ask students to read the information in the Question charts box or read it aloud as students follow in their books. Students then work in pairs to write points 1–5 in the question chart to organize their thoughts. Allow 4 minutes for this, before inviting feedback from the class.

Answers

when? 1 who? 3 what? 5 where? 4 how? 2

3 Students work in groups of 3 or 4 and discuss the questions about problem solving. If appropriate, do the first question with the whole class before asking students to continue on their own. Allow 4 minutes for this, before inviting feedback from the class. This activity can be extended by putting students from different groups into pairs and asking them to discuss their ideas from their group with their new partner. Allow another 3 minutes for this, before inviting feedback from the class.

Possible answers

1 using flow charts (Units 3 and 5), advantages / disadvantages tables (Unit 4), consequence maps (Unit 6), ideas rakes (Unit 7), cluster diagrams (Unit 8), descriptions wheels (Unit 9), question charts (as here) and students' own ideas
2 Yes, because it will give your ideas more weight and make them more believable. Then you can argue your case convincingly.

SPEAKING

PREPARATION FOR SPEAKING

1 Tell students that when we are listening to someone talking, we generally make some movements or noises to indicate that we are interested in or bored with what they are saying. Students work with a partner to think of what we do to show we are interested or bored. Allow about 2 minutes for this, before inviting feedback from the class. You could ask students how someone would feel if they were talking to you and you did the actions that show you are bored.

Answers

Answers will vary but could include: **to show you are interested** – nodding your head, saying 'I see' or 'Mmmm' with a rising intonation; **to show you are bored** – looking around or out of the window, tapping your fingers, sighing

2 Students work in pairs to talk to their partner about the topics given. Allow 1 minute of silent thinking time for students to think of ideas and make very brief notes. The listening student has to show interest or boredom and the speaking student has to guess which it is. Allow about 6 minutes for this, to enable both students to talk about all the topics. Tell students to talk for no longer than half a minute about each. Circulate, monitor and give assistance where appropriate, before inviting feedback from the class. Find out who had the most interesting responses to each of the six topics.

3 Tell students that when we are talking with other people, we have some fixed phrases to help us manage the conversation. Ask students if this is the same in their language. The main functions are *inviting someone to speak, interrupting* and *continuing to speak.* Write these on the board and check

that students understand the meanings. For *interrupting*, you could ask two strong students to repeat some of their conversation from Exercise 2 out loud. When the second student starts to talk, you interrupt with the example phrase from the table. Students work individually to complete the table with the phrases. They could either write just the letters for each phrase or, preferably, copy the table in their notebooks and write the phrases in full. Allow about 8 minutes for this. Circulate, monitor and give assistance where appropriate. Ask students to check with a partner, before giving feedback to the class.

Answers

inviting someone to speak	interrupting	continuing to speak
a What is your opinion?	d Can I just cut in there?	b Can I finish?
f You haven't said much. What do you think?	e Sorry but I have to interrupt you and say …	c I'd like to finish my point.
g Why don't you start us off …?	h Sorry but can I just say …?	j Let me just finish what I was saying.
i Would anyone like to say anything else about …?		

4 Students work individually to complete the dialogue with phrases a–j from Exercise 3. Point out that more than one answer is possible in some places. Allow about 4 minutes for this. Circulate and monitor, giving assistance where appropriate. Ask students to check with a partner, before inviting feedback from the class.

Answers

1 a/g 2 d 3 b/c/j 4 i 5 f 6 a/i

5 Put students into groups of 5 and ask them to practise the dialogue. Students should swap characters three times. Allow about 5 minutes for this.

6 Tell students that just as we have some phrases for managing a conversation, we also have some phrases for starting and finishing a discussion. Students work in pairs to mark the phrases *S* or *F*. Allow about 2 minutes for this,

before inviting feedback from the class. While the students are doing this exercise, write the phrases on the board to assist with Exercise 7.

Answers

1 S 2 F 3 S 4 S 5 F 6 F

7 Ask students if they can remember any of the things they said about the topics in Exercise 2. Elicit as many ideas as possible. Put students into groups of 3 and ask them to look at Exercise 2 on page 189. Draw their attention to the phrases on the board from Exercise 6. Ask students to discuss the topics in Exercise 2, using the phrases on the board. Each student should contribute to each topic. Allow about 8 minutes for this. Circulate, monitor, note good language for feedback to the class at the end of the activity and give assistance where appropriate. Finish off by inviting feedback from the class to check whether every student used both a starting phrase and a finishing phrase.

SPEAKING TASK

Optional lead-in

Books closed. Ask students: 'Has anyone ever been to a conference?' If any of them have, ask them to tell the class what the conference was about, what they did during the conference and if it was useful. If no one has been to a conference, ask: 'What conferences have you heard about?' Possible answers could be teachers' conferences, conferences held by political parties, sales conferences.

PREPARE

1 Give students a minute to read the box and remind themselves of the Speaking task they are going to do. Students to work in pairs to discuss what happens at a conference. Allow 2 minutes for this, before inviting feedback from the class.

Answers

A conference is a large, formal meeting which can last a few days. People present and discuss their work, research or studies. It is an opportunity to meet other people who are interested in similar things.

2 👥 Read the list of things students have to do and check that they all understand each one. Students then work in small groups to think about the possible problems that might happen during the conference. They should make a list of them. Circulate, monitor and give assistance where appropriate. Allow 3 minutes for this but do not invite feedback at this stage.

3 👥 Students work in their groups to plan their conference. Allow 5 minutes for this but again do not invite feedback from the class at this stage.

DISCUSS

4 👥 Students work in their groups to discuss the order to put points a–d in. Allow 2 minutes for this, before inviting feedback from the class.

> **Answers**
>
> 1 b 2 a or d 3 d or a 4 c

PRESENT

5 👥 Put two groups together so that each group presents its ideas to the other group. Encourage the group which is listening to challenge the presenting group with the problems they thought about in Exercise 2. The students in the listening group should make notes about what the presenting group says and the possible problems. Allow 5 minutes for this but don't do any feedback at this point.

6 👥 The same two groups continue to work together to decide which ideas are the best for each part of the conference. Allow 5 minutes for this but don't do any feedback.

7 You could ask each group to choose a spokesperson or people to present the group's plan to the whole class. Students should make notes about similarities and differences as they listen. Allow each group 2 minutes to present their plans. Make notes of good language use to feed back to the class. Finally, there could then be a class vote to choose the best conference plan.

ADDITIONAL SPEAKING TASK

See page 143 for the Additional speaking task (*Have a discussion about opening a language school to teach your language in an English-speaking country*) and Model language for this unit.

Make a photocopy of page 143 for each student.

👥 Divide the class into 2 halves. Tell one half that they like the idea of opening a language school and the other half that they don't. Students work with a partner who has the same idea. They should think of ideas to support their argument: those in favour should find good reasons for opening the school and those against should think of as many problems and reasons for those problems as possible. They should make notes in the table on page 143 to help them structure their arguments.

👥 Put students into groups of four, two in favour of opening the school and two against. Groups discuss their ideas and decide how they will organize the school. They should use the notes they made in the table and the Model language to help them.

Finish off by inviting feedback from the class about how they will organize their schools.

TASK CHECKLIST AND OBJECTIVES
REVIEW

Refer students to the end of the unit for the Task checklist and Objectives review. Students complete the tables individually to reflect on their learning and identify areas for improvement.

WORDLIST

See Teaching tips page 10, section 6, for ideas about how to make the most of the Wordlist with your students.

REVIEW TEST

See pages 132–133 for the photocopiable Review test for this unit and page 107 for ideas about when and how to administer the Review test.

RESEARCH PROJECT

Create an eBook explaining space phenomena

Divide the class into groups and ask students to research one of the following space phenomena: black holes, star types, supernovas, comets or meteors. There are various sources on the internet (including lower-level language resources) which explain these phenomena. Students can use the Cambridge LMS as a central place to share information.

Tell the class they are going to create an eBook. You can find guides and eBook software by searching 'create eBook'. The class will need to decide on a title for the eBook. Each group can add the information they have collected on their space phenomenon to the eBook.

REVIEW TESTS ANSWERS AND AUDIO SCRIPTS

The *Review tests* are designed to be used after students have completed each unit of the Student's Book. Each *Review test* checks students' knowledge of the key language areas and practises the listening skills from the unit. The *Review tests* take around 50 minutes to complete, but you may wish to adjust this time depending on your class or how much of the Student's Book unit you covered.

Review tests can be given for homework as general revision. *Review test* audio is accessed from the Cambridge LMS. Use the *Additional speaking tasks* at the end of the Teacher's Book or in the Online Workbook to test your students' speaking skills. Photocopy one test for each student. Students should do the tests on their own. You can check the answers by giving students their peers' papers to mark, or correct the papers yourself. Keep a record of the results to help monitor individual student progress.

REVIEW TEST 1 ANSWERS

1 1 The house was built _in_1800.
2 Is_it_a bridge?
3 They built_a kind_of city above the sea.
4 Did you have your_own room when you were_a child?

2 A (in any order) ancient castle desert traditional
B (in any order) glass modern unusual

3 1F 2F 3F 4O 5O

4 1 heat
2 drive
3 store
4 chop
5 prepare

5 1 lived
2 did you go
3 recognized
4 collected
5 thought

6 1 traffic lights
2 coffee shop
3 wildlife area
4 ancient
5 route

REVIEW TEST 1 AUDIO SCRIPTS

(◀) **1.1** 1 The house was built in 1800.
2 Is it a bridge?
3 They built a kind of city above the sea.
4 Did you have your own room when you were a child?

(◀) **1.2** Hello, my name's Sultan and I'd like to tell you about two of my favourite buildings in my country, Saudi Arabia. A lot of people think that Saudi Arabia is such a new country that we don't have much history. This isn't true. We may not have such a long history as the Egyptians or Syrians, but we do have some very old buildings. My particular favourite is Masmak Fort. This is an ancient castle and is very important in our history. When it was built it was in the middle of the desert, but now it is in the middle of our capital, Riyadh. It is made of traditional materials: mud-bricks. It is important in our history because the future King won it in a battle and from this came the Kingdom of Saudi Arabia.
My other favourite building is one of the newest in the country. It's called Kingdom Tower, or Mamlaka, which means Kingdom in Arabic, Tower. It's got a really unusual design. Some people don't like it at all, but I love it as it is just so modern and exciting. The walls of the building are made of glass and look like mirrors and reflect the colour of the sky. At night the top part of the building is lit up with different colours and it just looks wonderful. And of course the views from the top of the building are amazing.

REVIEW TEST 2 ANSWERS

1 1 The film was really good but I didn't like the ending.
2 Are you enjoying the festival?
3 What time does the festival start?
4 Will you get a job after you finish school?

2 1 Wednesday
2 August
3 town
4 tomatoes

3 1 festival
2 the seasons
3 culture
4 biggest
5 the early 1940s

4 1 celebrates
    2 exchange
    3 envelopes
    4 costumes
    5 decorate

5 1 Do you like ice cream and cake?
    2 Are you feeling happy now?
    3 Are you good at English?
    4 Do you always do your homework?
    5 Are you enjoying the festival?

6 1 bride
    2 dried fruit
    3 firework
    4 interesting
    5 exam

REVIEW TEST 2 AUDIO SCRIPTS

🔊 **2.1** 1 The film was really good but I didn't like the ending.
2 Are you enjoying the festival?
3 What time does the festival start?
4 Will you get a job after you finish school?

🔊 **2.2** Here in Spain we have lots of festivals. We love to celebrate and are always ready to have a party. A lot of our festivals relate to the seasons and of course a lot of festivals are about food. Food is very, very important in our culture. My favourite festival is La Tomatina festival. Some people say that this is the biggest food fight in the world. I think it is a lot of fun. It takes place each year on the 4th Wednesday in August in a small town near Valencia called Buñol. In the afternoon thousands of people come to the centre of the town and throw tomatoes at each other. Nobody really knows how or why the festival started. Most people accept that the first time people threw tomatoes was sometime in the early 1940s. But no one knows why. Some people say that it was some young men fighting with police, others say that it was unhappy townspeople throwing tomatoes at politicians they didn't like.

I don't think it really matters that we don't know how or why it started. The most important thing is that it is a lot of fun. Everyone is welcome. No one gets hurt, because the tomatoes are so soft at the end of the summer. Just make sure that you wear a very old tee-shirt!

REVIEW TEST 3 ANSWERS

1 1 agrees enthusiastically
    2 disagrees
    3 disagrees
    4 agrees
    5 agrees
    6 disagrees

2 1T 2F 3F 4T 5T 6F 7T 8T

3 1 problem
    2 think
    3 with
    4 that
    5 disagree
    6 totally

4 1 martial arts
    2 education
    3 results
    4 train
    5 high

5 1 to leave
    2 playing (to play is also acceptable)
    3 to ask
    4 doing
    5 to go

6 1 d 2 a 3 e 4 b 5 c

REVIEW TEST 3 AUDIO SCRIPTS

🔊 **3.1**

1 **a:** Don't you think that students should be able to choose what subjects they want to study?
    b: Oh yes, I totally agree with that. (agrees enthusiastically)

2 **a:** I think students should be able to learn with just a book, pencil and paper.
    b: Yes, that's true but… . (disagrees)

3: **a:** I thought the course was great.
    b: It was Ok, I suppose but to be honest I didn't find it very helpful. (disagrees)

4 **a:** Everyone should be able to go to university.
    b: Yes, I totally agree with that. (agrees)

5 **a:** I never want to take an exam again.
    b: Oh yes, I agree. (agrees)

6 **a:** I don't think exams are the best way to test us.
    b: Well, that may be true but… . (disagrees)

Sultan: Hi guys, how are you enjoying the course?

Hussain: Well, to be honest, I'm enjoying the course but I don't like some of the rules here.

Sultan: What do you mean? Which rules? I think it's very relaxed here.

Hussain: Well, this rule about not being late for class. I find it so difficult to get up in the morning, and we get a mark against us if we are more than 10 minutes late.

Abdulatif: Yes, I have a problem with that as well. But I do understand it's important for the whole class to start on time.

Hussain: Surely, if I'm late it doesn't upset the rest of the class.

Abdulatif: Well, it does. If we are working together and someone comes in late we all have to stop.

Hussain: Yes, I see. Sultan, what do you think?

Sultan: I agree with Abdulatif. It's important for everyone that we start on time.

Hussain: Well what about the rule that we can't bring coffee into class? I really need my coffee in the morning.

Sultan: Yes, I agree with you on that! Coffee really helps me think in the morning.

Abdulatif: Well I disagree. If you want coffee, you should get up earlier. What I don't like is the rule that our homework marks are included in our final mark.

Sultan: I totally agree. I think that's totally wrong.

Hussain: Me too. I think we should complain.

Abdulatif: Yes, you're right. Let's do it now.

REVIEW TEST 4 ANSWERS

1 1 /s/ 2 /ʃ/ 3 /ʃ/ 4 /tʃ/ 5 /s/ 6 /ʃ/ 7 /s/
8 /ʃ/ 9 /ʃ/ 10 /tʃ/

2 1 clean
2 $499
3 tired
4 night
5 Robo-Filter.

3 1 in the corner (of the room)
2 all the hard work (for you)
3 saves time (as well)
4 your pool is as clean as new
5 clean (for us to breathe)

4 1 advertisements
2 encyclopaedia
3 company
4 invention
5 communities

5 1 to be able
2 Could
3 be able to
4 to be able to
5 be able

6 1c 2a 3e 4b 5d

REVIEW TEST 4 AUDIO SCRIPTS

🔊 4.1

1 On Fridays my father always goes to the mosque.
2 My sister always buys fashionable clothes.
3 On my uncle's farm there are cows and sheep.
4 When there is an important football match my brother gets very excited.
5 The bus will only stop if you press the button.
6 I wish we didn't have to do any exams.
7 I must go and wash my face.
8 I love the sound of the ocean.
9 We don't have to go to college on our national day.
10 I think I watch too much television.

🔊 4.2

Hi folks, and welcome to news from the Robot Shop. Your one-stop-shop for all your housework robots, and have we got some great new robots for you. Firstly new in from America is the Robo-Vac. This clever little robot will keep all your floors clean. All you need is a simple intelligent device in the corner of the room and away it goes. For only $499 this is a bargain. Second is the window-cleaning robot. Something to save your tired arms as it does all the hard work for you. As it can do the inside and outside at the same time it saves time as well. Fabulous value at $699. Now, for those of us who live in hot countries a swimming pool is an important part of our lives. But how many of us enjoy cleaning the pool? Yuk….not me. That's why I've bought the Pool Power-Vac. Set it to work at night and in the morning your pool is as clean as new. It's not cheap at $1099 but worth every cent. Finally for our air conditioned houses the air cleaning robot Robo-Filter is a must. This robot cleverly takes out all the pollution and toxins from the air in our home leaving it clean for us to breathe. Especially important if there are babies or old people in your home. So, that's it from this week's News from the Robot Shop.

REVIEW TEST 5 ANSWERS

1 The underlined words in 1, 4, 5, 6, 7 and 9 have a silent 'l'. In sentence 10, you can hear one 'l'.

2 1E 2A 3D 4B 5C

3 1 coffee
  2 Broomfield Hospital
  3 yes
  4 3
  5 a capital letter

4 1 Equator
  2 ancestors
  3 beach
  4 market
  5 mountains

5 1 'I'll call you at 8 pm.'
  2 'I'm unhappy at work.'
  3 'I don't like chocolate ice cream.'
  4 'You have to finish the work by the weekend.'
  5 'Have you got the correct tickets?'

6 1 picked up
  2 nose
  3 Deaf
  4 smell
  5 heads

REVIEW TEST 5 AUDIO SCRIPT

◀)) 5.1

1 Usually I get a bus to work but if the weather is good I walk.
2 If you're going to the shops please could you get me some milk.
3 I think it's important to get 7 hours of sleep every night.
4 When my sister and her friends meet at the coffee shop they never stop talking.
5 If he wants to pass his exams he should work harder in class.
6 I always feel calm when I'm by the sea.
7 My mother said I could borrow her earrings.
8 I always confuse the letters b and p.
9 I only did half my homework last night.
10 My father wants to sell his car.

◀)) 5.2

A We're here at Burger World to welcome you to the country's most exciting casual dining experience with fun food for all the family. Parents, bring your kids along on a Saturday morning and we will give them a free party pack with games and ice cream to keep them happy all day. And for you parents we offer free coffee with every special meal deal. See you soon!

B This is Dr Peter Gibson. I'm sorry I am not able to take your call at the moment, please leave a message after the beep. If your call is urgent, please contact Broomfield Hospital on 634 951.

C ……..and here in the Egyptian Room we have the jewels from the Pharaohs. As you can see, this is an amazing collection. Of course all the gold you see here is real, together with many rare and precious stones such as diamonds, rubies and lapis lazuli……now… moving on……

D Welcome to the 10 o'clock news. Our headlines today - storms continue in the west of the country causing serious flooding in the region. The Minister for Education announces 3 more universities to open in the next 5 years……

E Firstly, here are your essays from last week. Generally very good, but please, please take care with your spelling and punctuation. Remember, sentences begin with a capital letter and end with a full stop or a question mark. OK, now can you all open your books at page 34….

REVIEW TEST 6 ANSWERS

1 1 interested
  2 interested
  3 bored
  4 bored
  5 interested
  6 bored
  7 interested
  8 bored
  9 interested
  10 bored

2 1F 2F 3T 4T 5F

3 1 effects
  2 enough
  3 more
  4 difficult
  5 rising

4 1d 2c 3a 4e 5b

5 1 it's going to start
  2 I'm playing
  3 I'm going to go / I'm going to
  4 We're having
  5 are you doing

6 1 dull 2 chilly 3 humid 4 upset 5 calm

REVIEW TEST 6 AUDIO SCRIPTS

🔊 6.1

1 **A:** The film was great. Thank you for taking me.

   B: Good, glad you liked it.

2 **A:** Did you know that more countries are having water shortages?

   B: Really?

3 **A:** It's our country's national day today.

   B: Is it?

4 **A:** This weather really is lovely, isn't it?

   B: I suppose so.

5 **A:** Thank you so much for letting me borrow your book.

   B: You're welcome. I hope you found it helpful.

6 **A:** We have to do something about environmental pollution.

   B: Do we?

7 **A:** Did you know how important the rainforests really are?

   B: No, are they?

8 **A:** I think climate change is the most important issue in the world today.

   B: Do you really?

9 **A:** Next week people are meeting to talk about rainforests.

   B: Oh really?

10 **A:** I love it when it rains a lot. It's great, isn't it?

   B: I suppose so.

🔊 6.2

Son: Hi Mum, I'm home.

Mother: Hello there! Did you have a good day at college?

S: Yes, it was really interesting. We learned about global warming and its effects on the weather.

M: Oh that, haven't we heard enough about it on TV? I'm so tired of it.

S: It's really important you know. It isn't something you can just forget.

M: I know, but it's always the same: more rain, less rain; more sun, less sun; more snow, less snow. The weather has always changed. What's so special about this?

S: OK, I understand why you get so confused. But global warming affects places in the world differently. So it isn't the same place that is getting more rain or less rain but the places that have a lot of rain are getting even more rain….

M: …And the places that have a little rain are getting even less.

S: Yes, that's right. But can you see what is now happening in these places? If there is too much rain, then it is difficult to grow food…

M: And if there is no rain at all, then it is impossible to grow food.

S: Exactly, so many people in the world today do not have much to eat.

M: Mmm, yes that really is very serious indeed. And what else is happening?

S: Well, the ice at the North and South poles is melting and so sea levels are rising. This is ok for us here, but…

M: …for big cities near the sea....

S: …and small islands with no hills…

M: …it could be terrible.

REVIEW TEST 7 ANSWERS

1 1 going to
   2 Do you want to
   3 do you
   4 going to
   5 want to
   6 Do you want to
   7 going to
   8 Do you, going to
   9 going to
   10 Do you want to

2 1 Spain
   2 1-3
   3 The number 7 from Manchester United
   4 He can run faster than the Spanish players.
   5 No

3 **England** (any 3 from) fantastic, exciting, better [team / side], amazing
   Spain (any 2 from) boring, slow, worst [game]

4 1 neighbourhood
   2 excited
   3 disappointed
   4 dangerous
   5 worried

5 1 ever 2 already 3 just 4 still 5 yet

6 1 advantage
   2 football
   3 golf
   4 the best
   4 boxing

REVIEW TEST 7 AUDIO SCRIPTS

🔊 7.1

1 I'm <u>going to</u> go shopping this evening.
2 <u>Do you</u> <u>want to</u> come to the football match with me?

3 Which car <u>do you</u> think you'll have next year?

4 Are you <u>going to</u> come to class tomorrow?

5 I <u>want to</u> get a good job with a bank.

6 <u>Do you</u> <u>want to</u> qualify to be a teacher?

7 Tomorrow I'm <u>going to</u> watch the match with my friends.

8 <u>Do you</u> think it's <u>going to</u> rain tomorrow?

9 I'm <u>going to</u> study sports science when I go to university.

10 <u>Do you</u> <u>want to</u> try chess boxing?

🔊 7.2

Now to last night's semi-final between England and Spain, what a match! England were fantastic. I've never seen such exciting football. Spain may have won but in my mind, England were the better team. The final score of 3-1 to Spain doesn't really give a true picture of the game. For me the best player was the new number 7 from Manchester United. He played with such skill, was able to run faster than any of the Spanish players. The new Spanish team was boring to watch and played with no interest in the game at all. Indeed, their game was very slow. The fact that they scored 3 goals doesn't mean that they played well. It was the worst game I'd ever seen from the Spanish side. No, without doubt England were the better side and were far more exciting to watch. Does the result really matter that much? I don't think so. Yesterday we saw the new England side play some amazing football. Even if their only goal was from a penalty, they still played very well indeed. So, English football fans, we have a lot to be happy about and we can look forward to the next competition with hope for a better result.

REVIEW TEST 8 ANSWERS

1 1 13% 2 4232 3 $15,050 4 ¼ 5 40% 6 2,000
7 33.5% 8 60% 9 53 10 $ 76,700

2 1 36% 2 38% 3 90% 4 25% 5 60%

3 1T 2T 3F 4F 5F

4 1 most
2 more (popular) than
3 Fewer
4 More
5 least

5 1 started up
2 took up
3 taking part in
4 put up with
5 run out of

6 1 happy 2 bad 3 calm 4 excited 5 untidy

REVIEW TEST 8 AUDIO SCRIPTS

🔊 8.1

1 Nearly 13% of students never do their homework.

2 If you need to call me, my telephone extension number is 4232.

3 Yes, this is a lovely diamond ring; it's $15,050.

4 The company profits have increased by a ¼.

5 Research has shown that 40% of people are not happy in their work.

6 The Cape of Good Hope is a good place for fishermen because it has 2,000 types of fish.

7 Over 33.5% of people check their social networking sites while they are at work.

8 Most people spend over 60% of their time working at their desks.

9 At work, people spend nearly 53 minutes on the phone every day.

10 This car costs $ 76,700.

🔊 8.2

Prof: Well, Suzan, how did you get on with your survey? You were asking students about what they wanted to do after they left university.

Student: Yes, that's correct. I am trying to find out both what students want to do and if they think it is going to be easy to get a job.

P: OK, go ahead.

S: I knew that medicine is a very popular major at this university but I didn't know how popular it was. 36% of students want to be doctors. Interestingly, more women than men want to be doctors with 38% of women and 34% of men. Also, this group of students were the most positive about getting a job. 85% believe that it would be easy for them to find a job. With more men than women feeling positive, 90% of male medical students thought it would be easy to get a job, compared with 80% of female medical students.

P: Well they are both high numbers so that shows how confident the future doctors are.

S: Sadly, not all groups of students were so positive. If we think about engineering, 25% of male students want to be engineers compared to only 5% of female students. The situation is reversed, with only 50% of male engineering students thinking it will be easy for them to get a job. But 60% of the female students think it will be easy for them to get a job.

REVIEW TEST 9 ANSWERS

1 1 N; 2 N; 3 E; 4 N; 5 E; 6 N; 7 E; 8 N; 9 N; 10 E
2 1 electricity 2 pink 3 ice (cubes) 4 bed
5 cup of coffee
3 1 flavour 2 easy 3 kick 4 are relaxed
5 cup of coffee
4 1 remarkable 2 homeless 3 funeral
4 fascinated 5 emperor
5 1 excited 2 boring 3 interested 4 tired
5 relaxed
6 1T 2F 3T 4T 5F

REVIEW TEST 9 AUDIO SCRIPTS

◀) 9.1

1 I'm really looking forward to the class
tomorrow. I love grammar.
2 The teacher said we had 3 tests this term
instead of 4.
3 Our teacher really is amazing.
4 We are going on holiday tomorrow.
5 I'm really enjoying this essay I'm writing.
6 Do you think it will rain tomorrow?
7 We've almost finished this course.
8 My teacher said that my essay needs more
work.
9 Well, I think I understand everything.
10 He's feeling very good about his work.

◀) 9.2

Welcome to this week's 'best products'
programme. Today we have two fantastic little
gadgets to talk about. Firstly the 'ice cream
football'.
We all love ice cream, especially when the
weather is hot, but how often have you gone to
the shop to find that your favourite flavour has
sold out? With the ice cream football you will
always be able to have your favourite ice cream,
and not only that, the gadget doesn't use any
electricity, so it's very cheap to use. The ball
comes in two colours: blue and pink. It's so easy
to use. Just put in your favourite flavours – mine
is strawberry – at one end. Then, in the other end
put some ice cubes and now all you have to do is
play with the ball, kick it around and soon you will
have a pint of your favourite ice cream. Brilliant.
Now our next gadget is for people who are a little
more relaxed. This is a desk for working with your
tablet while still in bed. The 'Comfi-Desk' has a
space where you can put your tablet so it is easy
to read. The bottom of the Comfi-Desk is like a
cushion so it is comfortable on your legs and there
is enough space on the desk for a cup of coffee
and a plate of cake. Perfect for those who work
better in bed!

REVIEW TEST 10 ANSWERS

1 1 whether 2 from 3 our 4 my 5 had 6 leaves
7 just 8 book 9 When 10 Look
2 [in any order] planets, exploration, results,
technology, sun
3 1 Whether 2 Now 3 the sun 4 as 5 mined
4 1 astronauts 2 diamond 3 solar system
4 couple 5 project
5 1 would 2 will 3 would 4 will 5 would
6 1 return journey 2 business trip 3 sea voyage
4 Mediterranean cruise 5 scheduled flight

REVIEW TEST 10 AUDIO SCRIPTS

◀) 10.1

1 Well, it depends whether or not the sun is
shining.
2 My taekwondo class is from four to six.
3 We have forgotten our books.
4 There are 8 students in my group.
5 Last night we had pizza.
6 I'm late. My plane leaves in an hour.
7 My sister's son has just started school.
8 It's a long time since I read such a good book.
9 When do we have to go to class?
10 Look, there's Marium.

◀) 10.2

So, what is the future for space travel and
exploration of new planets? In today's world we
have the knowledge and the technology. However
do we have the money or enough desire to
continue with the space exploration programme?
I would like to talk about some of the reasons
why I think we should continue. Whether or not
we continue is not my decision to make. Now our
nearest neighbour is Mars. It is closer to the sun
than the Earth and is known as the red planet.
Already, man-made vehicles are exploring Mars
and getting some very interesting results.
Most important are the types of material that may
exist on Mars. For example aluminium, copper
and zinc. Sometime in the future these important
minerals could be mined on Mars and then sent
back to Earth. We do not have the technology
for that yet. But as we use more and more of the
Earth's resources it is important to know that they
are there.
For these reason only I believe it is important that
we continue exploring other planets.

Name: .... **Date:** ....

LISTENING (20 marks)

LISTENING 1

1 (🔊 **1.1**) Listen to the sentences and draw the links between the consonants and vowels. You will hear each sentence twice. 2 marks for each correct answer.

1 The house was built in 1800.

2 Is it a bridge?

3 They built a kind of city above the sea.

4 Did you have your own room when you were a child?

LISTENING 2

2 (🔊 **1.2**) You are going to listen to someone talking about the two photographs. Before you listen, predict which words in the box will be used to describe each building. Some words are not used. Listen and write the correct words under the photos. 1 mark for each correct answer.

forest   ancient   glass   bridge   modern   castle   unusual   desert   cave   traditional

A Masmak Fort, Riyadh

B Mamlaka Tower, Jeddah

_____

_____

_____

_____

3 (🔊1.2) Listen again and mark the sentences F for fact or O for opinion. 1 mark for each correct answer.

1 But we do have some very old buildings.
2 This is an ancient castle.
3 It's got a really unusual design.
4 I love it as it is just so modern and exciting.
5 It just looks wonderful.

LANGUAGE DEVELOPMENT (15 marks)

4 Complete the sentences below with words from the box.

store prepare heat drive chop

1 In winter we need to ____________ our homes to stay warm.
2 Some people use the bus to go to work but others prefer to ____________.
3 It is important to ____________ food carefully in a fridge.
4 Before making soup you need to ____________ the vegetables into small pieces.
5 Busy people often ____________ their dinner in the mornings so they can eat it as soon as they get home.

5 Complete the sentences with the correct form of the words in brackets.

1 I ____________ (live) in Spain for 5 years from 2005 to 2010.
2 Where ____________ (do / go / you) for your holiday last year?
3 She ____________ (recognize) his face but couldn't remember his name.
4 When he was a child, he ____________ (collect) stamps and coins.
5 She ____________ (think) her keys were in her bag but they were on the table.

6 Choose the correct word to complete the sentence.

1 The car stopped at the *traffic lights / bus stop* as they turned red.
2 She likes to meet her friends at the *tourist information office / coffee shop* on Saturday morning.
3 There is a beautiful *traffic light / wildlife area* by the lake.
4 There is an *ancient / modern* castle near the top of the mountain.
5 The best *tour / route* to the hotel is over the bridge and along the road by the lake.

TOTAL ____ / 35

REVIEW TEST 2

Name: .... **Date:** ....

LISTENING (20 marks)

LISTENING 1

1 🔊 **2.1** Listen to the sentences and underline the stressed words. The numbers in brackets tell you how many words are stressed, and the number of marks per sentence.

1 The film was really good but I didn't like the ending. (4)

2 Are you enjoying the festival? (2)

3 What time does the festival start? (3)

4 Will you get a job after you finish school? (2)

LISTENING 2

2 🔊 **2.2** You are going to listen to someone talking about their favourite festival. Listen and complete the notes below with one word for each gap. 1 mark for each correct answer.

> **LA TOMATINA**
>
> Date: 4th (1)_____ in
>   (2)_____
>
> Place: Buñol: a (3)_____ near Valencia
>
> Activities: Throwing (4)_____

3 🔊 **2.2** Listen again and write words from the audio which have a similar meaning to the words in bold below. 1 mark for each correct answer.

1 La Tomatina is an important **celebration** in Spain. _____

2 A lot of celebrations are related to **spring / summer / autumn / winter.** _____

3 Celebrating food is a very important part of Spanish **tradition.** _____

4 La Tomatina is the **largest** food fight in the world. _____

5 The Festival started sometime **between 1940 and 1945.** _____

LANGUAGE DEVELOPMENT (15 marks)

4 Complete the sentences with the correct form of the words in the box.

| exchange   costumes   celebrate   envelope   decorate |

1 When a baby is born the family often _____ with a party.
2 In every culture there is a time when people _____ gifts.
3 In China parents give their unmarried children money in red _____.
4 In some festivals people wear beautiful _____ when they go out.
5 At New Year many people _____ their houses with lights.

5 Use the words to make questions in the Present tense. Use the correct auxiliary verb.

1 you / like / ice cream and cake?

_____

2 you / feeling / happy now?

_____

3 you / good / at English?

_____

4 you / always do / your homework?

_____

5 you / enjoying / the festival?

_____

6 Choose the correct word to complete the sentences.

1 The *bride / groom* wore a beautiful white dress.
2 The cake is decorated with *noodles / dried fruit* and cream.
3 At the end of the festival there was an amazing *celebration / firework* display.
4 She thought the lecture was very *interesting / interested*.
5 Before you take *an exam / care* it is a good idea to take some advice from your teacher.

TOTAL _____ / 35

REVIEW TEST 3

Name: .... **Date:** ....

LISTENING (20 marks)

LISTENING 1

1 (◄) **3.1** Listen to the conversations. Does the second speaker agree or disagree with the first speaker? Circle the correct answer. 1 mark for each correct answer.

1 agrees / disagrees
2 agrees / disagrees
3 agrees / disagrees

4 agrees / disagrees
5 agrees / disagrees
6 agrees / disagrees

LISTENING 2

2 (◄) **3.2** You are going to listen to 3 students talking about the rules in their college. Listen. Are the following sentences T (true) or F (false)? 1 mark for each correct answer.

1 Speaker 2 enjoys the course but not the rules.
2 There are no rules about when a student can arrive for class.
3 Students get a mark against them if they are 20 minutes late for class.
4 If someone comes late to a class, they all have to stop.
5 Everyone should start on time.
6 Students can bring coffee into class.
7 If you want coffee, get up earlier.
8 Homework marks are included in the final mark.

3 (◄) **3.2** Listen again and complete the sentences with one word. 1 mark for each correct answer.

1 Yes, I have a _____ with that as well.
2 Yes, I see. Sultan, what do you _____ ?
3 I agree _____ Abdulatif.
4 Yes, I agree with you on _____ .
5 Well, I _____ .
6 I totally agree. I think that's _____ wrong.

LANGUAGE DEVELOPMENT (15 marks)

4 Complete the sentences with words from the box.

| education   high   martial arts   results   train |

1 _____ such as taekwondo and kung fu are now popular all over the world.

2 Most people believe that the most important thing for a successful career is a good _____ .

3 He was very disappointed when he got his exam _____ . He had worked very hard but he didn't pass.

4 Companies usually have to _____ their workers so they can do their jobs well.

5 I wasn't very happy at my primary school but when I moved to my _____ school things got a lot better.

5 Complete the sentences with the correct form of the verb in brackets.

1 She decided _____ (leave) school after she passed her exams.

2 I started _____ (play) the piano when I was 12 years old.

3 He wanted _____ (ask) about places to visit but the tourist information office was closed.

4 When I've finished _____ (do) my homework, I'll give you a call.

5 He finally agreed _____ (go) with them to the cinema.

6 Match 1–5 with a–e to make sentences.

1 I agreed   a to learn English when I was 11 years old.
2 I began   b helping you with your homework, because I enjoy Maths.
3 Blended   c cooking the cake, but we enjoyed eating it more!
4 I don't mind   d to help with the cleaning.
5 We enjoyed   e learning is a mixture of online and classroom learning.

TOTAL _____ / 35

REVIEW TEST 4

Name: .... **Date:** ....

LISTENING (20 marks)

LISTENING 1

1 (🔊 4.1) Listen to the sentences and decide if the underlined letters are pronounced /s/, /ʃ/ or /tʃ/. Circle the correct sound/symbol. 1 mark for each correct answer.

  1 On Fridays my father always goes to the mo<u>s</u>que. /s/ /ʃ/ /tʃ/

  2 My sister always buys fa<u>sh</u>ionable clothes. /s/ /ʃ/ /tʃ/

  3 On my uncle's farm there are cows and <u>sh</u>eep. /s/ /ʃ/ /tʃ

  4 When there is an important football ma<u>tch</u> my brother gets very excited. /s/ /ʃ/ /tʃ/

  5 The bus will only stop if you pre<u>ss</u> the button. /s/ /ʃ/ /tʃ/

  6 I wi<u>sh</u> we didn't have to do any exams. /s/ /ʃ/ /tʃ/

  7 I must go and wash my fa<u>ce</u>. /s/ /ʃ/ /tʃ/

  8 I love the sound of the o<u>ce</u>an. /s/ /ʃ/ /tʃ/

  9 We don't have to go to college on our na<u>ti</u>onal day. /s/ /ʃ/ /tʃ/

  10 I think I wa<u>tch</u> too much television. /s/ /ʃ/ /tʃ/

LISTENING 2

2 (🔊 4.2) You are going to listen to a radio programme about new products for the home. Listen and circle the correct word to complete the sentences. 1 mark for each correct answer.

  1 The Robo-Vac will keep all your floors *clean* / *dry*.

  2 The Robo-Vac is a bargain at *$399* / *$499*.

  3 The window-cleaning robot can save your *tired* / *long* arms.

  4 The Pool Power-Vac cleans swimming pools during the *day* / *night*.

  5 For houses with air conditioning the *Robo-Filter* / *Robo-Airclean* is a must.

3 (🔊 4.2) Listen again and complete the sentences. 1 mark for each correct answer.

  1 The Robo-Vac floor cleaner needs an intelligent device _____

  _____.

  2 The window-cleaning robot will save your tired arms as it does _____

  _____.

  3 As the window-cleaning robot can do the inside and outside at the same time, it _____

  _____.

  4 If the Pool Power-Vac is set to work at night, in the morning _____

  _____.

  5 The Robo-Filter takes all the pollution and toxins from the air leaving it _____

  _____.

LANGUAGE DEVELOPMENT (15 marks)

4 Choose the correct word from the box to complete the sentences.

company communities advertisements encyclopaedia invention

1 These days we see a lot of _____ in the street.
2 When I need to find some information I use an online _____ as well as the one in my office.
3 The _____ I work for spends a lot of money on research.
4 Some people believe that the telephone is the greatest _____ in the history of technology.
5 One of the best things about the internet is how many people can become part of online _____ and share their interests with other people.

5 Complete the sentences by choosing the correct form of the verb *be able to*.

1 You have *to be able* / *can* to use a computer if you want to get an office job.
2 *Can* / *Could* you swim when you were 3 years old?
3 You will *be able to* / *can* fly to work in the future.
4 In the past you had *to be able to* / *can* use a typewriter, but now we normally use a computer keyboard.
5 You won't *can* / *be able to* save this file to your computer becuase it's too big.

6 Match the words (1–5) with their definitions (a–e).

1 battery   a what we do when we are looking around the internet for something we like
2 surf   b what we do when we write messages and send them to people on our phones
3 charger   c it provides power for small electrical items
4 text   d what we do when we get information from the internet and put it on our own computer
5 download   e what we use when we have no power left in our phone or tablet

TOTAL _____/ 35

Name: .... **Date:** ....

LISTENING (20 marks)

LISTENING 1

1 (◄) 5.1 Listen to the sentences below. Mark sentences with an S if the *l* in the underlined word is silent. 1 mark for each correct answer.

  1 Usually I get a bus to work but if the weather is good, I <u>walk</u>.

  2 If you're going to the shops, <u>please</u> could you get me some milk?

  3 I think it's important to get 7 hours of <u>sleep</u> every night.

  4 When my sister and her friends meet at the coffee shop they never stop <u>talking</u>.

  5 If he wants to pass his exams, he <u>should</u> work harder in class.

  6 I always feel <u>calm</u> when I'm by the sea.

  7 My mother said I <u>could</u> borrow her earrings.

  8 I always confuse the <u>letters</u> b and p.

  9 I only did <u>half</u> my homework last night.

  10 My father wants to <u>sell</u> his car.

LISTENING 2

2 (◄) 5.2 Listen to five extracts (A–E) and match the genres (1–5) with the extracts. 1 mark for each correct answer.

  1 Teacher   _____

  2 Radio advert   _____

  3 News report   _____

  4 Telephone message   _____

  5 Museum guide   _____

3 (◄) 5.2 Listen again and answer the questions. 1 mark for each correct answer.

  1 What can parents get free at Burger World?

    _____

  2 Which place do you need to phone if it is an urgent call?

    _____

  3 Is the gold in the Pharaohs' jewels real?

    _____

  4 How many new universities will open in the next 5 years?

    _____

  5 What type of letter do sentences begin with?

    _____

LANGUAGE DEVELOPMENT (15 marks)

4 Complete the sentences with words from the box.

ancestors market beach Equator mountains

1 There are no deserts on the _____ because there is always a lot of rain.
2 Some people enjoy researching the lives of their _____, finding out where they lived and what work they did.
3 For many people on holiday the most important thing is that there is a beautiful _____ near their hotel.
4 I prefer to get my fruit and vegetables from the local _____ as they are fresh and cheap.
5 Even in the summer the _____ have snow on them.

5 The sentences below use reported speech. Write what the person actually said.

1 He said that he would call me at 8 pm.

_____

2 She told me that she was unhappy at work.

_____

3 You said that you didn't like chocolate ice cream.

_____

4 The teacher told us we had to finish the work by the weekend.

_____

5 They asked us if we had got the correct tickets.

_____

6 Choose the correct word to complete the sentence.

1 When he went to France he *picked up* / *taught* the language really quickly.
2 The old man had a long white beard on his *nose* / *chin*.
3 *Deaf* / *Blind* people can learn to communicate using sign language.
4 The flowers in the shop have such a lovely *smell* / *taste*.
5 When they visited their grandmother she always gave them some money and patted their *palms* / *heads*.

TOTAL _____/ 35

REVIEW TEST 6

Name: .... **Date:** ....

LISTENING (20 marks)

LISTENING 1

1 (◄) 6.1) Listen to the conversations. Is the second speaker interested or bored? Mark the sentences I (interested) or B (bored). 1 mark for each correct answer.

  1   A: The film was great. Thank you for taking me.
      B: Good, glad you liked it.

  2   A: Did you know that more countries are having water shortages?
      B: Really?

  3   A: It's our country's national day today.
      B: Is it?

  4   A: This weather really is lovely, isn't it?
      B: I suppose so.

  5   A: Thank you so much for letting me borrow your book.
      B: You're welcome. I hope you found it helpful.

  6   A: We have to do something about environmental pollution.
      B: Do we?

  7   A: Did you know how important the rainforests really are?
      B: No, are they?

  8   A: I think climate change is the most important issue in the world today.
      B: Do you really?

  9   A: Next week people are meeting to talk about rainforests.
      B: Oh really?

  10 A: I love it when it rains a lot. It's great, isn't it?
      B: I suppose so.

LISTENING 2

2 (◄) 6.2) Listen to the conversation between a mother and son and mark the following statements T (true) or F (false). 1 mark for each correct answer.

  1   At first the mother is really interested in global warming.
  2   Her son thinks that global warming isn't important.
  3   The mother thinks that the news about global warming is always the same.
  4   Her son explains that global warming affects the weather differently all over the world.
  5   At the end the mother is really bored by global warming.

3 (◀ 6.2) Listen again and complete the sentences with the correct word. 1 mark for each correct answer.

1 At college the son learned about global warming and its *effects / reasons* on the weather.
2 His mother thinks that they've heard *enough / not enough* about it on the TV.
3 The son says that places that have a lot of rain are getting even *more / less* rain.
4 The mother realizes that both too much rain and too little rain can make it *difficult / easy* to grow food.
5 The son explains that because of melting ice the sea levels are *rising / falling*.

LANGUAGE DEVELOPMENT (15 marks)

4 Match the words 1–5 and a–e to make phrases.

1 bright	a change
2 extreme	b winds
3 climate	c weather
4 fossil	d sunshine
5 strong	e fuel

5 Complete the sentences using the correct form of the verb in brackets.

1 Look at those dark clouds. I think it's _____ (start) raining.
2 I've just finished my homework. I _____ (play) tennis with my brother in half an hour.
3 I'm _____ (go) to the supermarket. Is there anything you want?
4 I need to study. We _____ (have) a test tomorrow.
5 What _____ you _____ (do) at the weekend? Would you like to go to the cinema?

6 Complete the sentences using words in the box.

calm   dull   humid   chilly   upset

1 This television programme is so _____ . I'm really bored.
2 There's a _____ wind today. You should wear your coat.
3 It is difficult to feel energetic when the weather is so _____ . The heat and the rain are so tiring.
4 Please don't be _____ if your exam results aren't very good. You will do better next time.
5 When I'm lying on the beach listening to the sound of the sea, I feel really _____ and relaxed.

TOTAL _____/ 35

REVIEW TEST 7

Name: .... **Date:** ....

LISTENING (20 marks)

LISTENING 1

1 (🔊 7.1) Listen and complete the sentences. 1 mark for each correct answer.

1 I'm _____ go shopping this evening.

2 _____ come to the football match with me?

3 Which car _____ think you'll have next year?

4 Are you _____ come to class tomorrow?

5 I _____ get a good job with a bank.

6 _____ qualify to be a teacher?

7 Tomorrow I'm _____ watch the match with my friends.

8 _____ think it's _____ rain tomorrow?

9 I'm _____ study sports science when I go to university.

10 _____ try chess boxing?

LISTENING 2

2 (🔊 7.2) You are going to listen to a report by an English football commentator about a match between England and Spain. He is very biased! Listen and answer the questions. 1 mark for each correct answer.

1 Which team won the game?

_____

2 What was the score?

_____

3 Who did the commentator think was the best player?

_____

4 What was special about this player?

_____

5 Does the commentator think that the result is important?

_____

3 (🔊 7.2) Listen again and complete the table with 3 adjectives the commentator uses to describe the English team and 2 adjectives he uses to describe the Spanish team. 1 mark for each correct answer.

England	Spain
1 _____	1 _____
2 _____	2 _____
3 _____	

LANGUAGE DEVELOPMENT (15 marks)

4 Complete the sentences with words from the box.

worried   neighbourhood   excited   dangerous   disappointed

1 Our house isn't very big but it's in a very good _____.
2 My brother always gets so _____ before a big football match.
3 My mother was very _____ when I told her I didn't want to be a doctor.
4 It is important to tell children that it is _____ to play with fire.
5 You shouldn't get so _____ before your exams. You've done plenty of revision.

5 Choose the correct adverb to complete the sentences.

1 Have you *ever / still* been to the United States of America?
2 I've *yet / already* seen that movie. Can we go and see another one?
3 I'm so happy. I've *just / ever* heard that I've got a place at university.
4 She's *still / already* reading the book she started last month.
5 Have you finished your homework *yet / still*?

6 The words in bold are in the wrong sentences. Write them in the correct sentence and then cross out the wrong words.

1 One **the best** _____ of playing sport is that it is good for our health.
2 The most popular sport in almost every country in the world is **boxing** _____ .
3 One disadvantage of **football** _____ is that it is very expensive to buy all the equipment.
4 I think **advantage** _____ way to get fit is to walk, cycle and go swimming.
5 A lot of people think that **golf** _____ is a very dangerous sport.

TOTAL _____/ 35

REVIEW TEST 8

Name: .... **Date:** ....

LISTENING (20 marks)

LISTENING 1

1 (🔊 8.1) Listen to the sentences and circle the correct number. 1 mark for each correct answer.

  1 Nearly *30% / 13% / 33%* of students never do their homework.

  2 If you need to call me, my telephone extension number is *4232 / 4323 / 4332*.

  3 Yes, this is a lovely diamond ring; it's *$15,500 / $1500 / $15,050*.

  4 The company profits have increased by *⅓ / ¼ / ⅕*.

  5 Research has shown that *40% / 44% / 14%* of people are not happy in their work.

  6 The Cape of Good Hope is a good place for fishermen because it has *200 / 2,000 / 20,000* types of fish.

  7 Over *31.5% / 30.5% / 33.5%* of people check their social networking sites while they are at work.

  8 Most people spend over *60% / 50.6% / 60.5%* of their time working at their desks.

  9 At work, people spend nearly *35 / 45 / 53* minutes on the phone every day.

  10 This car costs *$76,000 / $67,700 / $76,700*.

LISTENING 2

2 (🔊 8.2) Listen to a conversation between a student and her professor. Choose the correct number to complete the sentences. 1 mark for each correct answer.

  1 *36% / 38%* of students want to be doctors.

  2 More women than men want to be doctors, with *38% / 36%* of female students studying medicine.

  3 *90% / 80%* of male medical students think it will be easy for them to get a job.

  4 *25% / 5%* of men want to be engineers.

  5 Female engineering students are more positive than male engineering students, with *50% / 60%* thinking it will be easy for them to get a job.

3 (🔊 8.2) Listen again and mark the following sentences T (true) or F (false). 1 mark for each correct answer.

  1 Medicine is the most popular major at this university.

  2 More women than men want to be doctors.

  3 Female medical students are more positive about getting jobs than male medical students.

  4 More men than women study medicine.

  5 Male engineering students are more positive about getting a job than female engineering students.

LANGUAGE DEVELOPMENT (15 marks)

4 Look at the information about how young people spend their free time and complete sentences 1–5.

activity	percentage of young people
Watching television	95%
Surfing the internet	80%
Social media	75%
Going to cafés with friends	60%
Playing sports	43%
Reading books	35%

1 The _____ popular activity is watching television.

2 Surfing the internet is _____ popular _____ going to cafés with friends.

3 _____ young people play sports than go on social media sites.

4 _____ young people surf the internet than read books.

5 Reading books is the _____ popular activity.

5 Complete the sentences with the correct form of the multi-word verbs in the box.

run out of   start up   take up   take part in   put up with

1 After he left university he _____ his own business and became very rich.

2 Last year my sister _____ tennis to help her get fit.

3 I love _____ team games. It's great fun to play sport with other people.

4 My mother finds it really difficult to _____ the noise of all her grandchildren.

5 My mobile phone always seems to _____ power just when I have to make an important call.

6 Look at the groups of words below and circle the word that is different.

1 worried anxious happy

2 good bad excellent

3 calm nervous upset

4 unhappy sad excited

5 confident positive untidy

TOTAL _____/ 35

REVIEW TEST 9

Name: .... **Date:** ....

LISTENING (20 marks)

LISTENING 1

1 (◀» 9.1) Listen to the sentences and mark those which show enthusiasm with an E. 1 mark for each correct answer.

1 I'm really looking forward to the class tomorrow. I love grammar.

2 The teacher said we have 3 tests this term instead of 4.

3 Our teacher really is amazing.

4 We are going on holiday tomorrow.

5 I'm really enjoying this essay I'm writing.

6 Do you think it will rain tomorrow?

7 We've almost finished this course.

8 My teacher said that my essay needs more work.

9 Well, I think I understand everything.

10 He's feeling very good about his work.

LISTENING 2

2 (◀» 9.2) Listen to part of a radio programme about new household products and complete the notes. 1 mark for each correct answer.

Ice cream football

1 Makes ice cream without _____ so it is very cheap.

2 Comes in two colours: blue and _____ .

3 Put flavours in one end and _____ in the other.

Comfi-Desk

4 Use it to work with a tablet when in _____ .

5 There is enough space for a _____ and a plate of cake.

3 (◀» 9.2) Listen again and complete the sentences by circling the correct word. 1 mark for each correct answer.

1 Sometimes you go to the shops and your favourite *flavour / ice cream* has sold out.

2 The ice cream football is very *easy / difficult* to use.

3 To make ice cream, you have to *throw / kick* the ball.

4 The Comfi-Desk is for people who *work hard / are relaxed*.

5 The desk has a space where you can put your *book / cup of coffee*.

LANGUAGE DEVELOPMENT (15 marks)

4 Complete the sentences with words from the box.

homeless   funeral   fascinated   remarkable   emperor

1 My grandmother was a _____ woman. She had 5 children and went to study at university when she was 45.
2 Many people can be left _____ after natural disasters like storms and floods.
3 After the popular President's death many thousands of people attended his _____.
4 I'm absolutely _____ by the history of ancient Egypt.
5 I think that Japan is the only country that still has an _____.

5 Complete the sentences by choosing the correct form of the adjective.
1 She was so *excited / exciting* when she passed her university exams.
2 He always found his classes so *bored / boring*. That's why he didn't do well at school.
3 She's been *interested / interesting* in history since she was a child.
4 I was very *tired / tiring* after studying so hard for my exams.
5 It is difficult to feel *relaxed / relaxing* just before a visit to the dentist.

6 Mark the following sentences about shapes T (true) or F (false).
1 A square has four sides of equal length and the corners are all the same size.
2 A rectangle has four sides of equal length and the corners are of two different sizes.
3 Two semi-circles make a whole circle.
4 Eggs are oval shaped.
5 The pyramids of Egypt are diamond shaped.

TOTAL _____/ 35

REVIEW TEST 10

Name: .... **Date:** ....

LISTENING (20 marks)

LISTENING 1

1 (◀) 10.1 Listen to the sentences and circle the correct word. 1 mark for each correct answer.

1 Well, it depends *whether / wither* or not the sun is shining.

2 My taekwondo class is *from / form* four to six.

3 We have forgotten *are / our* books.

4 There are 8 students in *my / may* class.

5 Last night we *had / hid* pizza.

6 I'm late. My plane *lives / leaves* in an hour.

7 My sister's son has *just / jest* started school.

8 It's a long time since I read such a good *book / buck*.

9 *Win / When* do we have to go to class?

10 *Look / Luck*, there's Marium.

LISTENING 2

2 (◀) 10.2 You are going to listen to an extract from a university lecture about space travel. Which words do you think the professor will use? Choose 5 words from the box that you expect to hear and write them in 1–5. Then listen, check and correct any of your words that are wrong. 1 mark for each correct answer.

planets cars computers exploration results weather technology winds sun water

1 _____

2 _____

3 _____

4 _____

5 _____

3 (◀) 10.2 Listen again and circle the correct words to complete the sentence the professor says. 1 mark for each correct answer.

1 *Whether / Wither* or not we continue is not my decision to make.

2 *Know / Now* our nearest neighbour is Mars.

3 It is closer to *this on / the sun* than the Earth …

4 … and is known *as / us* the red planet.

5 Sometime in the future these important minerals could be *mend / mined* on Mars.

LANGUAGE DEVELOPMENT (15 marks)

4 Complete the sentences with the words in the box.

diamond   solar system   project   astronauts   couple

1 _____ are the men and women who explore space.

2 My sister's husband bought her a very expensive _____ necklace.

3 There are 9 planets in our _____ .

4 My aunt and uncle only got married two years ago. Everyone says they are a great
_____ .

5 Our class has worked hard on this _____ for so long.

5 Choose the correct word to complete the sentences.

1 If I came with you, *will / would* you buy my ticket to the cinema?

2 If it rains tomorrow, we *will / would* have the party indoors.

3 If you could go anywhere in the world, where *will / would* you go?

4 If she has a daughter, she *will / would* call her Sara.

5 If he had enough money for a car, he *will / would* buy a sports model.

6 Correct the incorrect collocations by moving the words in bold.

1 return **cruise** _____

2 business **flight** _____

3 sea **trip** _____

4 Mediterranean **voyage** _____

5 scheduled **journey** _____

TOTAL _____/ 35

ADDITIONAL SPEAKING TASK 1

DESCRIBING AN INTERESTING HOME

1 You are going to describe an interesting home. Work with your group and read the information your teacher has given you. Decide what you are going to say about your home and how you will organize your talk. Fill in the table. Use the Model language below to help you.

Introduction	
General facts	
Advantages	
Disadvantages	
Summary	

2 Work in groups of 3 (A, B, C). Take turns to present your 3 homes. Give as much detail as you can. Ask each other questions about your homes. Use the Model language below to help you. Then decide which is the best home and why. Be ready to present your group's best home to the class.

MODEL LANGUAGE

TALKING ABOUT PEOPLE

Presenting information

I'd like to talk about / I'd like to tell you about …

First of all / Firstly, let's look at the advantages.

I'd also like to talk about / I'd also like to give you some disadvantages.

In summary / Finally …

Describing places

For giving facts
This house / building has (*number or type of rooms*).
It was built in (*year*).
It is (*number*) years old.
Obviously …
As we know …

For giving opinions
I think …
I believe …
In my opinion …
I personally feel that …
It is interesting, because …

A	B	C
Place: Germany	**Place:** Spain	**Place:** Australia
Year built: 1870	**Year built:** 2012	**Year built:** 2003
Made of: stone and brick	**Made of:** glass and cement	**Made of:** wood
Interesting fact: not finished	**Interesting fact:** next to sea	**Interesting fact:** good for the environment
Price: $24,500,000	**Price:** $6,000,000	**Price:** $800,000

ADDITIONAL SPEAKING TASK 2

ORGANIZING A FESTIVAL

1 Your class is going to organize a festival about an important aspect of your country's culture. Work in your group to make a list of the reasons why you want to hold this festival. Use the table below and the Model language below in your discussion.

What?	
When?	
Where?	
Who?	

2 Work in your new group. Take turns to present your 4 festivals and ask each other questions. Then decide which is the best festival and why. Be ready to present your ideas to the class.

MODEL LANGUAGE

TALKING ABOUT FESTIVALS AND CELEBRATIONS

Making suggestions

At this festival you can try …

Do you like the arts / sports / music / cars …?

You could …

Why not …?

Shall we …?

How about …?

I'd suggest …

Responding to suggestions

Negatively

Oh, I'm not sure that is a good idea.

Can we think about it?

I'd rather not.

Well, I don't think that's a good idea.

No, I don't want to do that.

Positively

Yes, fantastic.

OK. Good idea.

What shall we do after that?

I'd like to …

I would like to …

Yes, that sounds good.

Yes, I'd love to.

That's a great idea.

ADDITIONAL SPEAKING TASK 3

A DEBATE

1 You are going to hold a debate. The topic is: *Should schools and universities prepare young people for the world of work by training them to do jobs or should they focus only on academic skills?* Your teacher will tell you if you are for or against the topic. Work with your partner and fill in the table with reasons for your opinion. Then fill in the reasons your opponents might give against your opinion. Use the Model language below to help you.

	education for jobs	education for academic skills
for		
against		

2 Work in groups of 4 (2 who support education for jobs and 2 who support education for academic skills). Take turns to give your opinions and your reasons. Agree or disagree with each other. Then decide which is better. Use the Model language below to help you.

....

MODEL LANGUAGE

TALKING ABOUT SCHOOL AND EDUCATION IN A DEBATE

Giving your opinion	**Agreeing**	**Disagreeing**
I think …	I totally agree.	Yes, but …
It seems to me …	That's true.	It's good but …
In my opinion …	I agree.	I am not really sure …
I feel …	Yes, that's right.	I don't think so.
For me it's better because…	Exactly!	I don't agree with that.
	You're right.	Yes, but on the other hand …
		Well, it was OK I suppose, but to be honest …
		Yes, I see what you are saying but …

ADDITIONAL SPEAKING TASK 4

A REPORT ON A PIECE OF NEW TECHNOLOGY

1 You are going to present a report about a piece of new technology. Work in with your group to think of as many positive features of one of the ideas for new technology below. Your teacher will tell you which one to focus on. Use the Model language below to help you plan your report.

ideas for new technology	what they do
1 3D headset with all around virtual reality	Let you get inside a game. Can be used for training soldiers, doctors, sports people etc.
2 Driverless car	This uses GPS to move without a driver.
3 Memory implants	Help people with long-term memory loss and can also make our brains remember things better
4 Smart watches	Have all the advantages of smartphones on your wrist

2 Work in your new group and take turns to present your reports on your new pieces of technology. Ask each other as many questions as you can.

MODEL LANGUAGE

TALKING ABOUT THE WORLD OF TECHNOLOGY

Language for giving a report

… are important because …

We are able to … because of …

In conclusion, it seems that …

… can help people …

… assist people with …

Giving additional information

… and …

… as well as …

… too …

… also …

Giving contrasting information

… but …

… whereas …

However …

On the other hand …

Giving reasons and examples

… due to …

… thanks to …

… because of …

… instead of …

For example …

DESCRIBING A PROCESS

1 You are going to describe a process. Work in your group to describe the process your teacher has given you. Use the Model language below. Make sure you talk about every step of the process. Be ready to describe your process to other students in the next part of the class.

2 Work in your new group. Take turns to describe your process but do not say what it is. The other students must guess what process you are describing.

MODEL LANGUAGE

DESCRIBING A PROCESS

Start	**Middle**	**End**
So first of all, put …	Next, put your …	At the end …
Firstly …	It should look like …	Finally …
First of all …	Next …	To finish …
To start with …	Then …	
	After that …	

1 Preparing your favourite meal	2 Taking a photo on your phone and sharing it with friends	3 Making the bed	4 Washing your clothes in a washing machine
First, take some rice / meat / cheese …	First, touch the camera icon …	First, take the clean sheets and pillow case …	First, open the door of the washing machine …

ADDITIONAL SPEAKING TASK 6

PRESENTING A SURVEY

1 You are going to create a survey about the effects of hot, cold and wet weather. Work in pairs. Read questions 1–5 in the survey and then write 5 more questions.

A survey on weather and climate

1 Do you prefer hot or cold weather?

2 Is it cold in your country in the winter?

3 How many seasons do you have in your country?

4 Do you feel more energetic in the summer or winter / hot or cold weather?

5 Which sports or hobbies do you do in a) hot weather, b) cold weather and c) wet weather?

6 ....

7 ....

8 ....

9 ....

10 ....

2 Go round the class and take turns to ask and answer the questions in your surveys. Make a note of the answers. When it is your turn to answer, remember to use the Linking words and phrases to explain the reasons and consquences in the Model language below.

3 Work with your partner from Exercise 1. Summarize the results of your surveys so that you can present them to the class. Use the Model language for Presenting survey results below.

MODEL LANGUAGE

Some countries are very hot and don't get much rain. **As a result,** there isn't enough water for plants, drinking and washing.

The plants died **because** there wasn't enough rain this summer.

The village flooded **due to** the heavy rainfall.

It is more difficult to work in high humidity **so** our concentration drops.

People feel more energetic in the summer. **Therefore** they can get a lot of things done if the sun is shining.

PRESENTING SURVEY RESULTS

Introducing your survey results

My survey was about …

I'm going to tell you about the results of my survey.

There were (20) students in my survey.

My questions were on the topic of (weather and climate).

Talking about the results

My (first / second / third / last) question was …

You can see here that (80%) of the students prefer hot weather and (20%) prefer cold weather.

You can see that half of the students don't do sports in hot weather and half do, because it depends on which country they are from.

You can see here that 'yes' is 60% and 'no' is 40%.

You can see here that the results are interesting.

ADDITIONAL SPEAKING TASK 7

A PANEL DISCUSSION

1 You are going to have a panel discussion about whether sport in schools should be compulsory. Work in your group to think of all the advantages of the position your teacher has given you (agreeing or disagreeing with the topic). Think also about the disadvantages of your position and the questions the other group will ask you about them. How you will respond to these questions? Fill in the table and use the Model language below.

2 Work in your new group to discuss both sides of the topic. Take turns to present your positions and to ask questions about the advantages and disadvantages.

I agree / disagree that sport in schools should be compulsory.	
ADVANTAGES	....
DISADVANTAGES	....
RESPONSES TO DISADVANTAGES	....

MODEL LANGUAGE

TALKING ABOUT SPORT AND COMPETITION

Asking for clarification	**Advantages**	**Disadvantages**
Can you explain what you mean?	An advantage of this is …	A drawback of this is …
I'm afraid I didn't get that.	A benefit of this is …	The worst thing about this is …
I'm sorry but I don't understand.	The best thing about this is …	A disadvantage of this is …
Would you mind giving me some examples?	One good thing is …	One bad thing is …
Sorry, I don't follow.		

ADDITIONAL SPEAKING TASK 8

GIVE SOLUTIONS TO PROBLEMS

1 You are going to give solutions to the work or study problems in the table. Work in your group to think of solutions to these problems. Make notes of your solutions in the table.

I don't like my job.	
I have to work too many hours to get my work done.	
I'm not very good at job interviews.	
I never have enough time to study.	
I find revising boring.	
I have to revise but I want to see my friends.	

2 Your teacher will give you one of the problems. Go round the class and talk to at least 4 students. Tell them about your problem and ask for their advice. Ask them about their problems and give them your advice. Use the Model language below to help you.

MODEL LANGUAGE

TALKING ABOUT PROBLEMS AND SOLUTIONS

Giving advice

I think you should …

I don't want to upset you but …

OK, I understand what you are saying.

If you want to do better, you need to …

I know it's difficult but at least you know …

If I were you, I would …

I think you should …

Be careful not to …

You should try (not) to …

I can help you.

Shall we …?

Why don't you …?

ADDITIONAL SPEAKING TASK 9

DESCRIBE AN OBJECT AND OTHERS GUESS WHAT IT IS

1 You are going to describe an object for other students to guess what it is. First of all, make sure you know what each of these household items is.

tin opener	calculator	weighing scales
scissors	stapler	kettle
door keys	torch	ice cube tray
light bulb	pen	chair

2 Work with a partner and decide how you will describe the object your teacher has told you to focus on. Use the Model language below to help you plan what to say.

3 Work with your partner and describe your object to the class. Can they guess what it is?

MODEL LANGUAGE

DESCRIBING OBJECTS

It lets you …
It's used to do the …
It's a thing used for …
It's a thing used for …
It's made of …
It has … main parts
It's usually made of …
It's used for …

Asking about objects

What's it used for …?
What does this part let you do?
What is this thing used for?
What does it look like?
What is this part used to do?
What's this thing for?

ADDITIONAL SPEAKING TASK 10

HAVE A DISCUSSION ABOUT OPENING A LANGUAGE SCHOOL TO TEACH YOUR LANGUAGE IN AN ENGLISH-SPEAKING COUNTRY

1 You are going to have a discussion about opening a language school to teach your language in an English-speaking country. Your teacher will tell you f you are in favour of the idea or against it. Work with a partner who has the same idea as you. Make notes in the box to support your argument.

Your company is going to open a language school to teach your language in an English-speaking country Think about: • The students • Times of the classes • Location of the school: city centre or in a residential area • Prices for the courses • Classes e.g. children, adults, business etc. • Anything else	....

2 Work in your new group and have a discussion about opening the school. How will you organize it? Use your notes in the table and the Model language below in your discussion.

....

MODEL LANGUAGE

HAVING A DISCUSSION

Starting
Would you like to start us off?
Why don't you start us off?
Let me begin by asking …
We'll begin today's discussion with a look at …
Would anyone else like to say anything about …

Inviting someone to speak
You haven't said much. What do you think?
What is your opinion?
Let's get your thoughts on this.

Interrupting
Can I just cut in there?
Can I just say something here?
Sorry, but I have to interrupt you and say …
Sorry, but can I just say …

Continuing to speak
Can I finish?
Let me just finish what I was saying.
Can I finish my point?
Please allow me to finish.
We are discussing the best way to …
For me it is definitely …
I'd like to finish my point.

Finishing
Let me finish this off by saying …
So to conclude …
Finally …

ACKNOWLEDGEMENTS

With thanks to Nick Robinson, agent extraordinaire. Also to Caroline Thiriau and Kate Hansford from CUP, especially to Kate for her consistently helpful responses to my avalanche of questions. Finally, and most importantly, to Richard Patterson for his constant good humour and endless patience.

Alison Ramage-Patterson

Publisher acknowledgements

The publishers are extremely grateful to the following people and their students for reviewing and trialling this course during its development. The course has benefited hugely from your insightful comments, advice and feedback.

Mr M.K. Adjibade, King Saud University, Saudi Arabia; Canan Aktug, Bursa Technical University, Turkey; Olwyn Alexander, Heriot Watt University, UK; Harika Altug, Bogazici University, Turkey; Laila Al-Qadhi, Kuwait University, Kuwait; Tahani Al-Taha, University of Dubai, UAE; Valerie Anisy, Damman University, Saudi Arabia; Anwar Al-Fetlawi, University of Sharjah, UAE; Ozlem Atalay, Middle East Technical University, Turkey; Seda Merter Ataygul, Bursa Technical University Turkey; Kwab Asare, University of Westminster, UK; Erdogan Bada, Cukurova University, Turkey; Cem Balcikanli, Gazi University, Turkey; Gaye Bayri, Anadolu University, Turkey; Meher Ben Lakhdar, Sohar University, Oman; Emma Biss, Girne American University, UK; Dogan Bulut, Meliksah University, Turkey; Sinem Bur, TED University, Turkey; Alison Chisholm, University of Sussex, UK; Dr. Panidnad Chulerk , Rangsit University, Thailand; Sedat Cilingir, Bilgi University, Istanbul, Turkey; Sarah Clark, Nottingham Trent International College, UK; Elaine Cockerham, Higher College of Technology, Muscat, Oman; Asli Derin, Bilgi University, Turkey; Steven Douglass, University of Sunderland, UK; Jacqueline Einer, Sabanci University, Turkey; Basak Erel, Anadolu University, Turkey; Hande Lena Erol, Piri Reis Maritime University, Turkey; Gulseren Eyuboglu, Ozyegin University, Turkey; Sam Fenwick, Sohar University, Oman; Peter Frey, International House, Doha, Qatar; Muge Gencer, Kemerburgaz University, Turkey; Dr. Majid Gharawi and colleagues at the English Language Centre, Jazan University, Saudi Arabia; Jeff Gibbons, King Fahed University of Petroleum and Minerals, Saudi Arabia; Maxine Gilway, Bristol University, UK; Dr Christina Gitsaki, HCT, Dubai Men's College, UAE; Neil Harris, Swansea University, UK; Vicki Hayden, College of the North Atlantic, Qatar; Joud Jabri-Pickett, United Arab Emirates University, Al Ain, UAE; Ajarn Naratip Sharp Jindapitak, Prince of Songkla University, Hatyai, Thailand; Aysel Kilic, Anadolu University, Turkey; Ali Kimav, Anadolu University, Turkey; Bahar Kiziltunali, Izmir University of Economics, Turkey; Kamil Koc, Ozel Kasimoglu Coskun Lisesi, Turkey; Ipek Korman-Tezcan, Yeditepe University, Turkey; Philip Lodge, Dubai Men's College, UAE; Iain Mackie, Al Rowdah University, Abu Dhabi, UAE; Katherine Mansfield, University of Westminster, UK; Kassim Mastan, King Saud University, Saudi Arabia; Elspeth McConnell, Newham College, UK; Lauriel Mehdi, American University of Sharjah, UAE; Dorando Mirkin-Dick, Bell International Institute, UK; Dr Sita Musigrungsi, Prince of Songkla University, Hatyai, Thailand; Mark Neville, Al Hosn University, Abu Dhabi, UAE; Shirley Norton, London School of English, UK; James Openshaw, British Study Centres, UK; Hale Ottolini, Mugla Sitki Kocman University, Turkey; David Palmer, University of Dubai, UAE; Michael Pazinas, United Arab Emirates University, UAE; Troy Priest, Zayed University, UAE; Alison Ramage Patterson, Jeddah, Saudi Arabia; Paul Rogers, Qatar Skills Academy, Qatar; Josh Round, Saint George International, UK; Harika Saglicak, Bogazici University, Turkey; Asli Saracoglu, Isik University, Turkey; Neil Sarkar, Ealing, Hammersmith and West London College, UK; Nancy Shepherd, Bahrain University, Bahrain; Jonathan Smith, Sabanci University, Turkey; Peter Smith, United Arab Emirates University, UAE; Adem Soruc, Fatih University Istanbul, Turkey; Dr Peter Stanfield, HCT, Madinat Zayed & Ruwais Colleges, UAE; Maria Agata Szczerbik, United Arab Emirates University, Al Ain, UAE; Burcu Tezcan-Unal, Bilgi University, Turkey; Scott Thornbury, The New School, New York, USA; Dr Nakonthep Tipayasuparat, Rangsit University, Thailand; Susan Toth, HCT, Dubai Men's Campus, Dubai, UAE; Melin Unal, Ege University, Izmir, Turkey; Aylin Unaldi, Bogaziçi University, Turkey; Colleen Wackrow, Princess Nourah bint Abdulrahman University, Riyadh, Saudi Arabia; Gordon Watts, Study Group, Brighton UK; Po Leng Wendelkin, INTO at University of East Anglia, UK; Halime Yildiz, Bilkent University, Ankara, Turkey; Ferhat Yilmaz, Kahramanmaras Sutcu Imam University, Turkey.

Special thanks to Peter Lucantoni for sharing his expertise, both pedagogical and cultural.

Special thanks also to Michael Pazinas for writing the Research projects which feature at the end of every unit. Michael has first-hand experience of teaching in and developing materials for the paperless classroom. He has worked in Greece, the Middle East and the UK. Prior to his current position as Curriculum and Assessment Coordinator for the Foundation Program at the United Arab Emirates University he was an English teacher for the British Council, the University of Exeter and several private language institutes. Michael is also a graphic designer, involved in instructional design and educational eBook development. His main interests lie in using mobile technology together with attractive visual design, animation and interactivity. He is an advocate of challenge-based language learning.

Text and Photo acknowledgements

The authors and publishers acknowledge the following sources of copyright material and are grateful for the permissions granted. While every effort has been made, it has not always been possible to identify the sources of all the material used, or to trace all copyright holders. If any omissions are brought to our notice, we will be happy to include the appropriate acknowledgements on reprinting.

p.8:(1) © Eric Limon/Shutterstock; p.8: (2) © szefai/Shutterstock; p.8: (3) © Steven Vidler/Eurasia Press/Corbis; Review Test 1, p.114 (left): Alamy/© Grapheast; Review Test 1, p.114 (right): Corbis/© Eric Lafforgue/ArabianEye.

All video stills by kind permission of © Discovery Communication, LLC 2014

Dictionary

Cambridge dictionaries are the world's most widely used dictionaries for learners of English. Available at three levels (Cambridge Essential English Dictionary, Cambridge Learner's Dictionary and Cambridge Advanced Learner's Dictionary), they provide easy-to-understand definitions, example sentences, and help in avoiding typical mistakes. The dictionaries are also available online at dictionary.cambridge.org. © Cambridge University Press, reproduced with permission.

Corpus

Development of this publication has made use of the Cambridge English Corpus (CEC). The CEC is a multi-billion word computer database of contemporary spoken and written English. It includes British English, American English and other varieties of English. It also includes the Cambridge Learner Corpus, developed in collaboration with Cambridge English Language Assessment. Cambridge University Press has built up the CEC to provide evidence about language use that helps to produce better language teaching materials.

Typeset by Integra.